DEFINING, LOCATING, AND ADDRESSING BULLYING IN THE WPA WORKPLACE

DEFINING, LOCATING, AND ADDRESSING BULLYING IN THE WPA WORKPLACE

EDITED BY
CRISTYN L. ELDER
BETHANY DAVILA

UTAH STATE UNIVERSITY PRESS
Logan

© 2019 by University Press of Colorado

Published by Utah State University Press
An imprint of University Press of Colorado
245 Century Circle, Suite 202
Louisville, Colorado 80027

The University Press of Colorado is a proud member of the Association of University Presses.

The University Press of Colorado is a cooperative publishing enterprise supported, in part, by Adams State University, Colorado State University, Fort Lewis College, Metropolitan State University of Denver, University of Colorado, University of Northern Colorado, Utah State University, and Western State Colorado University.

∞ This paper meets the requirements of the ANSI/NISO Z39.48-1992 (Permanence of Paper).

ISBN: 978-1-60732-815-5 (paperback)
ISBN: 978-1-60732-816-2 (ebook)
DOI: https://doi.org/10.7330/9781607328162

Library of Congress Cataloging-in-Publication Data

Names: Elder, Cristyn L., editor. I Davila, Bethany, editor.
Title: Defining, locating, and addressing bullying in the WPA workplace / edited by Cristyn L. Elder, Bethany Davila.
Description: Logan : Utah State University Press, [2018] I Includes bibliographical references and index.
Identifiers: LCCN 2018034319 I ISBN 9781607328155 (pbk.) I ISBN 9781607328162 (ebook)
Subjects: LCSH: Writing centers—United States—Administration. I Writing centers—Social aspects. I Writing centers—Psychological aspects. I Bullying in universities and colleges. I Bullying in the workplace.
Classification: LCC PE1405.U6 D44 2018 I DDC 302.34/3—dc23
LC record available at https://lccn.loc.gov/2018034319

This collection is dedicated to those who have been bullied and the allies who have stood up to this form of injustice.

CONTENTS

ACKNOWLEDGMENTS

The editors would first like to thank the authors in this collection who bravely agreed to lay bare their experiences with bullying so we can all learn how to begin to address this issue head-on. We'd also like to thank our survey participants and interviewees who have trusted us with their stories. At USU Press, Michael Spooner deserves considerable appreciation for believing in this project since the day we cold-called him and pitched the idea, and appreciation also goes to Kylie Haggen and Laura Furney for guiding us through production. We are also grateful to our colleagues who talked about this project with us at different stages along the way, including Seth Kahn, Chuck Paine, and Ryan Skinnell.

Cris would like to thank Stella Aschenbrenner, who listened with great care to the frustration Cris was feeling in the face of her bully. She also thanks her Purdue crew, Elizabeth Angeli, Ehren Pflugfelder, and Megan Schoen, who with their levity and humor brought friendship and light during a dark time. And always thank you to Tyler and the kitties for creating a warm, loving, and safe space to come home to. Finally, an outpouring of wholehearted gratitude goes to Beth, an incredible colleague, friend, and ally who helped Cris understand what she was experiencing and helped her realize that it wasn't about her but about her bully. B, I'm so grateful to have worked alongside you on this project, which I hope will go on to help so many more.

Beth wants to thank the many people who provided support both throughout the process of editing this collection and when she was dealing with her own experiences with bullying: Jesse Alemán for his astute advice; Hannah Dickinson, Staci Shultz, and Stephanie Moody for their empathy and humor; and Frank, Julius, and Kai for their patience and regular reminders of what really matters in life. And last but certainly not least, a huge heartfelt thank you to Cris for suggesting this project as a way to gain agency, which made a shitty situation a little less shitty.

FOREWORD

Shirley K Rose

You probably think this book is not about you. But chances are good that you have been bullied by a coworker or colleague or that you have bullied a coworker or colleague—intentionally or not, knowingly or not—or that you have witnessed or otherwise become aware of one of your coworkers or colleagues bullying another. Targets of bullying often don't recognize the abuse directed at them for what it is. Bullies often lack the self-awareness to acknowledge that their behavior is abusive. And bystanders often have difficulty acknowledging that a colleague they respect and admire is either the target or the perpetrator of bullying because it doesn't align with their beliefs about their colleague or their workplace. This may be especially so in the academy, where we live the "life of the mind," quite distant from the stereotypical scene of the "schoolyard bully."

That is why we need this collection of essays.

This collection of essays about workplace bullying experienced by writing program administrators and writing programs contributes not only to writing program administration studies but also to an important conversation about bullying in academia as a whole. This is a difficult subject to discuss because people are often unwilling or afraid to discuss their own experiences, which makes it difficult to do the kind of comparisons across instances that allow for drawing generalizations and theorizing. Silence about these incidents can also have the result of isolating those who have experienced bullying.

The editors have assembled a diverse set of contributors from varied institutional backgrounds with varied institutional power (tenured, pre-tenure, non-tenure track) as well as various groups that are often subjected to harassment, which editors and authors are careful to distinguish from bullying. Many readers will recognize their own experiences

DOI: 10.7330/9781607328162.c000a

in these chapters—for some, the chapters will help them develop a frame of reference for understanding their experience as targets of bullying, and perhaps a few others will recognize their own bullying behavior and consider ways they could change, since not all bullies are aware of the effect of their behavior. The chapters offer a mix of personal narrative and theorizing, with each chapter suggesting one or more general principles or lessons to be drawn from the individual experience. However, the primary contribution of the collection is not the individual narratives but the theoretical grounding of these experiences.

In addition to providing theoretical frames on bullying, this collection will serve as a useful complement to other work on writing program administration, taking a different perspective on experiences of pre-tenure WPAs. The editors and contributing authors make the point that in cautioning against taking a WPA position before tenure, more senior scholars sidestep their responsibility for advocating for a change in the behaviors that make pre-tenure faculty vulnerable. By dismissing bad behavior as "politics," we normalize and even excuse it when we should be calling it out.

Even as a very experienced senior scholar and WPA, I found the collection helpful in understanding some recent professional experiences of my own that have troubled me. Though I initially picked up this collection because I thought it could be a valuable resource for students in the graduate WPA seminars and graduate professionalization courses I teach, by the time I had read it through and put it down, I understood that this book was about me. I trust that other readers will also find themselves here.

DEFINING, LOCATING, AND ADDRESSING BULLYING IN THE WPA WORKPLACE

INTRODUCTION: BULLYING
Not Just Politics as Usual

Cristyn L. Elder and Bethany Davila

Right out of graduate school, we, Cris and Beth, the editors of this collection, individually and collectively found ourselves faced with unexpected difficult situations.[1] At the time, we called it departmental "politics," but, in actuality, it was a pattern of incivility. It was bullying. We found many ways to explain to ourselves what we witnessed and experienced. For example, during a department meeting, when a senior faculty member called our research "suspect" and "a subject of concern" (research, by the way, that has been well received in our field, resulting in multiple publications and a national award), we tried to explain it away as professional insecurity. When we saw a full professor yell at a lecturer in the hallway, chastising him and calling him insubordinate, we recoiled at the lack of professionalism. When a pre-tenured[2] colleague repeatedly snapped at us, telling us we shouldn't be at an R1 if we were so committed to teaching, we reasoned that a combination of ego and insecurity might be manifesting as aggression.

While these examples (from multiple institutions) detail specific occurrences we have experienced, they also represent patterns of behavior tied to individuals as well as patterns of bullying documented in this collection. In our own case, our interpretations of the situation were (somewhat) helpful frames that cast our colleagues' behavior as not personal; however, our explanations did not help us formulate agentive responses that would improve our workplaces. In fact, as we now realize, we were falling into the practice of using coded language to conceive of workplace bullying as simply *politics*. Although some may consider it impolite or bad form to talk about departmental politics outside of one's institutional home, when we do so with close friends and mentors we are struck by how accepted—and expected—certain behaviors are, especially in regard to writing program administration (WPA) workplaces. Institutional politics are presented as regrettable but assumed *working conditions*—a term we take up in greater detail below. As *Defining, Locating, and Addressing Bullying in the WPA Workplace* demonstrates, a culture of silence—including the use of coded

DOI: 10.7330/9781607328162.c000b

language—discourages our talking about bullying and making it more visible rather than discouraging the behaviors or the bullies.

In fact, the culture of silence is part of what inspired this collection, as it made it difficult for us to respond productively to the bullying we were experiencing. In response to the silencing and in an effort to try to understand the motivations of her bully, Cris began reading Robert I. Sutton's (2007) *The No Asshole Rule: Building a Civilized Workplace and Surviving One That Isn't.* At the same time, Cris and Beth attended the 2015 Conference on College Composition and Communication (CCCC) in Tampa, Florida—the theme of which was "Risk and Reward." There we listened to a discussion on the "role of racialized and gendered bodies as WPA practitioners" and the accompanying risks. As each speaker (including one of the contributors to this collection) described the patterned abuse they[3] had faced, we began to think of bullying as a social justice issue, with already-marginalized groups facing the highest risk. Therefore, it was this confluence of events—Cris's and Beth's own experiences with bullying, Cris's reading of *The No Asshole Rule* (Sutton 2007), the serendipitous theme chosen for CCCC 2015, and the presentations in response to that theme—that collectively gave birth to the idea for this collection.

When we issued the CFP for this collection, we were struck by how many people contacted us directly to thank us for taking on this work and often to express regret at not being able to contribute, given the possibility for retribution on their campuses. Faculty from all sorts of institutions, with varying levels of field-wide recognition, with and without tenure, worried about what it would mean to publish their experiences with bullying. We quickly learned that while this collection is an important project, it is also difficult to break the culture of silence and fear that surrounds workplace bullying. As a particularly poignant example, one of our contributors who had decided to publish under a pseudonym later withdrew from the project based on the advice of a mentor at her institution.

In acknowledgment of the risks associated with this topic, we designed a research project using surveys and interviews to capture as many experiences as possible and to give a collective voice to those who find it too risky in their current situations to speak out individually. We present the results of the survey in chapter 1. Because of limitations of space, we leave the interview data for a separate, forthcoming article in the journal *WPA: Writing Program Administration.*

We are continually inspired by and grateful to everyone who has contributed to this collection or who has encouraged us as we ventured forth in this project. In particular, we are thankful to the chapter authors; in addition to the risks of exposing oneself as having been bullied, these authors have also been forced to revisit feelings of angst, frustration, fear, anger, and sadness as they've shared their stories. We hope that by sharing these experiences, theirs and ours, we can help others name the bullying they may be experiencing for what it is. Only then can it be addressed.

However, this book is not a collection of "victim narratives." Rather, this book itself has become a form of agentive response to the bullying the chapter authors, the survey/interview participants, and we ourselves have faced. This book draws on the experiences of individuals of varying status, in different types of WPA programs, across many kinds of institutions, in order to define and locate bullying in the WPA workplace. The authors use these locations as points of departure to further theorize bullying and to provide clear advice about agentive responses. We expect this book to be useful to WPAs and other actors within the WPA workplace, including instructors, faculty who mentor graduate students, and faculty who might move into other kinds of administrative positions (e.g., department chair or dean). Graduate students will also benefit from this collection, as it works to disrupt normalized, systemic bullying often introduced in graduate school and to offer models for creating and participating in workplace civility.

As we worked on this collection, our definition of bullying evolved. We began to see as a form of bullying the common, particularly nasty reviews that are sometimes part of the peer review process. We now read the genre of Facebook posts that belittle students or disparage certain kinds of scholarship as bullying. Moreover, we discovered that it no longer feels acceptable—or ethical—to leave bullying unchecked when we witness it, even when addressing the behavior puts us at professional risk. Indeed, since beginning this project, we have worked to protect graduate students from bullying by a tenured faculty member, and one of us—despite her pre-tenure status—has taken considerable professional risk to do so. Ultimately, we hope this book will encourage and empower all of our readers to take an active role in defining, locating, and addressing bullying in their own workplace.

BULLYING IN THE WORKPLACE

According to Gina Vega and Debra R. Comer (2005, 104), "Various studies report between 38% and a terrifying 90% of the [US] workforce has experienced bullying at some point in their work lives." The large span between these figures illustrates the difficulty many scholars have faced when attempting to identify the prevalence of workplace bullying—in part because of the different terms used to describe this phenomenon, including mobbing, emotional abuse, incivility, and microaggressions, to name a few. Although the bullying described in this collection takes multiple forms—incivility, mobbing, systemic bullying—we use the overarching term *bullying* to include all of these actions and behaviors because it is the term most commonly used in reference to the academic context and because formal definitions of bullying often include the different terms listed above. In addition, US K–12 schools have begun implementing zero-tolerance bullying policies, and the media has condemned what was once normalized as a part of childhood. Our hope is that this collection will elicit similar ethical responses when it comes to bullying in the WPA workplace.

While many different behaviors can constitute bullying, they must meet the criteria that the behaviors persist over a period of time and negatively impact the target to be considered bullying. For example, one list of bullying behaviors includes harassment, social exclusion or isolation, rumors, criticism, and verbal abuse (Keashly and Neuman 2010, 49; Salin 2003, 1215). To be considered bullying, these behaviors must represent a pattern of behavior that spans a period of time, with most scholars using six months as the example time frame (Fox and Cowan 2015, 124; Keashly and Neuman 2010, 49).

Some definitions of bullying include a statement about an imbalance of power where the bully holds some sort of power over the target. However, many scholars recognize the shifting and varied nature of power, noting that bullying involves "*a perceived power imbalance*" (Salin 2003, 1214–15; original emphasis) or that regardless of power relations prior to bullying, targets lose power through the bullying interaction (Einarsen, Hoel, Zapf, and Cooper quoted in Keashly and Neuman 2010, 49). Finally, multiple scholars point out the connection between power in the workplace and power dynamics in our society writ large. In other words, people who have a minority status (for whatever reason) in our larger culture are likely to have a minority status in academia. Denise Salin (2003, 1219) notes that regardless of workplace positions and titles, "organizational power differences are . . . often connected with societal power differences and bullying often overlaps with related phenomena such as sexism or racism in the workplace."

All scholars who study bullying agree that workplace bullying has myriad negative consequences for the targets, spanning economics and mental and physical health. Vega and Comer (2005, 106) list among the consequences "depression, anxiety, aggression, insomnia, psychosomatic effects, stress, and general physical and mental ill health." Suzy Fox and Renee L. Cowan (2015, 116) list a similar set of adverse effects but also note that targets can suffer post-traumatic stress disorder and "emotional damage such as humiliation, doubt and stress; and vicious cycles of counterproductive work behavior." Bullying affects more than just the target, though, as institutions suffer costs associated with "people leaving . . . reduced productivity, and a loss of creativity and innovation" (Fox and Cowan 2015, 106). In addition, there is consensus that witnessing unchecked bullying leads to more bullying (McDaniel, Ngala, and Leonard 2015, 599; Salin 2003, 1217).

There is some contention regarding whether and how bullying is measured or assessed. Many scholars are careful to point out that it is the target who decides when bullying has occurred (Hoel, Einarsen, and Cooper 2003; Twale and DeLuca 2008). Others suggest that bullying should pass a reasonable person test, in that behaviors count as bullying when "a reasonable person would find [them] abusive" (Fox and Cowan 2015, 124). Likewise, scholars in the field of human resources are working to create objective measurements for identifying bullying to rule out the possibility that targets could be misreading a situation (e.g., Fox and Cowan 2015). The field-specific discrepancies surrounding identifying and naming bullying are likely related to the stakes associated with these acts. For human resources, jobs are on the line, so they need objective measures for bullying. In contrast, researchers who study the consequences of bullying understandably focus on the target(s) and their experiences.

Indeed, the issue of who decides what counts as bullying shows up in many of the chapters in this collection, and we can attest to at least two instances we know of personally where both the bully and the target claim to have been bullied, putting institutions in the difficult position of having to determine whose claims hold more truth—or, more commonly, whether to get involved at all. This points to the importance of documenting bullying as it occurs, particularly to establish a pattern of behavior by the bully. In this collection, our goal is not to argue the validity of the narratives included in each chapter. Instead, the narratives offer an opportunity to locate bullying, allowing the authors to further theorize their experiences and, importantly, to offer suggestions for how others can respond when facing similar situations.

BULLYING IN ACADEMIA

A growing body of research suggests that bullying is especially prevalent in higher education institutions. Leah Hollis (2012, 36) estimates the incidence of workplace bullying in higher education to be approximately 62 percent. Jamie Lester (2013, viii), in the introduction to *Workplace Bullying in Higher Education*, cites studies (Keashly and Neuman 2008; Goodyear, Reynolds, and Both Gragg 2010) that put incidence rates anywhere from 32 percent to over 80 percent. As with the research on the prevalence of workplace bullying more generally, research on workplace bullying in higher education often relies on small population sizes and a mix of terms—factors that leave us with little ability to accurately estimate the size of this problem.

Although we may not know how many people directly experience workplace bullying in academia, Loraleigh Keashly and Joel H. Neuman (2010) identify features of the academic work environment that could make bullying more likely in this context. Perhaps the most expected factor is tenure. The tenure structure ensures that it can be hard to fire someone who has tenure and creates a possibility that people will work together for long periods of time, which increases the likelihood for conflict and interpersonal aggression (Keashly and Neuman 2010, 53). In addition, because it is hard to fire someone with tenure, colleagues might turn to bullying as a way to get an unwanted colleague to leave on his or her own (Taylor 2013, 27). The tenure structure is also a competitive one that can make space for bullying. According to Salin (2003, 1223), faculty may bully other faculty members whom they perceive to be more competent so as to gain limited merit-based rewards for themselves. Finally, bullying seems to thrive in hierarchical environments, "characterized by rank structure" (Salin 2003, 1220), which the tenure structure ensures. These highly structured environments enable bullying in part by creating strict reporting lines that simultaneously make it difficult for a target of bullying to report the behavior to anyone outside their own department and allow upper administration to assume that someone else—a department chair, for example—should handle the situation. However, as authors in this collection and those we have surveyed can attest, having tenure or a higher status in the hierarchy does not necessarily protect one from being bullied.

Additional risk factors for bullying are perceptions of unfairness and frustration within one's institution more broadly. For example, faculty may find student evaluations and merit and promotion processes to be unfair, which can lead to anger, aggression, and bullying (Salin 2003, 1222; Keashly and Neuman 2010, 55–56). There might also be growing frustration related to budget cuts, which affect both class sizes and salary increases (Keashly and Neuman 2010, 58). In fact, the restructuring that accompanies budget cuts and changes in administration can be a trigger for bullying (Salin 2003, 1224–25). According to Lester (2013, xi), "Bullying is known to be highly correlated with leadership changes and resource shortages."

Finally, Salin (2003, 1220) notes that large institutions seem to provide safety for bullies because of their size and the lack of willingness by upper management to respond to bullying. This last point cannot be overstated, as it shows up in many of the chapters in this collection and was a constant thread in our interviews. In our own personal experiences, it is not just upper management that chooses not to respond to bullies; other colleagues in positions to support us have responded with empathy, not action. For example, we have been advised "to choose your battles," which really means the person who could be an ally is not choosing *this* battle; "to keep our heads down," which suggests that we should not defend ourselves; or "to put on our big-girl pants," advising us to develop thicker skin so we can endure the bullying these colleagues choose not to address. Our point in offering these examples is to highlight the endemic problem and the likely familiar language that allows bullying to continue on our campuses, in our departments.

BULLYING IN THE WPA WORKPLACE

While the research on bullying in academia does not focus on administrative positions specifically, some scholarship suggests that administrators—such as WPAs—may be at a higher risk for being targets of bullying (Fratzl and McKay 2013, 61). Furthermore, according to Karen Rogers McDaniel, Florence Ngala, and Karen Moustafa Leonard (2015, 600), administrators who see their work as filling a social need or contributing to a social good are especially vulnerable, as being bullied while doing this kind of work "adds to the emotional strain already inherent in the work." (Of course, as some of our survey participants and contributors to this collection acknowledge, WPAs themselves are sometimes the bullies.)

The concept of bullying is not new to the field of WPA, although we may not have identified it previously as such. Much of WPA literature has addressed issues of power associated with WPA work (e.g., Bailiff, Davis, and Mountford 2008; Dew and Horning 2007; Edgington and Gallaher 2009; Enos and Borrowman 2008; George 1999). However, workplace bullying has not yet received focused attention in WPA scholarship. Despite acknowledgment of the challenges WPAs face, there has yet to be a collection that focuses on defining, locating, and addressing bullying in the WPA workplace—including perspectives from non- or pre-tenured WPAs,

WPAs from underrepresented social groups, and WPAs responding to the bullying of others (e.g., students, staff, faculty). This, we believe, leaves workplace bullying largely unnamed and under-theorized, forcing WPAs into the vulnerable position of having to seek out resources and advice on their own or to read between the lines of what has been published.

One location where this reading between the lines seems to be necessary is in Debra Frank Dew and Alice Horning's *Untenured Faculty as Writing Program Administrators: Institutional Practices and Politics* (2007). For example, in the preface to the collection, Edward M. White (2007, vii) describes the only recent valuing of WPA work among "traditional English departments" and how, still, "on a few campuses, writing programs have left indifferent or hostile English departments and established new homes in more friendly territory for teachers and administrators." While not explicitly framing it as bullying, White (2007) hints at the lack of respect generally shown to WPAs as individuals and to the field more broadly. This lack of respect and the hostility referenced can be forms of bullying and are not only risks for pre-tenured WPAs, as this current collection will show. As Horning (2007, 4) herself writes, "Even those with tenure do fall into political disfavor and are subsequently released from their WPA duties, despite the success of their programs."

Of course, this hostility or bullying does not take place only in traditional English departments where literature colleagues may have more power in numbers. As this collection reveals, our own rhetoric and composition colleagues can be among the worst perpetrators. Horning (2007, 7) argues that "senior faculty, department chairs, and other mentors need to help jWPAs negotiate the turbulent waters of running a program," but how does one respond when these are the same people, within our own programs, who stir up those waters?

However, the more senior colleagues that Horning (2007) suggests one turn to may themselves be among the bullied. Joseph Eng (2007), for example, offers an at-times-painful look at what WPA life can be like at two different institutions for a non-white, non-native English–speaking administrator when colleagues and graduate students make assumptions about his knowledge of grammar (good or bad), offer unsolicited opinions about which discipline he should be working in (e.g., ESL), and scrutinize his formal and informal written communication. Eng examines these inappropriate, unwanted acts in relation to his identity, but he does not at the time of writing in 2007 refer to these acts as microaggressions or patterns of bullying, as we might today.

Other publications also hint at or describe experiences within WPA work that may be recognized as bullying but weren't identified as such in the context in which they were written. In *Kitchen Cooks, Plate Twirlers, and Troubadours: Writing Program Administrators Tell Their Stories*, editor Diana George (1999, 64) refers to the challenges of "sexual politics and disciplinary lines drawn in the sand." In the same collection, Nancy Barbara Conroy Maloney Grimm (1999, 14) likens her status to that of an Irish maid relegated to the downstairs quarters, as she is "marginalized and excluded from decisions that have a direct impact on [her] work." Mara Holt (1999, 27) writes of her own questioning "about the validity of my 'oppression'" in the face of "gender politics." As stated above, "politics" can simply be a euphemism for bullying, which is often accompanied by the doubt Holt expresses about her own experiences and how to characterize them.

Another seemingly common euphemism for bullying in WPA scholarship is *working conditions.* Or, perhaps better said, clear patterns of bullying are often inappropriately conflated with the material circumstances of WPA work when narrating our working conditions. In his foreword to *The Promise and Perils of Writing Program Administration*, John Trimbur (2008, ix), in reference to George (1999), lists "meetings, e-mail, mentoring, phone calls, public relations, networking, annual reports, and daily multitasking" as examples of WPA material circumstances at the same time he refers to WPAs as "mid-level managers" who perform these tasks while caught "between the staff they manage and the supervisors they report to." It's this casual reference to being "caught in the middle" (Trimbur 2008, ix) or being part of "a beleaguered group" (Bruffee quoted in Rose 2008, 28) that we take issue with, as it is this aspect of our "working conditions" that is largely assumed and unaddressed, as the following narrative from Randall McClure (2008, 104; original emphasis) illustrates: "For example, a senior faculty member once took offense in a department meeting to my use of the term *composition program* to describe our developmental and FYC [first-year composition] courses. She quipped, 'We do not have a composition program, just some courses.' The idea, I think, was to make it clear that I, as a junior faculty member, was not in charge of any program, and if I were in charge of anything, it was *just* a course or two in *comp* [as opposed to *real* writing]."

The material circumstances of McClure's situation are the actions he took to improve the TA program at his institution and his consequential strengthening of the composition program. His colleague's derisive attitude in response to this work, in contrast, is not a material circumstance. It is not something to be expected. Or accepted. It is just plain incivility—and if part of a larger pattern, it is workplace bullying. It is this aspect of a WPA's working conditions that is rarely addressed and that gets hidden—and protected—by our coded language.

Other material circumstances that WPAs might unfortunately expect include budgetary constraints, a lack of transparency in the tenure and promotion process, and what is often perceived as the paternalistic hierarchy maintained in academia. WPA scholarship has collected a number of narratives about the special challenges these circumstances bring to our work lives (see Dew and Horning 2007; Enos and Borrowman 2008; George 1999). However, rarely do these narratives separate out from one's material circumstances the aggressive attitudes of others that can accompany this work. Elizabeth Hodges's narrative is a rare exception. In her chapter "At the Pleasure of the Chair: A Cautionary Tale from the Private Side of the Public Story," Hodges (2008, 232) recounts the patterns of abuse she experienced over a period of years in a new faculty/WPA position, ranging from colleagues' attacks on her character to their open disregard for her work and her discipline to the anonymous grievance(s) made against her, "thus denying the alleged guilty [party the opportunity] to face [her] accuser." Hodges (2008, 232) identifies her patterns of experiences within the department as "workplace mobbing," a form of bullying.

It is a grave mistake not to separate out from one's material circumstances within WPA work the deliberate actions performed by others that aim to impede or disparage that work. By not identifying patterns of bullying for what they are, we not only make it all the more difficult to address bullying, but we also end up normalizing these patterns as something that comes with the job, as something to be expected as a part of "working conditions."

Perhaps even worse is when we problematize not the working conditions but the WPAs themselves. For example, Shirley K Rose (2008, 21) admits that her initial response to jWPA (junior WPA) narratives about the promises and perils of doing WPA work pre-tenure was to characterize the jWPAs as "naive and uninformed" rather than "powerless or overworked" and perhaps deaf to the "well-meaning and sound advice of would-be mentors," only then to acknowledge that these initial responses were not merited. As Rose might, we ask our readers to reconsider the ways we have unjustly characterized individuals, particularly jWPAs and gWPAs (graduate student WPAs), in the literature and through the "common sense" advice we have offered WPAs in response to what could be identified as bullying.

When we simply advise junior faculty and graduate students not to take WPA positions because they are unprepared for the "working conditions" and "politics" they are likely to face, we participate in a type of victim blaming that is already so prevalent in rape culture, discourses of whiteness, and other forms of systemic oppression and violence. We blame the bullied for their lack of preparation (or experience/status/tenure) in attending to the "politics" of the situation rather than blaming the perpetrator for inappropriate, unprofessional, and unethical behavior. And, as within rape culture, we rarely see the perpetrators of bullying in academia held accountable.

With this collection, by identifying bullying for what it is, we hope to stop the recursive cycle that in the past has been perpetuated even by our own scholarship when we don't recognize bullying for what it is.

BULLYING IN THIS COLLECTION

The following chapters provide a comprehensive description of bullying in the WPA workplace: they define bullying within specific institutional contexts, showing how many actions can become bullying when they represent a pattern of behavior that creates professional and personal harm; they describe various forms of bullying, including microaggressions, incivility, mobbing, and emotional abuse; they define bullying as institutional racism, "academic systemic incivility," a crisis of insularity, and faculty fundamentalism; they locate bullying in research institutions, small liberal arts colleges, community colleges, and in writing programs and writing centers. Of course, not all contexts and circumstances of bullying may be covered in this collection, and we do not address matters of sexual harassment, which is distinct from, though often accompanied by, bullying behaviors. However, we hope readers will find the defining, locating, and addressing of bullying discussed within to be useful and applicable to other instances of bullying in the WPA workplace.

The narratives in each of the chapters outlined below represent the authors' memories and interpretations of their experiences. While it is possible, even likely, that other people involved in these situations would characterize them differently, that is not of utmost importance to the aims of this collection. The primary contributions of this collection are not necessarily the narratives themselves—as engaging as they are; the major contributions are the theoretical grounding of the experiences, the naming of patterns of behaviors as bullying, the resistance against ideologies of normalcy, and, most of all, the agentive responses to bullying that readers can apply to their own contexts.

In the opening chapter, Bethany Davila and Cristyn L. Elder report on survey data collected from stakeholders in WPA workplaces across the United States on their experiences with bullying. The authors use these data to establish the scope and patterns of bullying in the WPA workplace, to define various behaviors linked to bullying, and to contextualize the scholarship on bullying in our field.

Chapter 2 is a reprinted manuscript by Harry Denny with a new coda. The chapter argues that while we are able to recognize very public and tragic instances of bullying, most of the time workplace bullying has become so normalized that we fail to recognize it. Denny, who situates his experiences of bullying within the writing center and in response to his sexual identity, calls for us to learn to identify this form of everyday oppression so we can be allies for those in need. He leaves us with a perhaps now familiar refrain but important reminder: we cannot wait until "it gets better."

In chapter 3, Aurora Matzke, Sherry Rankins-Robertson, and Bre Garrett suggest that the everyday nature of bullying is attributed to a culture of bullying embedded in academia that begins in graduate school and extends across institutions and designations of tenure. They locate bullying in their experiences as three female WPAs at different institutions and at various stages of tenure, complicating traditional notions of power that center on top-down bullying between tenured faculty or administrators and pre-tenure WPAs. Finally, they provide specific strategies for counteracting and surviving bullying in the WPA workplace.

Sarah Allen, in chapter 4, offers an explanation for one way bullying becomes part of the culture of a department. She draws on Sharon Crowley's (2006) *Toward a Civil Discourse: Rhetoric and Fundamentalism* to define academic fundamentalism as a precursor to bullying. Allen draws parallels to the political context of the Trump presidency, in which citizens are polarized, dissenting voices cannot be heard, we are haunted by threats of violence, and individuals no longer choose to participate in democratic practices. In addition, Allen shows how complicated bullying can become when sometimes the bullied bully back. She then offers recommendations on how to work toward civility under such circumstances in the WPA workplace.

In chapter 5, Dawn Fels demonstrates that in addition to being part of the academic culture, risk factors for being bullied are often related to other systems of oppression—in this case, contingent labor. Fels examines the experiences of contingent writing center directors, which she has collected over a three-year period through interviews. She uses these data to highlight the particular difficulty this group faces in finding "justice" when bullied, the effects this bullying has, and what can be done about it.

Another system of oppression that can result in bullying is institutional-ized racism. In the sixth chapter, Andrea Dardello combines the political genre of testimonial with academic research to illustrate the importance of resisting silence, which she argues has the power to erase bullying and "forfeit the change that can happen if I but dare to speak" (104). Dardello's experience—being publicly ridiculed and forced out of her administrative position at a community college because she resisted the department chair's characterization of her as hostile—in combination with scholarship, defines bullying as a manifestation of institutionalized racism used to disempower her, an African American female.

Staci Perryman-Clark, in chapter 7, continues to explore the relation-ship between bullying and race by locating bullying within racialized interactions and tactics steeped in white privilege. Specifically, she describes attempts by a graduate student teaching assistant, with the sup-port of a tenured faculty member, to undermine her authority and their efforts to remove her from her administrative position. By locating and defining bullying in terms of tenure, race, and gender, Perryman-Clark identifies the possibilities of white ally-ship to address the bullying of WPAs of color—especially those who are pre-tenure.

In chapter 8, Erec Smith teaches us that the combination of bully-ing and racism can lead to academic insularity and mobbing against the "other." Smith describes the bullying he experienced as a form of insularity and racism while a writing center director, "diversity worker," and single academic in rhetoric and composition at a former institution. As Smith writes, "The insularity that creates a disdain for rhetoric and composition also creates a xenophobia that discourages cultural diver-sity within academia. As a black man—one carrying a torch for diversi-fication to boot—I was a reminder of the outside world that was always threatening" (146). Smith argues that these forms of insularity, which in his case manifested as bullying, are a crisis that must be addressed.

Mobbing is again taken up in Amy Heckathorn's chapter. Heckathorn examines bullying as it relates to a familiar disciplinary divide that arises with the lack of acknowledgment of rhetoric and composition as a field and the expertise that academics in the field represent. However, she shows that, in her experience, the mobbing extended beyond the department and quickly cut the writing program off from all available resources to address the situation. As a solution, Heckathorn calls for independent writing programs, providing an overview of the benefits and challenges this response to bullying can bring.

While Heckathorn describes bullying that spans an institution, in chapter 10, W. Gary Griswold locates bullying at the level of a university system. He defines the bullying he (and many other faculty members in the California State University [CSU] system) experienced as "Academic Systemic Incivility" (ASI), describing tactics used by administrators in the CSU system to enforce a mandated remediation program the faculty vehemently opposed. Ultimately, Griswold suggests that WPAs can counteract ASI by becoming—or recognizing their role as—servant leaders, thereby creating a model of civility.

NOTES

1. The authors contributed equally in the writing of this chapter.
2. In this collection we use *pre-tenure* to indicate those on the tenure track who have not yet gone through tenure, whereas *non-tenured* refers to those not on the tenure track.
3. This collection follows the NCTE (2012) recommended *Guidelines for Gender-Fair Use of Language* at http://www2.ncte.org/statements//genderfairuseoflang.

REFERENCES

Bailiff, Michelle, Diane Davis, and Roxanne Mountford. 2008. *Women's Ways of Making It in Rhetoric and Composition.* New York: Routledge.

Crowley, Sharon. 2006. *Toward a Civil Discourse: Rhetoric and Fundamentalism.* Pittsburgh: University of Pittsburgh Press. https://doi.org/10.2307/j.ctt5hjng7.

Dew, Debra Frank, and Alice Horning, eds. 2007. *Untenured Faculty as Writing Program Administrators: Institutional Practices and Politics.* West Lafayette, IN: Parlor.

Edgington, Anthony, and Robin Gallaher, eds. 2009. *Junior Faculty and Graduate Student Administration Issues (WPA-CompPile Research Bibliographies, no. 1.).* Council of Writing Program Administrators and CompPile. http://comppile.org/wpa/bibliographies/Bib1/Edgington_Gallaher.pdf.

Eng, Joseph. 2007. "Demystifying the Asian-American WPA: Location in Writing, Teaching, and Program Administration." In *Untenured Faculty as Writing Program Administrators: Institutional Practices and Politics,* ed. Debra Frank Dew and Alice Horning, 153–71. West Lafayette, IN: Parlor.

Enos, Theresa, and Shane Borrowman, eds. 2008. *The Promise and Perils of Writing Program Administration.* West Lafayette, IN: Parlor.

Fox, Suzy, and Renee L. Cowan. 2015. "Revision of the Workplace Bullying Checklist: The Importance of Human Resource Management's Role in Defining and Addressing Workplace Bullying." *Human Resource Management Journal* 25 (1): 116–30. https://doi.org/10.1111/1748-8583.12049.

Fratzl, Jae, and Ruth McKay. 2013. "Professional Staff in Academia: Academic Culture and the Role of Aggression." In *Workplace Bullying in Higher Education,* ed. Jaime Lester, 60–73. New York: Routledge.

George, Diana, ed. 1999. *Kitchen Cooks, Plate Twirlers, and Troubadours: Writing Program Administrators Tell Their Stories.* Portsmouth, NH: Boynton/Cook.

Goodyear, Rod K., Pauline Reynolds, and Janee Both Gragg. 2010. "University Faculty Experiences of Classroom Incivilities: A Critical-Incident Study." Paper presented at the American Educational Research Association annual conference, April 30–May 3, 2010, Denver, CO.

Grimm, Nancy Barbara Conroy Maloney. 1999. "'The Way the Rich People Does It': Reflections on Writing Center Administration and the Search for Status." In *Kitchen Cooks, Plate Twirlers, and Troubadours: Writing Program Administrators Tell Their Stories,* ed. Diana George, 14–25. Portsmouth, NH: Boynton/Cook.

Hodges, Elizabeth. 2008. "At the Pleasure of the Chair: A Cautionary Tale from the Private Side of the Public Story." In *The Promise and Perils of Writing Program Administration*, ed. Theresa Enos and Shane Borrowman, 225–37. West Lafayette, IN: Parlor.

Hoel, Helge, Ståle Einarsen, and Cary L. Cooper. 2003. "Organisational Effects of Bullying." In *Bullying and Emotional Abuse in the Workplace: International Perspectives in Research and Practice*, eds. Ståle Einarsen, Helge Hoel, Dieter Zapf, and Cary Cooper, 2–30. New York: Taylor and Francis.

Hollis, Leah. 2012. *Bully in the Ivory Tower: How Aggression and Incivility Erode American Higher Education*. Wilmington, DE: Patricia Berkly LLC.

Holt, Mara. 1999. "On Coming to Voice." In *Kitchen Cooks, Plate Twirlers, and Troubadours: Writing Program Administrators Tell Their Stories*, ed. Diana George, 26–43. Portsmouth, NH: Boynton/Cook.

Horning, Alice. 2007. "Introduction: What Is Wrong with THIS Picture?" In *Untenured Faculty as Writing Program Administrators: Institutional Practices and Politics*, ed. Debra Frank Dew and Alice Horning, 3–12. West Lafayette, IN: Parlor. https://doi.org/10.1053/sonc.2003.50036.

Keashly, Loraleigh, and Joel H. Neuman. 2008. *Final Report: Workplace Behavior (Bullying) Project Survey*. Mankato: Minnesota State University. https://www.mnsu.edu/csw/work placebullying/workplace_bullying_final_report.pdf.

Keashly, Loraleigh, and Joel H. Neuman. 2010. "Faculty Experiences with Bullying in Higher Education: Causes, Consequences, and Management." *Administrative Theory and Praxis* 32 (1): 48–70. https://doi.org/10.2753/ATP1084-1806320103.

Lester, Jaime, ed. 2013. *Workplace Bullying in Higher Education*. New York: Routledge.

McClure, Randall. 2008. "An Army of One: The Possibilities and Pitfalls of WPA Work for the Lone Compositionist." In *The Promise and Perils of Writing Program Administration*, ed. Theresa Enos and Shane Borrowman, 102–9. West Lafayette, IN: Parlor.

McDaniel, Karen Rogers, Florence Ngala, and Karen Moustafa Leonard. 2015. "Does Competency Matter? Competency as a Factor in Workplace Bullying." *Journal of Managerial Psychology* 30 (5): 597–609. https://doi.org/10.1108/JMP-02-2013-0046.

National Council of Teachers of English (NCTE). 2002. *Guidelines for Gender-Fair Use of Language*. http://www2.ncte.org/statements/genderfairuseoflang.

Rose, Shirley K. 2008. "'Creating a Context': The Institutional Logic of the Council of Writing Program Administrators' Development of the Evaluator Service." In *The Promise and Perils of Writing Program Administration*, ed. Theresa Enos and Shane Borrowman, 21–46. West Lafayette, IN: Parlor.

Salin, Denise. 2003. "Ways of Explaining Workplace Bullying: A Review of Enabling, Motivating, and Precipitating Structures and Processes in the Work Environment." *Human Relations* 56 (10): 1213–32. https://doi.org/10.1177/00187267035610003.

Sutton, Robert I. 2007. *The No Asshole Rule: Building a Civilized Workplace and Surviving One That Isn't*. New York: Business Plus.

Taylor, Susan. 2013. "Workplace Bullying: Does Tenure Change Anything?" In *Workplace Bullying in Higher Education*, ed. Jaime Lester, 23–40. New York: Routledge.

Trimbur, John. 2008. "Foreword." In *The Promise and Perils of Writing Program Administration*, ed. Theresa Enos and Shane Borrowman, ix–xiv. West Lafayette, IN: Parlor.

Twale, Darla J., and Barbara M. De Luca. 2008. *Faculty Incivility: The Rise of the Academic Bully Culture and What to Do about It*. San Francisco: Jossey-Bass.

Vega, Gina, and Debra R. Comer. 2005. "Sticks and Stones May Break Your Bones, but Words Can Break Your Spirit: Bullying in the Workplace." *Journal of Business Ethics* 58 (1–3): 101–9. https://doi.org/10.1007/s10551-005-1422-7.

White, Edward M. 2007. "Preface." In *Untenured Faculty as Writing Program Administrators: Institutional Practices and Politics*, ed. Debra Frank Dew and Alice Horning, vii–ix. West Lafayette, IN: Parlor.

1

"SHOCKED BY THE INCIVILITY"
A Survey of Bullying in the WPA Workplace

Bethany Davila and Cristyn L. Elder

In their opening chapter to *The Promise and Perils of Writing Program Administration*, Jillian Skeffington, Shane Borrowman, and Theresa Enos (2008) identify ways writing program administrators (WPAs) (most of whom are women and many of whom, whether male or female, are junior faculty) fight to do their jobs.[1] They provide examples of both the professional and personal challenges WPAs can face and share the results of their "Web survey of WPAs," designed "to profile the work of writing program administrators in broad strokes" (Skeffington, Borrowman, and Enos 2008, 8). The authors begin their discussion by listing the questions they did *not* ask, including, as they note, the most important yet implicit question "are you okay," a question to which "many junior faculty with administrative duties cannot respond positively on either a personal or professional level" (Skeffington, Borrowman, and Enos 2008, 9). In many ways, we designed our survey—the focus of this chapter—to address an aspect of that unstated question ("are you okay?") by asking WPAs and those who work in the WPA workplace whether they have experienced bullying and, if so, to describe the details of those experiences. Through the results of our survey, we identified bullying as a common peril in the WPA workplace. In addition to contributing to WPA scholarship on what has heretofore been termed *working conditions* or *politics* (phrases we take issue with in the introduction to this collection), this chapter also contributes to scholarship on bullying in higher education by defining the categories of the Negative Acts Questionnaire–Revised (NAQ-R)—a research instrument used to collect data on workplace bullying in primarily Anglophone settings—and by identifying an additional category that is relevant to and perhaps beyond the WPA workplace.

Ultimately, this chapter describes the scope of bullying in the WPA workplace as well as the prevalent patterns within the broad term *workplace bullying*. Through this work, we aim to draw attention to

DOI: 10.7330/9781607328162.c001

unacceptable behaviors that have been largely normalized and often go unaddressed. By showing the unacceptable prevalence of bullying in the WPA workplace, we will not only send the message to targets of bullying that they are not alone, but we also hope to inspire others to work against the behaviors and patterns described below. In other words, we intend for this chapter to serve as a call to action for our field.

THE SURVEY

To investigate the extent of bullying in the WPA workplace, we surveyed and interviewed self-identified stakeholders in writing programs at colleges and universities across the United States. In this chapter we will share the results of this survey, which sought to answer these questions: what does bullying in the WPA workplace look like, and how often does it occur?

We began the anonymous online survey by asking participants (recruited through professional academic listservs, namely, WPA-L, BW-L, WAC-L, and SLW-L) if, based on the one definition of bullying we provided,[2] they had been bullied in relation to their work in the WPA workplace. For participants who answered "yes," we asked them to describe their experiences. In addition and alternatively, participants were given the option to provide their contact information so we could interview them about these experiences.[3] Our goals with these first two questions were to identify the scope of bullying in the WPA workplace and to collect information about the kinds of bullying people have experienced.

The next section of our survey followed an established method of measuring workplace bullying: asking participants to read a list of acts or behaviors and to indicate how frequently, if at all, they had experienced each of those acts in the previous twelve months. The list we used was a slightly adapted version[4] of the NAQ-R, which is "a reliable, valid, comprehensive, yet relatively short scale, tailor-made for use in a variety of occupational settings" (Einarsen, Hoel, and Notelaers 2009, 27). The full list of the acts and behaviors is included with our findings in this chapter. We followed the protocol tested in association with the NAQ-R and asked participants to limit their responses to a specific time frame (the previous twelve months). This time frame helps distinguish between bullying, which involves "repetition (frequency), duration (over a period of time) and patterning (of a variety of behaviors involved)," and other negative but isolated workplace experiences (Einarsen, Hoel, and Notelaers 2009, 25). However, a few respondents specifically stated either that they did not follow those directions or that if they hadn't done so, their answers would have been considerably different, as their experiences with bullying happened at prior institutions and didn't fit within the twelve-month time frame. Participants' answers to this section of the survey help us better understand the kinds of bullying WPAs might face and the frequency of specific acts of bullying.

Finally, the survey collected demographic information and (again) asked participants to provide contact information if they were willing to participate in a follow-up interview.

PARTICIPANTS

A total of 124 people answered at least one question in the survey. However, only 114 participants provided demographic information by answering one or more of the questions at the end of the survey, and 104 of those respondents also reported having experienced bullying. Because the rest of the chapter focuses on the responses of those who both completed the survey and experienced bullying and because 50 percent of those who did not report bullying also did not provide demographic information, we report only on demographic information for the 104 participants who reported on their bullying experiences. See Appendix 1.B for data from the ten respondents who did not report experiencing bullying but did provide demographic information.

Of those who reported experiencing bullying, the majority (74%) of respondents were between the ages of thirty and sixty, indicating that the issue of bullying spans careers, from early to late. Sixty-five percent identified as female, 22 percent as male, 1 person as transgender, and 1 person as "cis"; roughly 11 percent did not respond. Approximately 80 percent identified as white, Caucasian, or Anglo. The remaining respondents identified as Asian (2%), Hispanic (2%), African American (less than 1%), multi-racial (2%), or "other" (less than 1%); nearly 13 percent did not respond to this question.

The combined majority of respondents to our survey had tenure (38%) or were on the tenure track (19%), indicating that for this group tenure did not offer foolproof protection against experiencing bullying. Fifteen percent were non-tenure-track administrators, just under 4 percent were lecturers, 3 percent were graduate students, and nearly 11 percent noted that their positions either spanned these categories or weren't represented in the options we provided; approximately 11 percent did not provide this demographic information.

Most of our respondents were employed at research institutions (39%) and liberal arts colleges (28%). Nearly 7 percent worked at community colleges, and just under 3 percent were at technical/professional colleges. About 13 percent worked at institutions that do not fit those categories, and approximately 11 percent did not provide this demographic information.

FREQUENCY AND TYPES OF BULLYING IN THE WPA WORKPLACE

Of the 123 people who responded to survey question #1 on whether they had experienced bullying in relation to their work in the WPA workplace, an initial 77 respondents (63%) indicated that they had. However, an additional 27 respondents who said no initially to question #1 and 1 person who didn't answer the question went on to report having frequently or occasionally experienced behaviors listed on the NAQ-R. Therefore, 105 respondents (85%) reported having experienced bullying in the WPA workplace. This figure is on the high end of the prevalence range (38%–90%) previously documented in higher education and US workplaces more broadly (Vega and Comer 2005, 104). Of course, we can't know if this accurately represents the prevalence of bullying in the WPA workplace; it could be that those who completed our survey did so because of their previous experiences with bullying. However, the responses we received do illustrate that bullying in the WPA workplace is an issue that needs to be addressed.

Among the 105 survey respondents who reported that they had experienced bullying in the WPA workplace, more than 50 percent indicated that they frequently or occasionally experienced this bullying in one or more of the following ways:

- Being ignored or excluded (67%)
- Someone withholding information which affects your performance (59%)
- Having your opinions ignored (59%)
- Spreading of gossip and rumors about you (52%)

Furthermore, 34%–45% or more of participants noted that they frequently or occasionally experienced these bullying behaviors:

- Being ignored or facing a hostile reaction when you approach (45%)
- Being humiliated or ridiculed in connection with your work (45%)
- Being exposed to an unmanageable workload (41%)
- Being shouted at or being the target of spontaneous anger (41%)
- Being ordered to work below your level of competence (40%)
- Excessive monitoring of your work (38%)
- Having insulting or offensive remarks made about your person, attitude, or your private life (36%)

- Having key areas of responsibility removed or replaced with more trivial or unpleasant tasks (34%)

Finally, fewer than 30 percent of respondents reported that they frequently or occasionally experienced the remaining behaviors/ responses:

- Persistent criticism of your errors or mistakes (28%)
- Repeated reminders of your errors or mistakes (26%)
- Having allegations made against you (24%)
- Being given tasks with unreasonable deadlines (22%)
- Pressure not to claim something to which by right you are entitled (sick leave, travel expenses, etc.) (20%)
- Hints or signals from others that you should quit your job (18%)
- Intimidating behaviors such as finger-pointing, invasion of personal space, shoving, blocking your way (17%)
- Being the subject of excessive teasing and sarcasm (14%)
- Threats of violence or physical abuse or actual abuse (2%)
- Practical jokes carried out by people you don't get along with (0%)

These results tell us that in addition to the high prevalence of bullying in the WPA workplace recorded in this survey, the respondents most often experienced behaviors that held them or their work at a distance and maligned them or their work.

EXPERIENCES OF BEING BULLIED IN THE WPA WORKPLACE

In survey question #2, we asked participants to describe their experiences of being bullied in the WPA workplace (or to provide contact information so we could interview them about these experiences, or both). Because the NAQ-R categories listed above are not defined in the literature on workplace bullying, the fifty-two qualitative responses that describe participants' experiences with bullying (which includes all responses to question #2 except for the responses that only provided contact information) allowed us to define these categories through examples and by differentiating categories. In addition, these responses revealed an additional category that does not appear in the NAQ-R—threats to job security—which we discuss with the other categories below. To put the responses to question #2 in conversation with the NAQ-R, we first coded the data according to the NAQ-R categories listed above and then used respondents' language and specific experiences to provide dimension to those categories. It is important to note that we sometimes coded experiences in multiple NAQ-R categories. For example, when respondents described a pattern of behavior in which their bully or bullies "demanded reports immediately," we coded this in the categories "being exposed to an unmanageable workload" and "being given tasks with unreasonable deadlines," as that kind of behavior fits both categories equally well. Coding qualitative data in multiple categories reflects our belief that forcing a behavior or interaction into only one category would involve privileging one interpretation over another. In addition, coding data in multiple categories allows us to better understand the related and overlapping relationship among the categories of the NAQ-R.

Below, we define the NAQ-R categories and group them according to the effect of the bullying behaviors on respondents: exclusion and isolation, undermining individuals and programs, exerting control over individuals and programs, and verbal and physical intimidation.

Exclusion and Isolation

As noted above, survey respondents reported that they experienced *being ignored or excluded* (67%) frequently or occasionally in the past twelve months. This behavior is very similar to the behavior *having your opinions ignored* (59%). To distinguish between the two, we coded responses related to silencing or dismissing a person under the first behavior and the dismissal of someone's expertise or authority under the second. Examples of *being ignored or excluded* include participants being told that they "weren't supposed to speak" or weren't allowed "to bring up concerns" in various meetings. One participant even noted that the individual was "deliberately left out of meetings." In some instances colleagues or administrators wouldn't talk to the respondent at all. Behaviors in this category ignore people through exclusion. *Having your opinions ignored*, in contrast, involves silencing, demeaning, or undermining a person's ideas. Multiple respondents described experiences with taking on an intensive project, presenting results, and then "learn[ing others] had gone behind my back to reverse the decision or put something else into place." In another example, a respondent noted that the person's dean had told them that "WPA work was less important (and less intellectual) than that of my colleagues." In this case, the person's entire field had been ignored because it was perceived as "less important and less intellectual" in comparison to the other fields represented in the department. A third, related category, *being ignored or facing a hostile reaction when you approach* (45%), places emphasis on physical interactions and the moment of encounter. There are no examples of this type of bullying in the qualitative data.

The category *someone withholding information which affects your perfor-mance* (59%) includes experiences with withheld resources as well as information. Sometimes bullies blocked respondents' access to infor-mation, meetings, or data. Other times they "stole" from WPA budgets, changed reporting lines, or denied support when respondents came to them for help with unethical situations and behaviors. In all of these examples, the withholding of information and resources had negative consequences for the targets' work performance and efficacy. Because the participants had the right to access the withheld information and resources, this category—in the context of the WPA workplace—overlaps almost entirely with the category *pressure not to claim something to which by right you are entitled* (20%). This latter category also included an example of a respondent being bullied into not claiming the right to "teach for another program."

Undermining Individuals and Programs

Although the category *spreading of gossip and rumors about you* (52%) might seem self-evident and does include gossip and rumors about individuals, most of the responses that fell within this category had to do with gossip and rumors related to a writing program. For example, two respondents noted that faculty members spoke poorly of their rhetoric and composition graduate program or courses to students. Another WPA cited an experience with a department administrator in which the individual was coerced into agreeing with the administrator or he would "raise caps on comp courses and tell people it was [the WPA's] fault." Several respondents noted that gossip and rumors were used as a method of undermining their authority within their depart-ment, college, or institution. As such, this category is similar to *hav-ing allegations made against you* (24%), in part because comments are made without the target present. However, the latter category includes descriptions of specific complaints or charges (even if inferred) as opposed to gossip and rumors that are more general. For example, some respondents were accused of "insubordination," of "changing policies and procedures," of not doing their jobs, or of being unquali-fied for their positions.

Another category, *being humiliated or ridiculed in connection with your work* (45%), also undermines a person's or program's authority; how-ever, the behavior in this category was directed at the target. In other words, instead of bullies talking to others about a WPA, the writing program, or both, the targets described bullies who confronted them *directly* to "belittle," "insult," "harass," "demean," "embarrass," "criticize," "admonish," "berate," and "humiliate" the targets, their programs, or both. Bullies also belittle people who work in the WPA workplace through *persistent criticism of your errors or mistakes* (28%). All of the descriptions in this category recount persistent criticism; however, we take issue with the notion that the criticism is warranted, as may be implied by describing the focus of criticism as "your errors or mistakes." Instead, this category would be more aptly titled *persistent criticism of your work or program*. Respondents described bullies "tak[ing] great pleasure" in these criticisms, which can focus on "work quality," "every idea the person presented," "the WAC [writing across the curriculum] program and the WC [writing center]," someone's teaching, or a person's "performance." We differentiate this category from *repeated reminders of your errors or mistakes* (26%), which also implies that errors and mistakes may have actually been made and includes an emphasis on repeated reminders. While this latter category is represented in the quantitative data, examples of it do not appear in the qualitative data.

Finally, bullies sometimes focus entirely on an individual as a being (in contrast to the individual in relation to his or her work or program, as described in the two categories above). Those behaviors fall in the category *having insulting or offensive remarks made about your person, attitude, or your private life* (36%). For example, one person wrote that the individual's bully, a supervisor, identified his or her personal flaw—according to a required personality quiz—as "boring" and identified a colleague's weakness as being "flaky." Another person described being belittled about more than just his or her work (including, for example, hobbies and interests) as a form of "repeated, sustained insult." Occasionally, respondents noted certain identity categories as the target of these insults, such as age (i.e., young or old) and gender (i.e., female or transgender).

Two other categories—*being the subject of excessive teasing and sarcasm* (14%) and *practical jokes carried out by people you don't get along with* (0%)— also result in undermining a person and the writing program. However, none of the respondents' qualitative examples fit into these categories.

Exerting Control over Individuals and Programs

Some respondents described experiences of *excessive monitoring of your work* (38%) that included being policed in terms of their hours on campus and who they were allowed to socialize with. Others described bullies who insisted on reviewing emails before they were sent and conference presentations before they were given. One respondent noted that she was given a list of terms she wasn't allowed to use when talking about writing and writers on campus. Another behavior that exerts control over those in the WPA workplace is *being exposed to an unmanageable workload* (41%). Despite the 41 percent of respondents who indicated that this happens frequently or occasionally in their workplace, there weren't many examples of these behaviors in the qualitative data. The few descriptions we have include being "deluge[d] . . . with unreasonably overwritten documents," which a participant labeled as "obstruction"; "being asked to take on a certain set of duties pre-tenure or without resources," which we interpreted to mean that the work was unmanageable; and a pattern of "demanding reports immediately." This last response we also coded in the related category *being given tasks with unreasonable deadlines* (22%), the only response coded in this category.

By and large, the responses that fit in the category *being ordered to work below your level of competence* (40%) describe experiences wherein people were not allowed to participate fully in the writing program. For example, one person described "being given orders as to how to perform" and not being "allowed to go into the campus sphere very much." Another person wrote of an enforced reading group during which lecturers with decades of experience were required to report on assigned composition articles to prove an awareness of the field. In both instances, these behaviors assumed a lower level of competence among these individuals and included a mandate in relation to that assumption. A similar category is *having key areas of responsibility removed or replaced with more trivial or unpleasant tasks* (34%). This category, however, doesn't indicate a directive about what a person must (not) do. Instead, the responses in this category described the loss of something—"a scheduled graduate seminar," "a pilot that I had been working on for the previous nine months"—or being left out of key program decisions.

A final category under this type of bullying is *threats to job security*, the one emergent category that is not part of the NAQ-R. This category references respondents' experiences in which bullies tried to actively get targets fired, joked about firing people, threatened jobs, or sabotaged tenure. We differentiated this new category from the existing NAQ-R category *hints or signals from others that you should quit your job*, as the first indicates a presumption of power that the bully can, in fact, influence someone's job security. The NAQ-R category, in contrast, encourages the target to quit on his or her own.

Verbal and Physical Intimidation or Attacks

Behaviors that were verbally abusive were coded as *being shouted at or being the target of spontaneous anger* (41%). Although there was some overlap between this category and *having insulting or offensive remarks made about your person, attitude, or your private life* (defined above), we distinguished between responses that specifically referenced anger or shouting as opposed to comments that mentioned demeaning or belittling communications but didn't provide details about the delivery of those damaging messages. Responses in this category described colleagues who "explode," "scream," "yell," "swear," "rant," "attack," and have other "outbursts." Most of the descriptions focused on face-to-face interactions; however, some respondents described attacking emails that demonstrated anger as well.

While the behaviors described above were verbal, the descriptions in the category *intimidating behaviors such as finger-pointing, invasion of personal space, shoving, blocking your way* (17%) were nearly all physical, such as being "followed" in the hallway or "pounding on desks." However, some respondents explicitly labeled threats of legal action and public humiliation as forms of intimidation, so we included them in this category, too. Finally, the category *threats of violence or physical abuse or actual abuse* (2%) is for behaviors that explicitly threaten individuals or include instances of abuse. Thankfully, only two responses fit into this category (though zero responses would have been better, of course). These responses included mention of a respondent being "threatened" and another respondent being "harassed," including "sexual harassment, verbal abuse and intimidation." Although sexual harassment is distinct from bullying, it could be one behavior in a pattern that constitutes bullying. Because of this potential overlap and because the respondent listed it as part of the individual's experience with bullying, we have included it here.

DISCUSSION

There were two key findings from this survey, the first was the newly identified category *threats to job security* described above. The second was that there is a distinction between the bullying described in the data summarized above and other scholarly descriptions of workplace bullying; specifically, in this study the target of the bullying often extends beyond an individual to include the writing program itself. The exclusion, belittling, attempts at control, and attacks often undermine the entire writing program, if not the field of writing studies. This focus on the program has been represented in WPA scholarship, particularly when describing tensions between literature programs and writing programs. These conflicts connect to multiple risk factors identified in the larger scholarship on bullying in higher education, most notably "resource shortages" (Lester 2013, xi) and competition over merit-based rewards (Salin 2003, 1223).

When bullying isn't directed toward the writing program or field but at the individual, the behaviors may be enabled by academia's insistence on hierarchical structures (Salin 2003, 1220). Susan Taylor (2013) notes that tenure—one aspect of the hierarchy in academia—contributes to bullying, in part by making it difficult to fire someone, which can result in bullying by colleagues as a way to get a person to leave an institution on his or her own. This, it seems, would fit with the NAQ-R category *hints or signals from others that you should quit your job* or countless other behaviors that would make one's working environment intolerable. The broader literature does not provide evidence for others' control over tenure; yet we do see evidence of this in participants' responses to our survey, including, for example, reports of "sabotage" and threats of not "support[ing a person] . . . for tenure." Indeed, the focus on tenure as both a system of stability and a hierarchical structure seems to obscure the multiple ways a bully could threaten a target's job security—whether the bully is in a position of authority, a peer, or even a subordinate. Importantly, almost 25 percent of respondents described bullying perpetrated *by the WPA or from others within our field.*

In addition to the hierarchy created by tenure, strict reporting lines are another hierarchical factor that can enable bullying in higher education, in part by limiting the opportunities for targets to secure allies (Salin 2003). For example, in our department, it is expected that if we experienced a problem, we would first go to someone in our own department (likely the chair) before going to the dean or other members of the college or university administration. If, however, as found at times in responses to our survey, the chair were the bully or had an allegiance to the bully, one could be blocked from assistance and support outside the department. In addition, even if one were able to seek support outside the department, administrators could simply refuse to get involved. In all of these instances, traditional (and often enforced) reporting lines enable the continuation of bullying.

CONCLUSION

As the collected responses to our survey indicate, bullying is a real and present peril in the WPA workplace. And as we surmise from individuals' stated hesitation to either complete the survey or be interviewed, the numbers of those bullied could be much greater than what we've been able to report here. If we are to continue the work of improving the lives of WPAs and other stakeholders in WPA programs, if we are to work toward increasing the promises of that work, the proverbial "getting there," as Skeffington, Borrowman, and Enos phrase it (2008, 19), then we cannot simply obfuscate experiences of bullying by referring to them as "working conditions." The result of this coded language is the normalization of bullying, making it an expected and accepted part of the job. Rather, we need to better understand how to define, locate, and address bullying.

In this chapter, we have attempted to further define bullying in the WPA workplace so that we can name it for what it is. The remaining chapters continue the work of defining while also offering specific examples of locating and addressing bullying. Taken together, we hope this collection will help our field make the WPA workplace a safer, more productive, and more enjoyable place for all stakeholders.

APPENDIX 1.A

SURVEY

1. According to one definition, bullying is the "repeated mistreatment of an individual(s) by verbal abuse, threatening, intimidating, humiliating conduct, or sabotage that creates or promotes an adverse and counterproductive [workplace] environment . . . [Bullying is not] occasional differences of opinion, conflicts, and problems in workplace relationships as these may be part of working life." (UNM [University of New Mexico] Faculty Handbook)

   Have you ever experienced bullying in relation to your work in the WPA workplace?

   ☐   Yes

   ☐   No

2. If you answered yes and would like to share the experience (or experiences), please write about the details here. If you would prefer to have us contact you for an interview so you may describe the experience (or experiences) that way, please provide your contact information (name, phone number, and email address) here. Note that if you provide your contact information, your name will be connected to your survey response. However, only the principal investigators of the study will see your name and responses. All identifying information will be removed when reporting survey results.

3. How many times (frequently, occasionally, once, never) have you experienced the following in the last 12 months?

	Fre-quently	Often	Once	Never
Someone withholding information which affects your performance.				
Being humiliated or ridiculed in connection with your work.				
Being ordered to work below your level of competence.				
Having key areas of responsibilities removed or replaced with more trivial or unpleasant tasks.				
Spreading of gossip and rumors about you.				
Being ignored or excluded.				
Having insulting or offensive remarks made about your person, attitudes, or your private life.				
Being shouted at or being the target of spontaneous anger.				
Intimidating behaviors such as finger-pointing, invasion of personal space, shoving, blocking your way.				
Hints or signals from others that you should quit your job.				
Repeated reminders of your mistakes.				
Being ignored or facing a hostile reaction when you approach.				
Persistent criticism of your errors or mistakes.				
Having your opinions ignored.				
Practical jokes carried out by people you don't get along with.				
Being given tasks with unreasonable deadlines.				
Having allegations made against you.				
Excessive monitoring of your work.				
Pressure not to claim something to which by right you are entitled (sick leave, travel expenses, etc.)				

Being the subject of excessive teasing and sarcasm.			
Being exposed to an unmanageable workload.			
Threats of violence or physical abuse or actual abuse.			

4. What is your age?

   ☐ 18–29

   ☐ 30–39

   ☐ 40–49

   ☐ 50–59

   ☐ 60–69

   ☐ 70 and above

5. How do you identify in terms of gender?

6. How do you identify in terms of race and/or ethnicity?

7. What is your rank?

   ☐ Non-tenure track administrator

   ☐ Full professor

   ☐ Associate professor

   ☐ Assistant professor

   ☐ Lecturer

   ☐ Graduate student

   ☐ Retired/emeritus

   ☐ Other

8. What kind of an institution do you work at?

   ☐ Research institution

   ☐ Liberal arts college

   ☐ Technical/Professional college

   ☐ Community college

   ☐ Other

9. Please provide any demographic information (noted above or other) that you feel is related to your experiences with workplace bullying.

10. At the beginning of the survey, we gave you an opportunity to provide contact information in case you would like to tell us more about your experiences with workplace bullying in an interview. If you did not provide that information earlier and would like to do so now, please write your name, email, and phone number in the box below.

APPENDIX 1.B

DEMOGRAPHICS OF RESPONDENTS WHO DID NOT REPORT BULLYING

Participants' Age	Number of Respondents
18–29	2
30–39	1
40–49	2
50–59	3
60–69	2
70+	0
No response	10
Total	20

Participants' Gender	Number of Respondents
Female	5
Male	4
No response	11
Cis	0
Transgender	0
Total	20

Participants' Race/Ethnicity	Number of Respondents
Asian	2
African American	0
Hispanic	0
Multi-racial	0
White	7
Other	0
No response	11
Total	20

Participants' Institutional Status	Number of Respondents
Assist. professor	1
Assoc. professor	2
Full professor	3
Graduate student	1
Lecturer	0
Non TT admin.	1
Retired/Emeritus	1
Other	1
No response	10
Total	20

Participants' Institution Type	Number of Respondents
Community college	1
Liberal arts college	3
Research institution	5
Technical/Professional college	0
Other	1
No response	10
Total	20

NOTES

1. The authors contributed equally in the writing of this chapter.
2. See the complete survey in appendix 1.A, which includes this definition of bullying.
3. Because of the amount of data collected, the interview results will be reported in a separate publication.
4. We changed spelling to match American conventions and removed "holiday entitlement" from a list of parenthetical examples.

REFERENCES

Einarsen, Ståle, Helge Hoel, and Guy Notelaers. 2009. "Measuring Exposure to Bullying and Harassment at Work: Validity, Factor Structure, and Psychometric Properties of the Negative Acts Questionnaire–Revised." *Work and Stress* 23 (1): 24–44. https://doi.org/10.1080/02678370902815673.

Lester, Jaime. 2013. *Workplace Bullying in Higher Education.* New York: Routledge.

Salin, Denise. 2003. "Ways of Explaining Workplace Bullying: A Review of Enabling, Motivating, and Precipitating Structures and Processes in the Work Environment." *Human Relations* 56 (10): 1213–32. https://doi.org/10.1177/00187267035610003.

Skeffington, Jillian, Shane Borrowman, and Theresa Enos. 2008. "Living in the Spaces Between: Profiling the Writing Program Administrator." In *The Promise and Perils of Writing Program Administration,* ed. Theresa Enos and Shane Borrowman, 5–20. Anderson, SC: Parlor.

Taylor, Susan. 2013. "Workplace Bullying: Does Tenure Change Anything?" In *Workplace Bullying in Higher Education,* ed. Jaime Lester, 23–40. New York: Routledge.

Vega, Gina, and Debra R. Comer. 2005. "Sticks and Stones May Break Your Bones, but Words Can Break Your Spirit: Bullying in the Workplace." *Journal of Business Ethics* 58 (1–3): 101–9. https://doi.org/10.1007/s10551-005-1422-7.

2

OF STICKS AND STONES, WORDS THAT WOUND, AND ACTIONS SPEAKING LOUDER

When Academic Bullying Becomes Everyday Oppression

Harry Denny

The fall semester of 2010 started off usual enough for New York City.[1,2] The sticky breezes of summer afternoons slipped toward chilled mornings and dozy evenings. Nervous excitement about new lives at college yielded to the grind of assignments, shuffling to classes, and the hum of teaching, tenure reviews, and everyday drama. The writing centers that I direct pulsed with new consultants shadowing veterans, class tours plodding through our spaces, and faculty seeking advice. The world beyond the local seemed like both a mirage and a welcome distraction. As the early September rush gave way to 9/11 commemorations and the buildup to the Jewish holidays, our routines were pierced. One by one, local news channels began to tune into the story of Tyler Clementi. What started out as a short segment on NY1, the metro cable news channel, quickly became a lead on network affiliates and national news coverage. Suddenly, it seemed, everyone everywhere was talking about him and how the epidemic of bullying had extended from high schools to college campuses. Clementi, a first-year student at Rutgers University in the Jersey suburbs, discovered his peers had conspired to broadcast on the internet his sexual encounters with another young man. Two days later, Tyler jumped to his death from the George Washington Bridge.

As the days, weeks, months, and years tick by since Tyler's death, even more young people have ended their lives, some with more attention, others with barely a notice. These deaths represent final, powerful, punctuated responses to experiences with oppression that were extreme and vulgar, experiences that stand in stark contrast to the ordinary experience of oppression as it happens in everyday life. Most encounters with bullying don't culminate with suicide or murder; rather, they pile up, one after the other[,] creating a voluminous reservoir of physical

DOI: 10.7330/9781607328162.c002

and emotional pain that's difficult to bridge or empty. The quotidian life with harassment doesn't happen as broadcast humiliation or public performances of hate speech and symbolic lynching. Quite the contrary, everyday oppression grinds on people's dignity and standing with the force and determination of any millstone and operates with a level of discretion and subtlety that rarely draws attention or resistance.

In the wake of public flashpoints of bullying, most visibly those directed at queer youth, Dan Savage, a tabloid sex columnist and celebrity commentator, launched a YouTube public service campaign designed to fill the vacuum of inaction to what seemed like an epidemic of suicides and instances of harassment. In reality, the only uptick was the widespread attention and concern. Savage's "It gets better" video series has sought to present role models who have overcome anti-queer bullying in adolescence and gone on to thrive as well-established, stable adults. Whether produced by celebrities or ordinary folks, the campaign has gone viral, raising awareness throughout popular culture and even extending to unexpected sectors like organized team sports, where professional athletes increasingly assure the wary, "It's okay to play." I don't doubt that these PSAs have saved lives or prevented suicides among kids in small-town America or in some forgotten corner of Brooklyn. But the campaign feels misdirected and ill fitting for the lived reality of everyday oppression.

Back on my campus, in the writing center, I was struck by the silence, what seemed to be a lack of any response to Clementi and what had become the subject of fierce talk and action, even protests, at other colleges. At St. John's, the quiet was unsettling because the institutional mission values advocacy around social justice. As a Catholic, I understood the theological reticence to address the sexuality dynamics at the heart of Clementi's suicide (even if I couldn't disagree more), yet I was drawn to the hypocrisy of an institution with a tradition of combating oppression appearing blind and silent to bullying, regardless of the identities and practices of those who are the objects of it. I also could look across my staff of seventy-some writing consultants, who represent a range of ages, races, cultures, and experiences. Some were queer. Others were on their own journeys of self-discovery, travels both similar to my own but surely just as unique and fraught. I knew still others had LGBTQ friends or were sympathetic to the cause of social justice around sexuality and gender. Regardless of identity, nascent or not, or allegiance to progressive politics, most of my students looked to futures where leadership would be a significant part of their personal lives and professional portfolios. What lessons were my institution or I teaching them if we remained silent, if we made no space to talk about Clementi or the everyday experiences of dealing with and combating oppression, if we didn't model an ethical or responsible form of leadership that held true to our common values?

I knew my own experiences as a gay man, a writing center director, and a pre-tenure faculty member at the time. It must have been during one of my hour-long commutes to campus that it all began to click for me, why I had a simmering rage about the silence on campus, the popular response to these suicides, and the inability to combat it. I realized I was, myself, immersed in a local culture of harassment whose roots were in homophobia and heteronormativity and also dovetailed with a repertoire of institutional and workplace bullying. The environment was so thick with the treatment that it was hegemonic, a natural term of existence in this space. My experience is a cautionary tale not just for queer people in academe, for junior faculty, or for those who find themselves in WPA positions. Most important, my experiences with a bullying workplace dovetail with the tensions inherent to Clementi's suicide and the mantra "It Gets Better." When our public rhetoric fails to match or address a moment and instead defers action to another time, such occasions inscribe crucial lessons about the shape oppression takes and its role in our society and culture, whether as abstractly or remotely experienced as a collective or a nation or as local as a community or profession.

In my years of negotiating my place at St. John's, I'd never named what was happening to me as harassment. I just always knew that this job, this context, was profoundly different from my prior workplaces because the resistance to my leadership had been so grudging and intractable. I figured I had to fumble and bumble to a new set of chops. But the combination of the college student suicides and the YouTube campaign spurred an epiphany: as our eyes and energies turn to the vulgar or grotesque instances of harassment, our gaze and action is blinded and blunted to oppression as it's practiced in our own backyards. My story began early in my career at St. John's when the scope of my position expanded from the fledgling branch campus writing center to include faculty direction of the larger one with a longer history. The bigger writing center had been a much smaller space that my colleague and its former director has written about (Owens 2008). Isolated and subversive, it had been a clubhouse with an identity deeply immersed in its home English department and a site where a collective of students and staff were deeply invested, even if not especially connected to a larger intellectual and academic community of practices around writing centers.

My directorship came on the heels of that writing center's expansion into a marquee space at the heart of campus, a higher profile, and an expanded mission to reach students throughout their college careers. The writing center went from working with hundreds of students to thousands, from a handful of disciplines to most on campus, from little accountability to tremendous scrutiny. It no longer could be a clique, bonded by a contradictory combination of academic elitism and marginality. The actors in this higher-profile writing center could no longer perform a collective identity that reveled in institutional subversion, because its new reality signified consummate privilege. The writing center was now venerated and a focal point of pride throughout the university. With its newfound visibility and cred, the writing center needed practices that matched its profile: it required a professional veneer steeped in the field's best practices and mechanisms to measure its efficacy and accountability. Since this culture shift was abstract and amorphous as much as it was palpable with pressure and pride, scapegoating became a natural response to changes that were inevitable, even if intractable and hard to resist. If, instead, frustration could be projected onto an individual—on me—then the collective resentment could have, at last, a tangible object and outlet on whom many could focus their energies.

This new writing center with its higher profile, new values, and different practices represented a rising tide against the still waters of an existing staff who drew inspiration from memories of the old, more intimate space they once inhabited. This old guard presented a critical mass that was wary of the corporatization of what the writing center had come to represent; it stood in stark contrast to the former iteration that was less formal, structured in looser ways, an outpost for poets, fiction writers, and other star students of the home English department's literary program. Suddenly, this writing center, along with its companion units for first-year writing and writing across the curriculum, had a profile, infrastructure, and resourcing that eclipsed, it seemed, the natural or hegemonic social and academic order and standing. This upstart writing center didn't know its place and needed to be brought into line. This story, the one of ongoing conflict within English departments around how they imagine themselves and how they stay relevant, along with the rest of the humanities, is the stuff of legends and clichés. In this instance, the narrative played out through multiple characters, scenes, and actions, so the details are less relevant than the shared bond forged through suspicion, recrimination, and doubt.

Such stock experience with academic rivalry and petty jealousy didn't stop at coveting physical space and symbolic status, an ongoing tango of who's more esteemed, how people are positioned vis-à-vis one another, who has which students, and what perks get parceled to whom. The particulars of the treatment in my context would only serve to identify the actors, all of whom no doubt have their own equally valid versions of the conflict, no doubt interpreted as benign and far less consequential and damaging as my own. One way to tell the narrative might be to speak into how faculty competed over students, or how conflict was manipulated or escalated in ways that made student and faculty interactions fraught with tension in a dynamic where people couldn't manage or repair reputations. Drama begat drama, factions formed and subdivided, and divisions morphed from the innocuous to the ideological and interpersonal. The side a person took came to have tangible consequences for the learning, working, and social environment within the writing center and beyond, wherever the interests came into contact with one another. My own personal tipping point came when one person in the department dubbed me "the Fag." On hearing that, I joked that I doubted that I was *the* fag but rather *a* fag because I knew that I wasn't the sole homosexual in the program. Turning to senior faculty in the department, I was waved off from pressing the issue of the environment, warned that someone on the cusp of tenure might not want to rock the boat too much. Besides, as I moved from one veteran colleague to another seeking counsel and support, the same refrain was intoned: it gets better.

By and large, society has a difficult time imagining oppression that happens on the everyday level, interaction that harms through passing words, averted eyes, whispered innuendos, and the general microphysics of formal and informal networks of mutual support mobilized to punish and ostracize. People aren't naturally inclined to see quotidian interactions and typical routines as sites and fodder for the Mean Girls in our midst. Instead, we're ginned up to only respond to horrific instances (or not): young boys being molested by men who ought to be their guardians, not their predators; a college man tied to a fence and beaten to death as a perverse lesson in gay panic for straight men; a black man dragged in chains by a pickup truck; a congresswoman and others shot in cold blood for being ideologically different. The list goes on, and we gather, we march, we denounce, we debate, pass, and implement laws, and then we move on until the next vulgar moment or incident. But the everyday practice of oppression is subtle, an art of coercion practiced with more finesse than gauche displays of individuals getting in one another's faces and business. It's proper, it's discreet, it's unrelenting in its ordinariness. Where Fred Phelps and his Westboro Baptist Church of Kansas or the Klan and Aryan/white power marches of yesteryear were obvious, messy, and unfiltered, the everyday practice of oppression has the crisp neutrality of middle-class America, where no-muss-no-fuss begets a political consciousness of the normative and hegemonic, even if the referents are mirages that dissipate with the slightest scrutiny. These practices aren't exercised through the public rhetoric of civics but taught through a political correctness turned toward cohesion and exclusion. From the puff of a hushed comment in passing or the slight touch to an arm, steering glance, and raised brow, these lessons are spoken and performed as well as engrained through the ordinary old-boys networks reinvented for postmodern times.

Not too long ago, the use of the vulgar forms of oppression to exercise power and domination was part and parcel of everyday life and the routines that maintain social order and its attendant hierarchies. Those practices were, at their core, public performances, demonstrations of power that act as object lessons for "correct" behaviors and beliefs and for a host of privileged subject positions—the dominant, the sovereign, the leader. Once people were lynched or brutally beaten as object lessons of power and the performance of oppression; today people still murder just as easily as they drive someone through harassment into suicide. Michel Foucault (1977) and Guy Debord (2002) would name these vulgar events as "spectacles," practices of power and domination that tie into the evolution of discipline as well as into the rise [of] contemporary media-saturated/initiated cultural obsessions. For Foucault, the spectacle emerged as a literal execution to demonstrate a sovereign's power, but today's society has dispersed the exercise of power through more subtle means of shaping and honing of bodies and minds as they pass through any number of institutions and everyday practices. That's not to say the pedagogical value of the spectacle has dissipated. Today, the spectacle still drives moral education. While we no longer gather at the town square to witness the beheading or quartering of someone, we still gather in front of televisions, computer screens, or wireless devices to virtually witness our spectacles.

In Tyler Clementi's case, the vulgar spectacle was initiated at the moment his peers broadcast moments of sexual intimacy and exploration, but the performance was intensified and magnified on multiple fronts and levels, from the internet to the media coverage. An individual trauma was made collective, and oppression gained a pedagogical power and proxy through its dissemination. While the immediate moment represented a relatively closed circuit and population, it gave birth to Tyler's suicide, a criminal investigation that became a salacious story that took on a life of its own in the media, inscribing and retelling the moral lessons embedded in the complex event—the violation, the death, and the prosecution. Just as the kids in the dorm room across from Tyler's couldn't resist looking, the media depends on the public's refusal to turn away, to switch off their screens. Tyler was being taught a lesson no less intense than the scrutiny that his tormenters were given, no more subtle than those of [us] who watched, who tuned in day after day, long after that night in September 2010. We were being inscribed as proxy witnesses, being taught lessons from that moment of outrage and scarred in ways that were supposed to approximate the horror that Tyler must have felt. Of course, we'll never know how he truly felt or whether our lessons are apt. But in those exercises, we gain teachable moments that are ironically illusive because they index experiences with harassment that are rarely duplicated.

Oppression on campuses and elsewhere rarely offers itself up as such searing displays of power that burn into collective experiences as shared rallying points. Campuses don't need to gird themselves for frequent outbreaks of rioting or gun-toting disaffected students. Instead, systemic harassment happens more frequently, tangibly, and with greater consequences on an everyday, hegemonic level. Research on bullying and that in the context of college campuses is relatively extensive. Darla J. Twale and Barbara M. De Luca (2008) have the most recent, comprehensive overview of the phenomenon in higher education in the context of intra-faculty incivility. Their research echoes the findings of workplace incivility in a broader college context, whether students are targeting faculty, or vice versus (DeSouza 2011). Peppered with sidebar narratives and reflections from individuals who have been harassed by colleagues, their overview suggests two major forms of pathological incivility in higher education: bullying is more individual, one-to-one in nature, whereas mobbing presents itself as a group form of bullying, often involving a faction attacking an individual through various means. Jeanmarie Keim and J. Cynthia McDermott's work carries forward those definitions and cites literature that defines the variables that contribute to people being targeted like frequency, intensity, duration, and power disparities. Generally speaking, the victims of academic workplace bullying and mobbing among faculty are seen to have skills, ethics, and independence, or they signify themselves (or are signified) in ways that threaten bullies or the mobbing group (Keim and McDermott 2010, 168). Often the trigger for the treatment can be as simple as possessing a "viewpoint [that] is beyond the invisible line of what is an acceptable opinion within the department" (Keim and McDermott 2010, 169).

The bullying and mobbing can become tangible through "verbal abuse, threatening and intimidating conduct, constant criticism, undermining work performance, exclusion, marginalization, overloading of work, and taunting" (Lester 2009, 445). All the research indicates that gender, race, and ethnicity can be contributing factors, though I ran across little hard data on the incidence and frequency of sexuality as a predictor or variable (it might be very well collapsed with gender). Gary Olson (2007) writes in *The Chronicle of Higher Education,* "No injustice, however great; no personal affront, however offensive; no decision, however wrongheaded, can justify abusive discourse—be it in print, in person, or in public." Piper Fogg (2008), also in the *Chronicle,* notes that bullying can be debilitating in academe, not just to the object's social standing in a department but also culminating in lasting psychological damage, from anxiety and stress disorders to clinical depression.

The consequences are stark for objects of departmental or academic bullying and mobbing. A person is driven to frustration, anxiety, isolation, and, if circumstance permits or forces it, departure. While retention is usually a huge concern around students, the loss of faculty or the risk of legal jeopardy and financial liability can be major by-products of hostile academic landscapes. Taking flight from hostile classrooms or offices or filing harassment lawsuits are culminations of environments that can be (and should be) challenged. These cultures of bullying or mobbing represent struggles over everyday landscapes by individuals and collectives, or, as Michel de Certeau (2002) argues, people acting on and through institutions in sense-making sorts of ways. De Certeau believes people navigate their worlds through what he calls tactics, while institutions try to hem people in, determine their actions, steer them in the "correct" ways by policing their use and activity. Tactics are subversive moves that enable actors to reclaim or work contrary to the institutional, the preferred, the dominant. We tend to think of the subversive as innocuous—scrawling graffiti on walls, jaywalking, speaking against the grain, occupying a public park to protest governmental connivance with industry and commerce.

However, resistance also can be about people oppressing one another, whether out of some misguided notion of leveraging for power [or] a move to gain greater control over conditions not entirely within one's purview. Though often more formally educated than blue-collar laborers, academic workers are no less susceptible to acting against collective interest, in misguided pathological competition with one another, through practices that don't challenge institutional relations and reify collective false consciousness. When academics factionalize ourselves, when cliques confound common interest, we further remove ourselves from critical understanding of our place as workers divided against one another instead of acting as a mobilized collective against institutional practices and systems that truly disempower and oppress in macro, global sorts of ways. In our jockeying with one another, in discovering new means to put one another down, actors are using tactics, to channel Pierre Bourdieu (1991), to compete over dominant visions and practices of local social and cultural fields, ultimately over status and privilege, regardless of formalized structures and dynamics that may officially be in place.   •

Bullying and mobbing are tactics of symbolic violence used to position, reposition, and dispossess individuals and groups for the benefit of others, all the while never contesting the official strategies that act on the dominant and marginal alike. In my case, as a pre-tenure faculty member, being an object of mobbing enabled my harassers to gain status and power in the short run—I was shut up, shunted, and ostracized—but my treatment didn't improve their chances for tenure, garner them greater perks beyond being more "popular," or transform anyone's institutional status (or any department's or unit's standing for that matter). It was a prolonged silly season, as our President termed his own taunting during his first national campaign. Rather than, for example, recognize the mechanisms that corporate higher education uses to create the conditions for petty rivalries to metastasize into toxic relationships, academic workers fall prey to being divided against one another, creating instances and episodes that self-inflict and perpetuate the very subordination and dissent that institutions require to maintain their standing as benevolent paternal figures, who can ultimately own mediation of troubles with their charges/children.

When I now look back, with the safety of tenure and the benefit of hindsight, I'm thankful that what I experienced wasn't a vulgar form of oppression. My harassment as a pre-tenure faculty member didn't involve someone spray painting "Die faggot!" on my office door. Nobody has ever physically abused any of my colleagues or me. Nobody has experienced the vulgar, like the night in Brooklyn when two Latino brothers, walking arm-in-arm, were brutally beaten, one to death, because a group of young men confused them for a gay couple. Instead, I now see the past few years as textbook mobbing, a form of bullying that was sustained through a variety of tactics, be it ostracizing, spreading false rumors, impugning a reputation, and mobilizing others to create a hostile environment—the silent treatment, exclusion, marginalization, forcing colleagues and students to ally (with or against). What drove my tormentors, subconsciously I'm sure, wasn't about homophobia or even me, perhaps; rather, it was about acting for power. By diminishing me, they were uplifted in their mental world. They came to control and exercise agency in a dynamic that temporarily benefited them but never foundationally challenged or undermined that larger system at work. The damage was no less real and felt than broken bones, a bloodied body, or even the loss of life; rather, it was inherently psychological in its traumatizing nature, and no compensation can recover or repair that hurt. I now worry that the experience could have, may have, in fact, changed me fundamentally, moved me away from a core of who I was before as an administrator, a teacher, a scholar, and an activist.

To survive, I shifted away from my impulse to protest and fight and instead became conciliatory, fearful of conflict, watchful of every action to stave off another round of harassment. It reminded me of how my own family members and myself would react to the alcoholics and domestic abusers in our lives: the edge and tension always rife and charged; the alertness to count drinks and wave off tipping points for when someone would grow out of control; to manipulate conversations away from flashpoints for fights that could escalate into slaps, kicks, and worse; to echo admonitions in our heads about not bringing conflict on ourselves. While I had long ago learned that it wasn't my fault or that I didn't cause my dad to hit me or my grandfather to drink or a former partner to overdose, I hadn't extended that lesson to my own workplace as a grown, hopefully mature, man. That is, by virtue of being, I didn't deserve to be humiliated, taunted, and made to feel less than or unworthy. Yet there it was; whether I was still ashamed on some level to be homosexual, whether I was still uncomfortable in my own skin, or whether I still doubted my chops as a WPA in a writing center, I still thought in the back of my mind, in my heart, that being bullied was all my fault, that I had brought it on myself, that I deserved to be treated badly. When I recognized that I had a right to be treated with dignity, that my learning and experience gave me expertise to do my teaching, scholarship, and administration, I began to heal myself and to stop internalizing the oppression, the everyday, the unrelenting and to begin to speak back and challenge. I discovered that I didn't need to wait for my academic life to get better; I needed to demand a different environment and turn a page. Yet even as I write these very words, I worry that the institutional and the system still wiggle free from contest, that any number of readers will focus only on the mob and the bullies. The lesson to me is that individuals and groups in tandem with abstract and intangible interests and structures (like institutions, disciplinarity, collegiality) demand scrutiny, challenge, and action.

When I now look back over the years, the refrain that "It gets better" echoes over and over in my mind. Clementi's tormentors have now inched through the criminal justice system and have paid their own debts through spectacle in their own right, and his parents have set up a foundation dedicated to building awareness of LGBTQ harassment. Is anyone better on the far side of that moment, that experience? More and more, these days I'm not sure getting better is the right frame. In my case, I'm now tenured and daily experience the autonomy that provides for me. This privileged position grants me the agency to speak without as much trepidation, yet the opportunity and willingness to do so is fleeting, even if the seductive potential of it all tickles the recesses of my imagination. Despite pulling my punches and holding back for another day to act on confrontations that have become the stuff of elaborate fantasies, the exhaustion of what's come before, of what's transpired, leaves me empty. I now wonder what advice I'd have on my own "It gets better" video, what I'd say to another Clementi or to a younger academic version of myself. My heart feels like it doesn't get better, that the tensions and minefields are inherent to the academic world in which I live, that they ebb and flow, that the targets or objects often shift over time, and that people just move on, physically, emotionally, or spiritually. My head thinks differently that it could get better if the very nature of the everyday were to shift, if the dynamics that make possible and reward harassment, bullying, and mobbing were to be contested. It could get better if activism were visible and local, not just remote PSAs and videos, but that learning and teaching extend beyond the conventional classroom to a whole host of fronts: institutional change; development for faculty, staff, and students; and consciousness raising about harassment and oppression in academic learning/teaching/working environments.

But could it get better, really? I need to hope that it does, but the reality is sometimes it doesn't. Sometimes it's pretty awful. Sometimes it helps to hear students, colleagues, friends, and family just confirm and recognize, not attempt to dismiss or fix. It does no service to the young student, the novice administrator, or the junior colleague to hear the message that safety and security are states of mind and existence best deferred to another time. It can get better, it should get better, it will get better. We just can't go it alone. We need allies, not just in name but in performance, too. We need to create a world where "It gets better" is supplanted by a reality of mutual respect and regard for the inherent dignity and worth of every person.

CODA

Looking back at this article is now a wistful, ironic experience considering that the United States has elected Donald Trump as its president. I'm not deluded to think that any of the presidential alternatives would have ushered in a halcyon era of widespread civility across the population. Still, as a country, we have legitimized oppressive voices once at the margins—post-truther asshole rhetorics, if you will—for which the essays in this collection offer cautionary case studies. We have rewarded and normalized conduct that warrants ad hominem attacks that make acceptable assaults on people's appearance, presence, and legitimacy to exist and that condone vitriol as comparable to reasoned debate. Our new normal testifies to the ubiquity of bullying, the need to name it, and the need to contest it. I can't argue, in the experience of my own mobbing in the workplace, that I was well equipped to understand it, mount a successful campaign to challenge it, or mobilize support in the face of it. If anything, my actions were typical: get beaten down, slink away, and tell my story as a "shoulda, coulda, woulda" narrative.

I wonder now whether the space itself contributed to the environment. The unique institutional dynamic—a free-standing writing institute—forced disparate groups of people with different stakes into close proximity. If former tutors turned tenure-stream writing faculty hadn't been on the same floor and shared the same offices as the high-profile writing center under new leadership, they might not have had the opportunity to do what they did. The ideal at the beginning of the institute was that such close contact between writing faculty and the writing center would enhance collaboration and naturalize interaction among students, consultants, and faculty. And it did. But proximity forced people together who had different histories with the institution, different relationships to the space, different professional trajectories, and different relationships within and across all those groups. At the same time, the physical, geographical separation of the writing institute from its disciplinary home in English contributed to another whole host of tensions—jealousies—that I write about in this chapter. The core of what I experienced was a toxic culture situated in a space where too many clashing stakeholders gained power and status from the dynamic. And for others, it involved relinquishing actual or perceived power. Some people's standing in the program was burnished when they played on the never-ending dynamic, and others, myself included, became further and further marginalized.

Connected to space and context, the mobbing I experienced might have been bigger than the physical space and the interpersonal conflict.

I remember one of the participants in an interview project Anne Ellen Geller and I conducted with mid-career writing center professionals sharing that one of her senior colleagues once advised her to learn how to "ignore" some of the knucklehead conflict that came her way. Embedded in that piece was the suggestion that we have the agency to engage and, just as important, not to engage (Geller and Denny 2013). I now wish I had internalized that lesson myself. Instead, I played into the dynamic, intent on winning over those whom I had no chance of winning over. But that's the toxic cycle of workplace bullying to which the chapters in this collection testify: objects of bullying find themselves self-blaming, constantly modulating interaction in a futile exercise to diminish the occasions of harassment and to enact a way out of the treatment. And the reality is, people deserve a workplace, a world that honors their dignity and enables them to work and be, without fear of harassment. There are just no grounds on which that principle should be, can be, ought to be negotiated or mitigated.

Toward the ending days at my prior institution, colleagues asked me whether they could have done something different, intervened, or otherwise been better allies. My inner voice said, "Of course, you could have stepped up." But my outer voice said, "I don't know." It was one last dishonest moment in a long string of difficult ones at that institution. I still chide myself for not having had the gumption to challenge my colleagues in the moment, to not stand on the sidelines but to jump into the fight. But at the heart of the situation is how we confront workplace harassment and how best our allies can help us address it. My head immediately goes now to the need to draw lessons from anti-oppression work. What do people in the cultural, social, and political majority do to support those of us at the margins? Surely we can't expect people of color, queer folks, women, religious minorities to confront every microaggression or rank experience with bigotry as teachable moments that are best performed with soothing voices and calm, reasoned action. Sometimes a person needs to address the moment with stank, crazy-ass, fierce outrage. But what's the responsibility of the majority? What to do as an ally? They need to step up when their inherent privilege allows them natural entrée where and when we can't challenge. Under what circumstances can we, myself included, leverage our status to address everyday bullying? Allies need to be somewhat prescient, I hate to say it, and just know when to step up. It means being empathetic and self-aware, knowing when one's privilege can be leveraged to speak on behalf of, in support of, in defense of or to intervene for a colleague, student, or anyone in need in the moment. It means having our backs. It means using this collection to learn how to identity, name, and respond to workplace bullying.

An earlier draft of my chapter had a conclusion in which I made an analogy between my experience living with skin cancer and the experience of workplace bullying. The draft suggested that the scars left behind from both are quite similar: some toughened, some very sensitive. I can no longer go out into a bright sunny day and not feel my uncovered scars tingle in reaction; I can't walk the hallways of a conference venue without a ghost from the past haunting me. Caught early, most skin cancer is easily treated with minimal discomfort; most people never have to fear loss of life. Both skin cancer and workplace bullying have a subtext, a wincing lesson about personal responsibility: a good measure of self-protection or self-care years earlier might protect someone from cancer happening, just as being more aware of the risk of workplace relationships might serve as a prophylactic. If I knew then what I know now, I would have been so much more careful about my exposure, but nobody can ever know whether it was all inevitable or how retrospection can avoid a pointless, hurtful cycle of victim blaming. Coming out as a survivor of either almost always elicits the question, What did you do? Nobody wakes up wanting a cancer diagnosis or to be harassed in the workplace, and nobody ever thinks too much exposure to the sun or misreading interpersonal dynamics will yield painful results. But they happen, often with little reason or prediction.

How we respond as objects, co-workers, supervisors, and leaders says volumes about everyone involved. Scar tissue is a cautionary lesson, a first step toward long-term healing. Today, running a finger across my collar-line or along my arm reminds me of what's come before: a lump of tough skin and a shallow spot of tender forearm. These tangible moments never let me forget that I have to be vigilant. Relationships and interactions with colleagues at school are now less open, more filtered; when conflict seems on the horizon, I step away or deflect. Years on now, relapse on any front is possible, but I know how to recognize, name, and respond in healthy ways that give me permission to persist and flourish. And perhaps that is the best outcome possible: to take this experience and the others documented in this collection as a collective guide and proxy support system as others search and find their own local versions.

NOTES

1.   The original version of this chapter was published as H. Denny, 2014, "Of Sticks and Stones, Words That Wound, and Actions Speaking Louder: When Academic

Bullying Becomes Everyday Oppression," *Workplace* (24): 1–8. Used by permission. All rights reserved by the original publisher.

2.   Thanks to my writing partner, Phyllis Conn, for encouraging and challenging me to move forward on this draft, to vent for argument's sake instead of venting for the sake of venting. Thanks also to my colleague Anne Ellen Geller, who spent many hours in coffeehouses and during walks in Paris helping me brainstorm and revise. Thanks to Joseph Janangelo, Pat Belanoff, and Michele Eodice for their critical readings, too.

REFERENCES

Bourdieu, Pierre. 1991. *Language and Symbolic Power*. Trans. G. Raymond and M. Adamson. Ed. J. B. Thompson. Cambridge, MA: Harvard University Press.

Debord, Guy. 2002. *Society of the Spectacle*. Detroit: Black and Red.

DeSouza, Eros R. 2011. "Frequency Rates and Correlates of Contrapower Harassment in Higher Education." *Journal of Interpersonal Violence* 26 (1): 158–88. https://doi.org/10.1177/0886260510362878.

Ferruci, Stephen A. 2001. "Composition's Professionalism vs. the Writing Center Director: Rethinking the Director as a Teacher." *Writing Instructor*.

Fogg, Piper. 2008. "Academic Bullies." *Chronicle of Higher Education*, September 12, B10.

Foucault, Michel. 1977. *Discipline and Punish: The Birth of the Prison*. New York: Vintage Books.

Geller, Anne Ellen, and Harry Denny. 2013. "Of Ladybugs, Low Status, and Loving the Job: Writing Center Professionals Navigating Their Careers." *Writing Center Journal* 33 (1): 96–129.

Keim, Jeanmarie, and J. Cynthia McDermott. 2010. "Mobbing: Workplace Violence in the Academy." *Educational Forum* 74 (2): 167–73. https://doi.org/10.1080/00131721003608505.

Lester, Jaime. 2009. "Not Your Child's Playground: Workplace Bullying among Community College Faculty." *Community College Journal of Research and Practice* 33 (5): 444–62. https://doi.org/10.1080/10668920902728394.

Olson, Gary. 2007. "How to Get What You Want in Academe." *Chronicle of Higher Education*, December 4. https://www.chronicle.com/article/How-to-Get-What-You-Want-in/46614.

Owens, Derek. 2008. "Hideaways and Hangouts, Public Squares and Performance Sites: New Metaphors for Writing Center Design." In *Creative Approaches to Writing Center Work*, ed. Shanti Bruce and Kevin Dvorak, 70–84. Cresskill, NJ: Hampton.

Twale, Darla J., and Barbara M. De Luca. 2008. *Faculty Incivility: The Rise of the Academic Bully Culture and What to Do about It*. San Francisco: Jossey-Bass.

3

"NEVERTHELESS, SHE PERSISTED"[1]
Strategies to Counteract the Time, Place, and Culture for Academic Bullying of WPAs

Aurora Matzke, Sherry Rankins-Robertson, and Bre Garrett

Some places treat WPAs as disposable. Use 'em up and get a new one.
Don't get used up. Make your own choices.

—Anonymous Advice

We can't tell you how often we've sat or stood in front of a crowd of sea-soned scholars at a professional conference and heard the refrain "that's why you don't take a WPA job until you're tenured." These voices are echoed by the scholarship we read while working as graduate assistants to writing program administrators (WPAs) (Bishop and Crossley 1996; Hult 1995; Gunner 1994; Schell,1998). And they are the voices we continue to hear in our formalized spaces. For example, in the 2016 *CCCC Statement of Best Practices in Faculty Hiring for Tenure-Track and Non-Tenure-Track Positions in Rhetoric and Composition/Writing Studies*, the first bullet under "Best Practices for Hiring WPA Administrators" states, "WPAs are hired with tenure at the rank of Associate or Full Professor." The formal position of the organization is clear (CCCC 2016).

The call to avoid WPA work until tenure has been acquired might not fully consider the academic landscape in which many of the younger professoriate now find themselves. After a Conference on College Composition and Communication (CCCC) presentation, Rita Malenczyk, former president of the Council of Writing Program Administrators, kindly spoke with one of the authors about working as a pre-tenure WPA, as Malenczyk has a known history as a pre-tenured administrator (see Malenczyk 1999). Malenczyk noted that many WPAs do not have the luxury of waiting for tenure to either take up the work of administration or do the tough job warranted by the WPA. Susan Meyers (2009, 152) describes the phenomena: "Many of us who have completed

DOI: 10.7330/9781607328162.c003

PhDs in rhetoric and composition in recent years . . . recognize the near inevitability of WPA work during the early stages of our careers. These voices . . . stand in sharp contrast to voices like Duane Roen, Ed White, and [Alice] Horning who consider [pre-tenured] WPA positions dangerous and perhaps even unethical. Many of them continue to issue a warning: New faculty members simply should not accept administrative work prior to tenure."[2] The authors of this chapter look back collectively at the first five years of our careers as pre-tenured WPAs who accepted positions as assistant professors with WPA responsibilities. Each of us has experienced being bullied while in WPA positions. The strain we've felt and often continue to face is, of course, linked to how protected and valued we may or may not believe our positions are. However, now that we have had the opportunity to theorize our experiences both individually and collectively, we know the landscape is significantly more complicated than we initially expected.

Near the beginning of our careers as new WPAs, each of us heard that tenure positions were a magical solution to a range of academic bullying behaviors present in higher education settings. Yet we are aware that while tenure may have allowed us to respond differently in some cases, it does not and would not have prevented the interactions; nor would tenure have taught us how to respond (positively) to bullying situations. If anything, the things that have kept us up at night and that play on a feedback loop during the in-between times are not only the challenges (and the bullies) we faced during our first few years but also the systemic issues bullies create for WPAs and the lack of scholarship that indicates how to address ongoing concerns.

Each one of us is a first-generation college graduate, a PhD earner, and an academic; all three of us are young(er) females (ranging from mid-thirties to early forties) in a predominantly (white) male workplace (higher education administration), and, as many administrators do, we speak our minds when confronted with adversity. While the academic bullying faced by the authors of this chapter has been primarily verbal, to say that bullying is "just words" (a statement an upper administrator made when one of the authors tried to report being bullied) does not acknowledge the complex systems in which these statements are spoken. In this chapter we dissect the physical, emotional, mental, and communal costs of doing the job of the WPA—which includes managing academic bullies—and then we offer on-the-ground strategies and a clear charge for cultivating local cultural change. We call for accountable reporting of bullied WPAs in higher education, opportunities for greater mentorship for both those who are pre-tenured and those in positions of power, and a stronger acknowledgment by the field that leaving the institution or stepping back from the administrative position isn't always the most useful solution when WPAs find themselves in academic bullying situations. Through a process of introspection and collective, interactive inquiry with each other, we have discovered some strategies for responding to our localized situations. Ultimately, we argue that WPAs may wish to apply a Venn of time, place, and culture to bullying interactions to allow for a critical look at the micro- and macro-aggressive embodied practices that slowly drain and then burn out WPAs over time.

IDENTIFYING AND DEFINING ACADEMIC BULLYING OF WPAS

As Elder and Davila address in this collection, bullying may begin as acts of incivility, shift into patterns of microaggression, and then manifest as sustained emotional abuse resulting in systemic bullying. Workplace bullying exceeds acts of unprofessionalism, moves into the realm of unethical behavior, and often stretches into areas of illegality (especially when involving individuals of a protected class) as it contributes to, among other things, a hostile work environment. Workplace bullying is inextricably linked to uneven power dynamics that are contingent on time, place, and culture. Suzy Fox and Renee L. Cowan (2015, 116) argue that "workplace bullying (WB) is . . . extreme, negative, and pervasive or persistent workplace abuse experienced by targets as an imbalance of power, and which can cause distress, humiliation, and other adverse consequences . . . WB covers a wide range of behaviours, from subtle incivilities to blatant threats, and has the potential to spiral into serious conflict."[3] Simply, bullying is abusive behavior that takes place in certain business settings when unequal power dynamics are in play.

Research on academic bullying notes that it is a widespread phenomenon, at times encouraged by the academic atmosphere: "Cultures where bullying flourishes have been characterised as competitive, adversarial and politicised. Academia . . . is more commonly competitive and political. Perhaps this is best illustrated by the bullying behaviours most cited within academic contexts—threats to professional status and obstructive behaviours, designed to inhibit employees achieving their goals" (Farley and Sprigg 2014). Academic bullying finds a ready home in the competitive cultures of many higher institutions, especially as resources, job opportunities, and dichotomous definitions of a stable university continue to abound. Calls for large-scale research studies of academic bullying have occurred in texts such as *Faculty Incivility: The*

Rise of Academic Bully Culture and What to Do about It (Twale and De Luca 2008), *Workplace Bullying in Higher Education* (2013), and *Bullying in the Ivory Tower: How Aggression and Incivility Erode Higher Education* (Hollis 2012). The existence of these texts shows the growing concern of not just workplace bullying but particularly the severity and rise of academic bullying. While these works share examples that identify academic bullying and offer suggestions for responding, little scholarship addresses the complex nature of WPA positions. Since the administrative role of the WPA may be unlike any other administrative role at the university and the pre- and non-tenured administrative ranks of WPAs continue to grow, more research directly addressing academic bullying connected to these two groups is needed.

The nature of WPA work requires high levels of engagement, communication, and, often, management of conflict. Sometimes these conflicts are part of a local system, as when a colleague disagrees with the pedagogical direction the WPA may be taking a writing program. And sometimes these conflicts are indicative of current larger concerns across higher learning, as when a WPA may work against unfair conditions present in part-time labor. As Stephanie Roach (2008, 111–12) describes, "Being a WPA is really about taking responsibility for student writing, the development of writing teachers, the design and delivery of writing instruction; it is about fostering allies for writing, communities of writers, and a campus-wide culture of responsible writing instruction; it is about educating others how writing is a way of knowing; it is advocacy for the power of language." The position of the WPA is often one of isolation and solitude, which may cause WPAs to be more vulnerable than other administrators at the same time the widespread duties associated with the job obviously create a very low threshold for encountering bullying behaviors.

When looking closely at the definitions of bullying alongside the responsibilities of the WPA, it is critical to acknowledge that along the spectrum of bullying, there are differences among academic dissonance, academic conflict, and academic bullying. Academic bullying relies on intention, severity, scope, and the ways power is present in the interaction, whereas dissonance and conflict may occur sporadically or be part of the larger rhythms present in the cultural web in which a WPA works. While disagreements and conflicts might include unprofessional behavior, they are not synonymous with academic bullying—even though the behavior may seem uncomfortable, unfair, or unwarranted. When we examined the nuances among the different incidents we have encountered, we observed a large breadth of interactions, ranging in scope, intensity, and dimension. However, consistent in all of the bullying encounters, as noted by Fox and Cowan (2015), is a recognizable imbalance in power. This imbalance can be slight, as when a more established colleague consistently makes ageist jokes at the expense of a newer, younger colleague, to a more extreme situation such as a dean threatening the WPA's position if the WPA does not "get in line." (And as other chapters in this collection point out, relational imbalance is not always directly connected to institutional or tenure status and may be more concretely related to resources or political positioning, among others.) Yet it is often at the root of the academic career that being bullied in the academy is first experienced and normalized. As we address in our next section, graduate school is a location where academic bullying often finds the first toehold in the professoriate.

DEVELOPING AS PROFESSIONALS AND FUTURE WPAS: FIRST ENCOUNTERS WITH ACADEMIC BULLYING

Here, we'd like to pause a moment and temporally locate some of the first instances of bullying or bullying-like behavior in academia that some may experience. We'd like to highlight *time* in the Venn of academic bullying. Graduate school is a time of learning how to become a professional, scholar, and colleague. While a person is in this middle space, struggles in performance can easily surface. Having strong mentor figures and close-knit peer relationships can help create smoother transitions. In addition, prospective WPAs often spend a significant portion of their graduate school time pursuing administrative roles. It is important to note that the experiences we share below were not isolated to any one institution; collectively, our graduate work extends to six separate institutions, spanning regions across the United States, from east to west and north to south. What we discovered about our collective reflections on graduate school experiences is that the early, more formative years have the potential to create expectations regarding normative patterns of behavior: patterns with the potential to twist and deepen as the years go on.

Graduate school is an active time of identification for developing WPAs. Personally, we each chose and sought out the professional lives we now hold when we entered the shaping experiences of doctoral student work. Graduate assistantships that provide the opportunity to serve in assistant director positions require close collaboration with writing program and writing center directors, as well as other faculty and students. Co-teaching with graduate teaching assistants, facilitating faculty training workshops, designing curricular materials, leading assessment initiatives, and essentially sharing the reins of many of the directors' daily tasks are common occurrences for those looking to engage in administrative work during their time in graduate school (Thomas 1991; Mountford 2002; Duffey et al. 2002). The authority thus garnered develops character and experience and paves the way for future positions, such as the ones we now hold (Corey and Caswell 2013). Collectively, our graduate work prepared us for these positions, in addition to forming lifelong mentor relationships that aid us weekly, if not daily. Graduate work, by and large, was an overwhelmingly positive, affirming educational endeavor for all three of us. However, it wasn't without moments of conflict, and for all of us it included some of the first experiences of being bullied in the academy.

While graduate students expect critique as part of emerging teacher and scholar experiences, what we observed suggested more pointed attacks on self-worth and ability. Negative critiques of teaching, writing, and administration hold the potential to extend beyond productive feedback and veer into the realm of attacks and accusations of bodily and mental weakness. In retrospect, we categorize personal attacks made by persons in positions of power against those in less powerful positions and linked to bodily disposition or identity as bullying acts or acts on a spectrum of bullying. In one instance, an esteemed female scholar shared that she had never believed in the ideas of Elizabeth Flynn's (1988) "composing as a woman" until she watched one of us formally present to a group of students. The female scholar's feedback came after she had made a public comment in a graduate seminar that "no one has any idea what you are talking about." Delivered just moments after the class, the faculty member's reference to Flynn was specific to the presenter, as she felt the presenter had not followed "a logical, rational order." She packaged insults under the guise of mentoring smiles, causing confusion and jarring confidence at a pivotal point in the developing WPA's candidacy. The argument could be made that it's important for faculty to forge ahead, to push students over the precipice of their own failures and inabilities; one might think these critiques were warranted or that handling feedback and critique is the nature of graduate school (and perhaps of further work in the academy). However, this encounter moved well beyond feedback and took advantage of the power imbalance present in the situation to demean and belittle. Unfortunately, moves such as these by faculty we may have hoped would be lifelong mentors may chip away confidence and lay the groundwork for the acceptance of personal attacks later in a person's career.

The interacting units of the educator and the educated highlighted in the example above (for beginning scholars and perhaps even more for first-time college graduates) are layered on a foundation of understanding particular places (higher education) as having cultural norms (bullying and belittling). It is difficult to extract one's oneself or to understand different possibilities when academic culture positions this particular time of development, within the space that should be a safe environment for such growth, as a place where bullying is normative. This sets up patterns in relationship dynamics, mentoring styles, and workplace ethos that we aim to counter in this chapter. The behaviors we seek to identify here are not limited to a few ill-chosen words delivered after a lecture; rather, they are indicative of widespread destructive patterns. They were layered, confined to a few individuals, always in an uneven power environment, and, when compared to the overwhelmingly positive responses to the majority of our work, completely out of step with our lived realities.

During another encounter, one of us mentioned to a graduate faculty member that she had been labeled a "basic writer" during her undergraduate experience, and the faculty mentor responded "I can tell." The faculty member then brought up this designation on more than one occasion while conversing with the student about her writing. When another one of the authors was discussing the budding stages of a research project she, as a graduate student, had planned to present at a conference, a faculty member and administrator asked, "What the hell are you doing? This is a mess." On another occasion, one of us was facilitating several graduate initiatives on campus and was often pulled aside by a faculty member and, contrary to feedback received by others regarding her leadership, told that she had poor time-management skills and should really consider whether "this" (academics) was a good fit. These various graduate student experiences ran parallel to us working on publications, speaking at conferences (both local and national), and mentoring peers while simultaneously enduring high levels of pressure to perform and be acknowledged for exemplary work—much like Johanna Atwood Brown's (1999) experiences reported in "The Peer Who Isn't a Peer—Authority and the Graduate Student Administrator." As Perryman-Clark discusses in chapter 7, these issues become even more complex when the target of bullying is a minority female.

To move through these experiences with an unscathed sense of self at one of the most formative times for a novice scholar was a challenge. Yet perhaps a more difficult reality to face was experienced when we confided in mentors about these negative experiences. In several instances, we were told to just "let it go" or "not take it so seriously," and in one particularly difficult conversation the mentor stated that "perhaps you're having a hard time because you are so much like X" (naming the professor who was often the source of bullying behaviors). The messages became clear: "If you can't cut it here, you won't cut it there," "If you cannot manage this, then perhaps this is the wrong business for you," and "You'll be more successful if you stop being so sensitive." What cultural patterns were developing in our administrative work across time and in these particular spaces?

What we realize now is that the types of interactions we describe above are problematic for three primary reasons. (1) Interaction with bullying behavior in graduate school normalizes bullying for emerging professionals who will one day be in situations where they might be encouraged to bully or believe that they deserve to be bullied, as graduate schools can be seen as the location to "haze" introductory members or to gate-keep certain individuals from joining the field. (2) Inaction by those in positions of power (WPAs, writing center directors, graduate coordinators, department chairs, graduate faculty members, and mentors) encourages a model for inaction. Witnessing this inactivity from leaders around you when you are a graduate student teaches you about the power infrastructures that are much stronger than the value of those without power. (3) Our own experiences and the larger literature would argue that bullying isn't limited to a few "bad seeds." If a budding WPA understands bullying as a normative part of the educational experience, it encourages inaction at best and participation at worst. In short, it's a self-perpetuating, self-sustaining, multi-institutional system that has to be acknowledged in both subtle and explicit ways to break the cycle. In the next section, we discuss *place* within the Venn diagram of time, place, and culture as we reflect on where we entered our new positions as new WPAs.

SURVIVING THE FIRST YEAR(S) AS THE WPA: LOCATIONS OF ACADEMIC BULLYING

As each of us reached the end of our graduate programs, we explicitly pursued and took administrative positions as assistant professors in our field. At two of our three institutions, there was an open acknowledgment that the composition programs needed and were, in fact, hungry for change. During contract negotiations, we were very careful to ask questions regarding administrative support, faculty support, available budgets, and promotion and tenure requirements.[4] Overall, we've been supported, mentored, and encouraged in these places; at the same time, we have also experienced the sharp strains of a song we have heard before—the melody of the tune that began playing in our graduate programs.

In one case, an upper administrator approached one of our department leaders and asked the leader to change the WPA's annual evaluation to report more negative comments than the department leader believed should have been made from working alongside the WPA. The department leader stayed silent and felt compelled to make the change to maintain the status quo with the upper administrator. And in another case, an upper administrator said the WPA position was one solely of service and stated in the same breath that the faculty appointment would not be secured if the WPA decided to step down from coordinating the composition program.

Pre-tenured WPAs may be vulnerable if they do their jobs in a way that builds a strong program because someone who has institutional history may decide he or she doesn't care for the changes made by the new WPA. Inherently, WPA work requires complex decision-making, mentoring faculty, facilitating the hiring and firing of faculty, implementing and changing curricula, vetting student complaints, pursuing budgetary constraint conversations, conducting programmatic assessment, developing custom textbooks, hosting symposiums and local conferences, and just all around participating in difficult work that never makes everybody happy. There's an old saying that nicely sums up the difficulty of WPA work: you can please some of the people all of the time, you can please all of the people some of the time, but you can't please all of the people all of the time. For many WPAs, complex decision-making processes exacerbate interactions where advancement, promotion, or program development is held slightly out of reach by a bullying authority—not necessarily at the same time.

Unfortunately, a common solution (and suggestion) offered to those who experience academic bullying is to leave the position or the institution: "Charlotte Rayner and Loraleigh Keashly estimate that 25% of victims and 20% of witnesses of bullying leave their jobs" (quoted in Sutton 2007, 125). In addition, what can complicate academic bullying is the functionality of the human resources and legal counsel in such encounters, a chorus that traps bullied colleagues into feelings of helplessness with the reminders that "university legal counsel fights for the institution" and "human resources protects the institution." The institution most often has an investment in maintaining the current system. Two of us were even told that we should *not* go to human resources, as doing so would mark our records. One of us was told by the university president, "Now is not the time to address this" because, as he justified to himself in the presence of the WPA when she requested that a bullying colleague be removed from her tenure committee, her tenure case was "too strong for any of this [bullying] to *really* matter." Simply put, he said, "Now is not the time to rock the boat" because the "vote would not hurt" the tenure outcome.

Let us be clear: we work diligently to maintain these positions, and we find these jobs, as many others (Roach 2008) have, incredibly fulfilling. We love the daily work of writing program administration; we thrive in these positions, which is why we not only accepted the appointments but sought them out. We actively invested time in graduate school taking WPA courses and studying the scholarship, and we continue to actively participate in the scholarly conversations surrounding WPA work. We all have colleagues and leaders who are good, kind, intelligent, hardworking, and socially responsible people. Our institutions, highly disparate though they are, have both personal and professional benefits. We are able to clearly identify where the work invested in our programs has paid dividends not only for our students and faculty but for the larger good of the institutions we call our academic homes. Yet the bullying persists, the faint strains play in the backgrounds of our days, and the silence regarding this behavior has been deafening.

For any WPA, regardless of tenure status, there are risks involved in speaking up, talking back, and naming abuses that occur within power imbalances. One seemingly simple risk is that those who are in positions of power (e.g., chairs, deans, provosts, and presidents) may not listen. Or, even worse, those with power do not speak up or respond/ act when they are informed of or party to bullying, and then the threat of retaliation (re)occurs. Our voices may resound against nothingness. Entire streams of higher education are union-free zones. Program funding may be slashed. Positions may be eliminated. Upper-administrative support is as easily redirected as the revolving door of the persons in upper-administrative positions. The space between the WPA, tenured or not, and decision-makers may be deep and impenetrable. Again, the places—both the positions and institutions—in which we find ourselves are different, and the moves available to WPAs are not the same.

We do not wish to flatten the rhetorical moves available to WPAs. We acknowledge that silence, as Cheryl Glenn (2002, 263) reminds us, "is not, in itself, necessarily a sign of powerlessness or emptiness; it is not the same as absence; and silencing[,] for that matter, is not the same as erasing." While silence is not a powerless rhetorical move, as Elder and Davila point out in the book's introduction, "A culture of silence . . . discourages our talking about bullying and making it more visible" rather than "discouraging the behaviors or the bullies." And while we will address responding positively with silence more concretely in our recommendations, we understand absolute silence in the face of academic bullying to have the potential to contribute to deeper, more restrictive risks that can scar livelihoods and jeopardize job security for those beginning their WPA careers. As Audre Lorde argued in her famous 1977 (41) MLA delivery, "Your silence will not protect you." Despite the numerous, real, and embodied risks that accompany one telling one's truth, we risk speaking up with the hope that the act of identifying and naming bullying will improve working conditions for other WPAs.

We also want to acknowledge that tenure (or the lack thereof) is an important part of the bullying conversation, especially in regard to WPAs. However, when positioned as a cure-all, achieving tenure undercuts the cultural nuances experienced by the bullied. In addition, it creates a non sequitur. If tenure is the solution, then the tenured should not be bullied. Yet we know this is not the case. For each of us, it was seasoned colleagues (with and without tenure) who acted out as bullies against us in our WPA appointments and graduate studies. There is no doubt that being bullied by fellow faculty *may not* affect a tenured colleague's career with the same severity as a bully on a pre-tenured WPA's promotion and tenure committee. That much is obvious. At the same time, this says nothing about those with more institutional authority than a tenured faculty member; nor does it allow for much discussion of what to do when one finds oneself in a pre-tenured or non-tenured bullying situation; nor does it account for institutions where upper administrators, who do not hold faculty lines but have a higher institutional rank, are not tenured and the faculty are (as was the case with one of the coauthors).

When we encountered difficulties, we were told by mentors in the field—time and again—to step down from our WPA positions and go on the market. But we have resisted those choices and persisted in these positions because no one has the right to take these jobs from us, to determine if we stay in our communities, or to dictate whether we retain positions as WPAs. Why does the answer seem to be wrapped up in narratives of escape instead of narratives of resistance or of transformation? The bigger issue, then, is how to stop the bullying tactics. Obviously, no one can ensure that we will not encounter bullying maneuvers at a new place, so what does a WPA really gain by departure? Academic culture, although localized, tends to reproduce the same systems of power struggles, and as one of us was told by a leading scholar in our field, "The devil's avatar will be everywhere you go." Again, the systematic structure of time, place, and culture is present when being bullied as the WPA; changing the place/location does not necessarily mean a WPA will encounter a different culture or time in regard to academic bullying.

What, then, is a bullied WPA to do? If time encourages bullying behavior and place may not limit bullying behaviors, how might culture play a role? Who can WPAs turn to for help, especially when those who are the bullies are also the supervisors or the supervisor is aware and refuses to intervene? By interacting with one another, we have reflected on the bullying we have either encountered, witnessed, or experienced; these reflections allow us to identify different cultural cycles of bullying that stretch beyond time and place, to name bullying based on varied definitions and behaviors, and to contribute to necessary change using different power dynamics.

PERSISTING THROUGH BEING BULLIED: RECLAIMING THE WORKPLACE CULTURE

The third sphere in the Venn diagram, *culture*, plays a significant role in understanding localized academic bullying and responding to being bullied. If, as Farley and Sprigg (2014) state, academic environments are breeding grounds for bullying because of their "competitive and political" nature, then opportunities for distributed leadership are paramount. In addition, workplace culture that is not only collaborative but also transparent will aid in reducing the target on the WPA.

One of the first lessons each of us learned as a new WPA and an important concept we encountered at the Council of Writing Program Administrators (CWPA) workshop held at the CWPA Conference was to build strong networks and to define a collaborative culture across any given institution. It's important as the WPA to have friendly partnerships, and often the greatest ally is the furthest distance away on campus. That was the case for one of us who was contending with a bully. One of the authors encountered a faculty member who had a decades-long reputation for silencing others through bullying. The author sought out mentorship from a seasoned veteran of the institution beyond her disciplinary faculty; the veteran helped her understand the culture of the institution into which the author was entering and in which the bully was thriving. What served the author most was the campus veteran's perspective that the WPA was simply the new(est) target in a long-standing bullying cycle—the bullying was not about the WPA. These conversations, in turn, strengthened the WPA's academic acumen within the context of her institution and then allowed her to pursue additional opportunities and establish a different kind of workplace culture.

In addition, naming and responding to the act of bullying in some documented way was significant for shaping the workplace culture for each of us. Rather than remaining silent out of fear or becoming paralyzed in toxic environments because of workplace bullying, what Elder and Davila label "the fear that surrounds workplace bullying," we argue for responding at some point in whatever capacity feels safe—even if to a colleague across the country—so you can hear validation of the injustice you are experiencing.[5] When you experience bullying, you may consider responding with "let me rephrase what I hear you saying" and provide a short recap of what you perceive the threat may be through a rhetorical move. You might ask to get a portion of a verbal conversation or a new requirement in writing to clarify any potential misunderstandings (or even to document the bullying). One of us recently encountered an unethical statement that was a perceived threat to her position, so she wrote a follow-up email to the meeting with this request: "So that I may better provide faculty with a framework of the plan you discussed with me, will you please provide me a clear understanding of how you see us moving forward?" This places the onus of explanation and follow-through on the shoulders of the offending party, helps clear up misheard or misunderstood moments, and helps the WPA get back on track with what really matters—understanding what is expected of him or her. You may, in fact, stay silent during the initial conversation and then re-initiate conversation regarding the situation once you've marshaled your thoughts, developed possible responses, and garnered some mentorship. Learn this response—"I need to think on that. When can we set a time to follow up?"—and then follow up but do not feel compelled to commit or respond in a moment. Control the desire to react in favor of planning a strategic and informed response: to talk across difference, to name and document instances of power imbalance or bullying and provide clear feedback, and to align program values with the department and the university in order to self-promote to cross-campus stakeholders.

In addition, we recommend that WPAs negotiate labor issues likely to exacerbate bullying as soon as they are able to, perhaps even before accepting the position. As the WPA comes to campus, he or she might want to consider:

- Reading the bylaws regarding reporting structure and how they outline, if at all, the position of the WPA or other faculty administrative roles

- Reviewing the contract for job responsibilities linked to promotion and tenure and, first and foremost, considering the feasibility of doing these tasks well while understanding how secure the faculty position may be outside of the administrative work[6]
- Determining how the university/college/department defines and quantifies WPA work as the equivalent of a particular number of course releases, extra compensation, twelve-month versus nine-month contracts, and titles
- Ensuring that all verbal agreements are in writing because the individuals who make agreements are often not in place when it comes time for application and recognizing that email is not the equivalent of "in writing" for legal matters
- Co-writing a Mutual Expectations Statement with a department chair or dean about expectations and responsibilities, including evaluative processes for the WPA.

While this information will not stop bullying, it will allow WPAs to operate with clear and cogent direction in the campus culture in which they find themselves. In our experiences, nothing has shut bullying down faster than when the WPA is in alignment with position expectations that are available to anyone who may have questions. Just as you aim to establish clear roles and expectations to be successful at work, it is equally important to impose boundaries for your work and carve out dedicated space and time to prioritize personal interests and relationships. If you are a new WPA, you will come to learn that you have to trade away your time. It's an exchange—when you give to work, you take from home.

Most experienced administrators would agree that the laborious work of administration can also take a toll on your personal life, let alone the added need to manage being bullied while doing administrative work. The three of us, like the eighty female respondents in a study conducted at the University of California supported by an NIH grant, are "deeply frustrated by a system that [we] they believe undervalues [our] their work and denies [us] them opportunities for a balanced life" (Jaschik 2008). In addition, the survey conducted by Davila and Elder and discussed in chapter 1 of this book indicates that 38 percent of respondents had experienced bullying comments that attacked them personally.

Scholarship shows that the price of being the WPA is often very high for our personal, physical, and intellectual selves. The personal costs of administration, as Douglas Hesse (1999) shares, can be so significant that ultimately the price paid for being married to our jobs eliminates the ability to sustain personal relationships at home. Yet these are the very relationships we must sustain if we are to remain productive contributors to our workplaces. During her first month as the WPA, one of the authors was reading Hesse's cautionary tale. She heard Hesse's voice as she carefully read and underlined his words on the page. She tearfully woke her husband to assert in that moment, at the start of her career as the WPA, that the life Hesse described would not be the life they would lead. Yet many of the warning signs identified by Hesse became reality for her, and her coauthors indicate similar signals in their lives and personal relationships.

Each of us has managed to deal with a range of serious health issues; collectively, these have included heart problems, high levels of anxiety, insomnia, spine issues, weight gain/loss, and miscarriages. As if these costs are not high enough on us as women, mothers, and partners, we have also endured public professional scrutiny as a result of the births of our children, and we have faced the private challenges of marital struggle because of the nature of administrative appointments in higher education. As Irene Ward (2002, 65) states, "WPAs have a right to jobs that are humane and that foster good health and emotional well-being. We have the right to healthy relationships in our families and communities that balance our working lives. However, we have to teach the University how to treat us." We urge readers to evaluate their job criteria and create a schedule in which rich home communities are as important as the work community—a daunting task for a new WPA, but as one department chair regularly told one of us, "Go home. The work will be waiting for you tomorrow . . . your family may not."

As WPAs often endure high levels of burnout, we should acknowledge that we do have choices about what we are willing to sacrifice. Hesse (2013, 411) further testifies that "life outside work benefits life inside it." He shares the importance to our intellectual selves of participation in physical activities and personal hobbies; he elaborates that WPAs "do your job better" when tending to a personal life because "going to the movies, concerts, and plays provides examples and ideas for teaching and also ice-breaking topics for talking to the provost or chancellor or meeting with community groups" (Hesse 2013, 411). We would add that a nourishing home life and close-knit friendships with one another have allowed us to thrive in our positions and to consider ways to reclaim and redesign the cultures we will exist within rather than to reify problems in the cultural places we entered.

Perhaps most important, we recommend modeling actions and behaviors that promote collaborative leadership models, making a conscious effort to avoid resorting to the same behaviors that many find belittling—in other words, making a conscious effort to shift the culture. Institute low-stakes reporting on your performance from those who work with you and those who report to you. When possible, provide small stipends for part- and full-time faculty to take up research related to the writing program. When working with graduate students, temper negative critiques with suggestions for improvement and strategies for greater success in the future. Create a composition/writing committee, council, or advisory board that assists in the decision- and policy-making of the program to change the dynamics of power within the writing program. These strategies, if coupled with distributed leadership, provide a firm support system and sounding board for WPAs who may find themselves in a bullying situation.

DEVELOPING STRATEGIES TO SUSTAIN AND THRIVE IN TIME, PLACE, AND CULTURE AS THE WPA

Not unlike most of our colleagues, each of us has had to make changes and adjustments, to varying degrees, to thrive at our institutions. Some of the alterations have included position changes and inter-campus relocations. Nonetheless, we have persisted, as these changes have required consciousness shifts that have enabled us to continue in good spirits, dedicated to the important work of student success. We each decided that the positives and importance of the contributions we are making at our respective institutions far outweighed the negatives we've encountered. We collectively acknowledge that part of the bullying might have been linked to growing pains of the institution(s) and the program(s) to which we were new (even though this does not excuse such behaviors). We have worked to develop ethical and equitable environments in which we can not only perform our jobs but also succeed with our colleagues to best serve the students.

In writing this chapter, we used memory as a visceral tool to re-search the past and remember recent past experiences. Memory unfolds reflection, raises questions, and provokes responses. Coming to a response provided us with a space to analyze with distance; our collaboration encouraged not only a double reviewing of previous events but also a triple resituating through our collective recollections. We have talked about the overlapping importance of time, place, and culture as critical ways of rereading, making sense of, and interpreting lived experiences. We have examined localized instances of workplace bullying in academic contexts to trace patterns of occurrence. And in this chapter we propose counter-bullying tactics we believe can open possibilities for productive change. Our suggestions can function as micro-moments of intervention or as habits of mind that yield more satisfactory responses over time.

While it's important to understand how individuals might work toward change, addressing institutional discrimination with policies and practices geared toward stopping bullying is likely to be more holistically effective in the long run. Consequently, we close with institutional strategies that speak to fostering a more inclusive bullying-free environment.

First, some bullying experiences may begin in graduate school, well before candidates take their first "real" (or high-stakes) administrative positions. The behavior to bully or to be bullied is often seen as a "rite of passage" because the students suffered under their teachers (chairs/administrators), so they believe it is their duty once they move into the position of teacher (or administrator) to "do unto others as was done unto them." Be mindful as you come into your position as the WPA that your role is to offer support and mentor those whose educations have been entrusted to you. Take into account that graduate students are often the most impressionable class, and you have a responsibility to model professional and ethical behavior for them. One of the authors remembers that during her graduate assistant days she was always referred to as property: "*My* graduate assistant will take care of that," "You can give that to *my* graduate assistant." Assistantships are first and foremost *mentor*ships.

Second, there are very few, if any, low-stakes structures designed to allow faculty to "report up." When we attempted to seek out help within our institutions, we discovered there was little infrastructure in place that would allow us to reclaim our own environments. It seemed, regardless of institution, that there was little to no assistance for us that did not mark our careers or the careers of the bully. In a place of higher learning, this absence seems especially troubling. Of course, each of our universities has a human resource department, but we were told that "building an HR case" would follow the academic who opened the file because our field is small. Of the three of us, only one had direct access to a dean, and none of us had access to any formal reporting structure that would have allowed for anonymous commentary that could have been used to generate thoughtful feedback to our immediate or upper-level supervisors. When WPAs have access to so many different work and administrative circles on campus and are measured left, right, upside down, and backward for their work, it makes little sense to us that larger institutional reporting designed to evaluate all administrators isn't available. In our experiences, we have not understood or witnessed department chairs (or higher) benefit from visible, ongoing inter-institutional mentorship along with clear and direct feedback from superiors. This seems to be a monumental gap that contributes significantly to unchecked bullying behaviors. We call for greater opportunities for accessible, on-the-ground mentorship for WPAs and those both directly and indirectly charged with leading the WPA.

Last, we write with the hope that more scholarship is developed for WPAs who face similar challenges so that as with best practices in assessment or classroom ratio, we as an academic community can respond with strategies and eliminate the ongoing cycles that exist for WPAs who are bullied. As Heckathorn states in her chapter in this collection, the telling of the stories allows us to see that "we are not alone in these toxic environments." We are aware that potential authors for this collection were concerned with being identified, which speaks to the continued retaliatory nature of identifying bullying in local contexts. We hope the strategies we have provided here and the narrative nature of the chapter, as well as the collection as a whole, will begin to fill this gap for WPAs. Being bullied may be common, but it should not be normalized. The presence of scholarship on this topic will allow others to see that they are not alone: this cycle of being bullied as the WPA is unacceptable and should not be tolerated.

NOTES

1. Mitch McConnell's 2017 comments on Elizabeth Warren, as she persisted in reading Coretta Scott King's letter as a response to Jeff Sessions's nomination.

2. For more on victim blaming of pre-tenured WPAs, see the introductory chapter to this collection.

3. Fox and Cowan use the work of C. Rayner, L. L. Keashly, S. Einarsen et al., and A. M. Freeman to arrive at this definition.

4. We recommend the same to any candidate interested in a WPA position. The more of these questions a hiring committee cannot answer, the more likely it is that incoming WPAs will have their work cut out for them.

5. Be careful about sharing bullying moments with on-campus colleagues in unofficial capacities. Unfortunately, this can foster problematic relationships and undercut a WPA's ethos over time.

6. Contracts may be vague. Ask for a job description. Know that if you take a faculty WPA position, you must work toward aligning your faculty and WPA responsibilities as much as possible.

REFERENCES

Bishop, Wendy, and Gay Lynn Crossley. 1996. "How to Tell a Story of Stopping: The Complexities of Narrating a WPA's Experience." *WPA: Writing Program Administration* 19 (3): 55–69.

Brown, Johanna Atwood. 1999. "The Peer Who Isn't a Peer: Authority and the Graduate Student Administrator." In *Kitchen Cooks, Plate Twirlers, and Troubadours: Writing Program Administrators Tell Their Stories*, ed. Diana George, 120–26. Portsmouth, NH: Boynton.

CCCC (Conference on College Composition and Communication). 2016. *CCCC Statement of Best Practices in Faculty Hiring for Tenure-Track and Non-Tenure-Track Positions in Rhetoric and Composition/Writing Studies*. Accessed August 1, 2017. http://cccc.ncte.org/cccc/res ources/positions/faculty-hiring.

Corey, Jessica Rose, and Nicole I. Caswell. 2013. "Just a Graduate Student: Doctoral Students in Writing Program Administrative Positions." *Doctoral Students in Writing Program Administrative Positions*. http://improgressjournal.net/archives/current-issue-2/just-a -graduate-student-doctoral-students-in-writing-program-administrative-positions/.

Duffey, Suellynn, Vic Mortimer, Ben Feigert, Jennifer Phegley, and Melinda Turnely. 2002. "Conflict, Collaboration, and Authority: Graduate Students and Writing Program Administration." *Rhetoric Review* 21 (1): 79–87.

Farley, Sam, and Christine Sprigg. 2014. "Culture of Cruelty: Why Bullying Thrives in Higher Education." *The Guardian*. November 3. https://www.theguardian.com/higher -education-network/blog/2014/nov/03/why-bullying-thrives-higher-education.

Flynn, Elizabeth. 1988. "Composing as a Woman." *College Composition and Communication* 39 (4): 423–35.

Fox, Suzy, and Renee L. Cowan. 2015. "Revision of the Workplace Bullying Checklist: The Importance of Human Resource Management's Role in Defining and Address-ing Workplace Bullying." *Human Resource Management Journal* 25 (1): 116–30. https:// doi.org/10.1111/1748-8583.12049.

Glenn, Cheryl. 2002. "Silence: A Rhetorical Art for Resisting Disciplines(s)." *JAC* 22 (2): 261–91. http://jaconlinejournal.com.

Gunner, Jeanne. 1994. "Decentering the WPA." *WPA: Writing Program Administration* 18 (1– 2): 8–15.

Hesse, Douglas. 1999. "The WPA as Father, Husband, Ex." In *Kitchen Cooks, Plate Twirl-ers, and Troubadours: Writing Program Administrators Tell Their Stories*, ed. Diana George, 44–55. Portsmouth, NH: Boynton.

Hesse, Douglas. 2013. "What Is a Personal Life?" In *A Rhetoric for Writing Program Administra-tors*, ed. Rita Malenczyk, 407–14. Anderson, SC: Parlor.

Hollis, Leah. 2012. *Bullying in the Ivory Tower: How Aggression and Incivility Erode Higher Education*. Philadelphia: Patricia Berkly LLC.

Hult, Christine. 1995. "Politics Redux: The Organization and Administration of Writing Programs." *WPA: Writing Program Administration* 18 (3): 44–52.

Jaschik, Scott. 2008. "'Quiet Desperation' of Academic Women." *Inside Higher Ed*. https:// www.insidehighered.com/news/2008/06/12/quiet-desperation-academic-women.

Lester, Jamie. 2013. *Workplace Bullying in Higher Education*. New York: Routledge.

Lorde, Audre. 1977. "The Transformation of Silence into Language and Action." Paper delivered at the Modern Language Association's Lesbian and Literature Panel, Chica-go, IL, December 28. First published in *Sinister Wisdom* 6 (1978) and *The Cancer Journals* (1980). San Francisco: Spinsters, Ink.

Malenczyk, Rita. 1999. "Productive Change in a Turbulent Atmosphere: Pipe Dream or Possibility?" In *Administrative Problem-Solving for Writing Programs and Writing Centers*, ed. Linda Myers-Breslin, 146–64. Urbana, IL: National Council of Teachers of English.

Meyers, Susan. 2009. "Power, Fear, and the Life of the Junior WPA: Directions for New Conversations." *WPA: Writing Program Administration* 33 (1–2): 152–62.

Mountford, Roxanne. 2002. "From Labor to Middle Management: Graduate Students in Writing Program Administration." *Rhetoric Review* 21 (1): 41–53.

Roach, Stephanie. 2008. "Why I Won't Keep My Head Down or Follow Other Bad Advice for Junior Faculty WPA." In *The Promise and Perils of Writing Program Administration*, ed.

Theresa Enos, Shane Borrowman, and Jillian Skeffington, 109–16. West Lafayette, IN: Parlor.

Schell, Eileen. 1998. "Who's the Boss? The Possibilities and Pitfalls of Collaborative Administration for Untenured Writing Program Administrators." *WPA: Journal of Writing Program Administration* 21 (2–3): 65–80.

Sutton, Robert. 2007. *The No Asshole Rule: Building a Civilized Workplace and Surviving One That Isn't.* New York: Business Plus.

Thomas, Trudelle. 1991. "The Graduate Student as Apprentice WPA: Experiencing the Future." *WPA: Writing Program Administration* 14 (3): 41–51.

Twale, Darla J., and Barbara M. De Luca. 2008. *Faculty Incivility: The Rise of Academic Bully Culture and What to Do about It.* New Jersey: Jossey-Bass.

Ward, Irene. 2002. "Developing Healthy Management and Leadership Styles: Surviving the WPA's Inside Game." In *The Allyn and Bacon Sourcebook for Writing Program Administration*, ed. Irene Ward and William Carpenter, 49–67. New York: Longman.

4

THE MAKING OF A BULLY CULTURE (AND HOW ONE MIGHT TRANSFORM IT)

Sarah Allen

Campus bullying [is] behavior at colleges and universities that tends "to threaten, to intimidate, to humiliate or to isolate members of the working university environment [and] that undermines reputation or job performance." It occurs frequently, and very often we who work in these environments are unaware of it.

—from "Prevention of Bullying
on Campus" at AAUP.org

In the fall of 2016, half of the nation (half of the people who voted, that is) elected Donald Trump, a bully, to the presidency. The rest of the nation (in fact, much of the world) is still wondering how this could have happened. Not long after his election, I received a revise-and-resubmit request from the editors of this collection on my draft of this chapter. I'm left wondering why I can't *manage* this piece. It's been one of the most difficult pieces I've written, in part because I've been hesitant about accusing my prior workmates of bullying but also because I've been too twisted up to see clearly how my unwillingness to name it has performed as a kind of complicity. In the last draft, I worked some of my worst conceptual acrobatics to avoid a direct accusation; I wanted instead to acknowledge my own tentativeness (even dodgy-ness) around the issue and to try to "move forward." The task comes to me again: to locate, define, and address bullying in the WPA workplace. For this chapter to do any work at all, I've accepted at last that I'll have to "lift the veil," as Henry Louis Gates Jr. (1998) said of his book *Colored People*.[1]

When I think of bullying, my mind leaps to Donald Trump. I think of his comments about women, which reporter Megyn Kelly sums up in the following list: that he's characterized at least a few different women he's encountered in his career(s) as "fat pigs, dogs, slobs, and disgusting

DOI: 10.7330/9781607328162.c004

animals" (quoted in Ross 2015).[2] My mind leaps again to a conversation with one of my workmates at my prior institution in which they tell me that we need to present a "united front" against the rest of the department. I say that I want time to get a sense of the department's history, of the political terrain. Sitting across from me, their body pressing into the table, their face reaching toward mine, their voice threatening, they whisper, "Then I will not support your tenure application." My mind leaps again to another workmate at the same institution who tells me behind the closed door and in the shrinking space of their office that they'll never support any proposal I bring to the department because they don't "like" me. My mind leaps once more to one of my classrooms this semester. I see myself at the front; I feel my heart pounding, the heat rising to my face. I'm panicking, folded into my anger and fear, trying to figure out how to manage them both in order to respond to a (large-in-stature, veteran, and male) student who bulldogs conversation in every class.

I don't think bullying is a rare occurrence. In my experience, it happens all the time. Still, my mother (a retired schoolteacher) told me recently, when I finally shared with her my frustrations with the student I mentioned above, that bullying is "passé," that there's no reason for me or the other students in the class to tolerate it, that I can and should shut it down—talk to my superiors, report his behavior, penalize him, whatever it takes.[3] I've been trying to figure out why I don't. The reasonable, morally responsible part of me would tell you that I don't because he's my student, because it's a rhetoric class, because our purpose is to hear each other and to negotiate with each other within whatever power dynamics emerge. To shut down a bully would be to dodge what is perhaps most at stake in my work with students on/in rhetoric.

The other part of me, the oldest part of me, doesn't shut him down, though, because she's scared. I don't know what he'll do if I try to silence or disempower him. Will he scream at me? Will he throw over a desk? Will he bring a gun to class? Or will he just keep showing up, registering his disapproval, his vitriol, in whatever ways he can? I think of Trump's accusations of a rigged election, his threats if he didn't win, his staff's continuing threats, post-election, to "throw [Hillary] in jail." Would my student try to find a way to shut me down—claiming, for example, that I am biased against him and filing a grievance against me—if I tried to put a stop to his tyrannizing of class discussion?

But then I think of the students in my other class this semester, about our discussion on the day after the election. Before it became a rally cry in the media, my students were saying, "We need to take care of each other. We need to protect each other. It's on us now." I wonder what it means to take care of each other in the face of bullies. What might taking care of ourselves look like when we are faced with a bully? This is the question I seek to address here, in this chapter. I address it by first tracing the relation between bullying and fundamentalism and then by offering a way to intervene in the "fundamentalist tendency" that is in part responsible for the making of a bully culture.

To hear bell hooks (1989) tell it, in the face of a bully, for example, the cultural bullies that are white supremacy and sexism, we must talk back; we must move from objects to liberatory subjects, which means we must take back our histories and our identities. We must "expose the false reality—to reclaim and recover ourselves" (hooks 1989, 3). In the same chapter she acknowledges, though, that "domination is not just a subject for radical discourse, for books. It is about pain—the pain of hunger, the pain of overwork, the pain of degradation and dehumanization, the pain of loneliness, the pain of loss, the pain of isolation, the pain of exile—spiritual and physical" (hooks 1989, 4). Every time I teach this text, I ask my students to reflect on this line, this passage. I've never been able to inspire an interesting conversation in response to it, though. Certainly, my students know the pain of domination. After all, as students at the University of Hawaiʻi at Mānoa (many of whom are local), they're living in a colonized state. Is the pain so normal, so profuse, that they don't even recognize it? Or is it too internalized to speak about?

I could dwell at length on each phrase in hooks's list of pains—structure this whole chapter around that list and thus add to the discourse about just how destructive this form of domination (bullying) is. I could trace a genealogy of my inadequate/impotent reactions to bullying in my life, using her work to explain how I've been so thoroughly disciplined, as a woman, into impotent reactions that inventing other possibilities becomes an Atlantean task. I could do that, and it might prove valuable. But I'm more interested, like much of the country, in figuring out, to quote John Oliver (2016), "what . . . we do now."

For many of us, bullying is a "you know it when you see it" affair. On the other hand, as I'll explain throughout this chapter, what counts as bullying for one person may count for another as an act of standing up for oneself, for one's own beliefs and values. To call on Trump again as an example, he has notoriously recast any acts of bullying committed by him (e.g., the piece of the hostile environment he has, at the very least, encouraged in our country with his hate speech toward women) as his refusal to participate in "political correctness." In the same exchange with Megyn Kelly that I refer to above, Trump says, "I've been challenged by so many people, and I don't frankly have time for total political correctness. And to be honest with you, this country doesn't have time either" (quoted in Ross 2015). He seems to see political correctness, which in this particular case is about using respectful language toward and about women, as a waste of the country's time, suggesting that there are far more pressing issues about which the country should be worried and that this particular issue (misogyny) is not a priority. In a sense, Trump is standing up for these more pressing issues, as he sees them—and no doubt for the American citizens who are also more concerned with other issues and who see political correctness as simply a series of liberal platitudes that distract the public from those issues. So even a bigoted and privileged white man can claim that he is "talking back" to what he perceives as the moral imposition of others rendered through the mores of political correctness.

In cases like this one, the impulse to stand up for our beliefs and values can come from a relationship to those beliefs and values that functions as a kind of fundamentalism. Historically, fundamentalism has been a term used to describe a form of religion (e.g., Islam or American Protestantism) that treats "some source of ideas, usually a text, [as] complete and without error" (Bruce 2008, 12). It is also a response to modernization, to change. Fundamentalists see "themselves losing control of their churches, their families, their working environments, their schools and their nation" (Bruce 2008, 71). To regain control, they promote an us versus them framework for understanding their beliefs and values in relation to different beliefs and values. In short, they promote the idea of value systems that exist in binary oppositions to each other, and they work to preserve and strengthen the one while diminishing the influence of the other (e.g., by not allowing members of the religious community to read texts that challenge their core beliefs).

Though bullying may seem justified if it is understood as standing up for ourselves against those "who represent everything that's wrong with . . . [X]," it comes at a terrible cost. As many chapters in this collection show, bullying has terrible consequences not only for the folks who are being bullied but also for the larger community to which those folks belong because prolonged and unchecked bullying can create a bully culture, in which bullying behavior is normalized.

According to the American Association of University Professors (AAUP) website, "Campus bullying [is] behavior at colleges and universities that tends 'to threaten, to intimidate, to humiliate or to isolate members of the working university environment [and] that undermines reputation or job performance'" (quoted in Wajngurt 2014, paragraph 1). At the beginning of this chapter, I made references to a couple of exchanges I had with senior writing faculty at a prior institution. Both seem to me to be clear instances of bullying, according to this definition. As much as I don't want to admit this, I think it's important to explain that in these moments, I didn't respond to the bullying itself. I remember that I tried to listen—that in both cases I asked perhaps another question or two, but I quickly stopped talking, let them finish, let the meeting end. I remember distinctly in both cases being both viscerally angry and scared. The two emotions, unfortunately, almost always come hand in hand for me, and the combination forces me into my go-to response—flight mode. "Fight mode," in contrast, always comes later. Point being, we can't always look to the bullied individual's response to an encounter for immediate evidence that bullying has indeed occurred. As I've learned in researching for and revising this chapter, we may not immediately want or know to identify bullying for what it is.

I have found that without the resources to identify and effectively address bullying, the bullied then become "ticking time bombs." I have seen too many colleagues bully each other to intervene in what they see as the other's bullying behavior. I've done it myself. Just yesterday, in the same class to which I referred earlier (with the student who bulldogs conversation), I went to class angry, deeply frustrated with the prior week's discussion—namely, with the domination of one or two white male students in class discussion and the consequent silence of several students of color and women. I had had enough, and I made an accusatory statement regarding the hegemonic consequences of privilege and what kind of person might be complicit in them that I'm now going to have to apologize for. If I'm lucky, my students will forgive me. But the truth is that what I did was inexcusable.

The two workmates I described above from my prior institution, who bullied me, have also been victims of bullying. I've heard a few of these stories, and I am sympathetic, even in the face of their bullying of me. But again, I think it would be a mistake to see the behavior as excusable. Still, this genealogy affirms what all the literature on bullying has told us for years (I remember hearing about this "moral" to stories about bullies when I was a child): that bullies are made—generally by other bullies. As explained at stopbullying.gov, "When kids are involved in bullying, they often play more than one role. Sometimes kids may both be bullied and bully others or they may witness other kids being bullied" (US Department of Health and Human Services 2016). It seems that members of campus communities, including faculty, can fall into the same multiple roles. Among faculty, though, contributing factors have less to do with the power imbalances grade school students face with regard to popularity, physical strength, and cognitive ability and more to do with competing values that perform like fundamentalisms as the result of an "us versus them" political framework.

In defining "General Fundamentalism," Grant Wacker (2000) explains that it "seeks to recover and publicly institutionalize aspects of the past that modern life has obscured. It typically sees the secular state as the primary enemy, for the latter is more interested in education, democratic reforms, and economic progress than in preserving the spiritual dimension of life. Generic fundamentalism takes its cues from a sacred text that stands above criticism. It sees time-honored social distinctions and cultural patterns as rooted in the very nature of things, in the order of creation itself. That means clear-cut and stratified roles for men and women, parents and children, clergy and laity." Of course, Wacker is describing religious fundamentalism here, but certain aspects of the description seem to leap off the page in their analogic relation to the political dynamics in my prior department.

For example, the privileging of the past over the modern would explain one of our fundamental disagreements: how we should have addressed student need. Many of my senior colleagues argued to me that we should uphold our old standards by having stricter grading standards, for example, harshly penalizing students who didn't obey the rules of "proper" writing. I argued (alongside a few of the department's untenured faculty who taught most of our first-year writing courses) that we needed to do more work to support struggling students, for example, by creating a supplemental instruction program, especially given that increasing numbers of students were showing up in our courses poorly prepared.[4]

There is also, though, the obvious analogy between the "clear-cut and stratified roles for men and women" from Wacker's (2000) definition. The senior faculty expected that junior faculty should defer to their expertise—should seek it out and submit to it. For example, a senior male colleague explained in a department meeting that junior faculty should be willing to "climb the mount" (which he explained was a reference to Moses climbing Mount Sinai) to seek the wisdom and guidance of the senior faculty; another senior male colleague once explained to a couple of other colleagues that junior faculty should "tremble in fear" of him. Both explanations were offered in conversations about the possibility of implementing a formal mentoring program for pre-tenured faculty—for predominantly female pre-tenured faculty, I should add.[5]

Of course, my peers and I (the junior faculty) were not above some of the symptoms of fundamentalism. In more frustrating moments, for example, I found myself referring to a few of my senior colleagues as placeholders at best and a drain on the department's resources at worst. If our senior colleagues weren't posing and implementing new ideas to reinvigorate our programs, if they spent too much time arguing over ideas and never agreeing to any compromise in order to move forward, then they were understood to be deliberately stymying efforts to make change. The assumption was that they did so to demonstrate their power and because they didn't want to do the work that would be required to make change.

Like fundamentalists who define their enemies according to "'those defects, weaknesses, corruption and naivetes' that believers feel they are 'under an absolute imperative to eliminate'" (Crowley 2006, 12–13), each faction saw the other as corrupt and somehow deficient. We worked against each other to diminish the "defects, weaknesses, corruption, and naivetes" of the other. We did so "by rendering opposing claims unworthy of consideration [and] by excoriating the character of people who [disagreed with us]" (Crowley 2006, 14). Both factions participated in the former during committee and department meetings—some going so far as to roll their eyes at each other. Both factions participated in the latter behind closed doors (in our offices, in Facebook exchanges, at dinners, and the like).

Sharon Crowley (2006) finds that liberals and fundamentalists, too, generally avoid working in the same discourse because their belief systems are fundamentally different, so much so that those belief systems are treated as inherently oppositional to each other. Drawing from Chantal Mouffe (2000), Crowley (2006, 2) explains the effects of that opposition:

> When citizens fear that dissenting opinions cannot be heard, they may lose their desire to participate in democratic practices . . . Something like this seems to have happened in America. Members of a state legislature flee the state's borders in order to avoid voting on a bill that will gerrymander them out of office. Other legislatures are unable to cooperate well enough even to settle on a method of deliberation. Authorized public demonstrations are haunted by the possibility of violence. Media pundits tell us that "the nation" is "polarized." Citizens do not debate issues of public concern with family, friends, or colleagues for the fear relationships will be irreparably strained in the process.

I find it alarming how much the last few sentences here perfectly describe the conditions that contributed to the election of a bully to the presidency. I also find it alarming that Crowley's examples sound a lot like the ways debate failed in my department—a community of people with PhDs who study, teach, participate in strategic, effective written arguments; who should be capable, then, of productive debate; and who are, for all intents and purposes, "liberal" in the ways Crowley defines but who function in debate like fundamentalists.[6]

One of the worst effects of this fundamentalism was that there was a major downturn in attendance at faculty meetings as a result of the same conditions Crowley describes above in relation to America. A few smart and especially hard-working (but absentee) faculty cited at least two reasons for avoiding them: the meetings were frustrating and stressful; they were pointless. I suspect that both of these reasons had something to do with the experience of being forced in meetings to witness the department's evasive ways of doing and talking about business. These evasive tactics developed in response to the unproductive polarization between the two factions that emerged during my tenure in the department, what I've been calling the "senior" and "junior" factions of faculty. We, too, were afraid to debate issues important in the department, but not because we were fearful that "relationships [would] be irreparably strained in the process." They were already strained. We simply didn't see the point in even trying.

Consequently, much of our departmental business was conducted behind closed doors and among groups of like-minded peers. Each group kept itself isolated, protecting itself from the other group and shoring up its defenses (or planning an offensive). Unfortunately, as Crowley (2006, 194) explains, there is a "single-mindedness that accrues to isolation and privilege." Though privilege worked in favor of my senior colleagues, that single-mindedness functioned in both factions: each anticipated the other faction's single-mindedness, so much so that when each faction would propose new policies and curricular or leadership changes, the reasons given often depended on whom the reasons were being offered to. Each faction played to its audience by appealing to the values the audience was understood to hold and by holding back reasons that would have explained the proposing faction's purpose and investment. We all knew we were working in such ways, and subsequently, a general state of suspicion toward each other set in. We no longer feared that dissenting opinions wouldn't be heard, as Crowley explains above; we knew it.

The question of privilege—who had it and how it contributed to the bully culture that was my department—is profoundly complicated. Given the power dynamics that are enabled simply by the tenure system and by faculty rankings, I would argue that departments must work very carefully, together, to prevent bullying from "naturally" emerging in senior-junior faculty exchanges. Of course, there are also gender dynamics, race relations, and similar factors. And, then there was for us the added complication of competing versions of expertise: one faction saw their time and experience, as tenured faculty, as the foundation of their expertise; the other saw their work as scholars as a significant (if not the predominant) part of their expertise. In the end, the former won out, as the latter were shamed into not publicly valuing their work as scholars too much—by often being accused of "not caring about students," of being selfish for dedicating too much energy to that work, or of being selfish for working on projects that didn't have a direct impact on our pedagogies and programs. The senior faction's efforts to win by shaming us were so powerful that they threatened to function like hegemony.

According to Mouffe and Ernst Laclau, "hegemony . . . involves the expansion of a particular discourse of norms, values, views and perceptions through persuasive redescriptions of the world" (quoted in Crowley 2006, 5), and if there is any value that might be shared across even the most divisive faculty in English studies, it's that hegemony should be challenged. But that's part of my point. We don't recognize hegemony (including the hegemonic practices of a bully culture) because we don't see it . . . until it is threatened. Even then, who wants to admit that they are a part of some hegemonic effort?

To be honest, I don't know that I can accuse the other faction of being malicious in their work to extend their "norms, values, views, and perceptions through persuasive redescriptions of the world." A faculty member in that faction once told me they believed we were trying to overthrow the department. If that's true, then the initial intent that enabled their hegemonic efforts may have been about self-preservation and self-empowerment. However, given the power dynamics (of senior versus junior faculty, of predominantly male versus predominantly female), I can't help but be reminded of the student to whom I referred above (the one who bulldogs class discussion) who volunteered the fact that he voted for Trump because "at least Trump is looking out for the white man who has been neglected for decades." As irrational as that belief might be, my student is thoroughly invested in it, and it's driven by a deep-seated anger toward those he perceives as having diminished his worth.[7]

Anger can mobilize people, and in the case of my prior department, it mobilized the junior faction against the hegemonic efforts of the senior faction. But it also enabled the very sort of fundamentalism I've been describing in this chapter. Brad Peters describes this mobilizing anger as "radical anger"—a kind of anger that "spurs an individual to act in a prolonged, extremely disruptive public manner against a policy, a practice, or often, another person whom [the individual] feels *symbolically represents* the social or political conditions that put [the individual] at a disadvantage" (2003, 136, emphasis in original). In our case, there was no "symbolic representation"; we saw the other as a direct threat—the enemy. Still, the following is an accurate description of the way a few of my peers and I functioned: "Radical anger is monomaniacal in its focus, yet megalomaniacal in its aims to search for all available means of persuasion. Its very zeal to assert its sources of pain demonstrates a compelling ethic and logic that can sometimes win over others whose *sensus communis* is shaped by similar pain. The radically angry . . . may collar those others—usually peers—in intensely private talks, creating an audience that is then familiar with [their] particular source of pain when [they speak] of it in more public settings" (Peters 2003, 139). Peters goes on to claim that this strategy, which he describes as "profoundly intuitive," grants the rhetor a kind of leverage not available to the ticking–time-bomb sort I described earlier, who simply look irrational when they finally speak back against the abusive behavior.

Similarly, a few of my peers and I talked in pairs, sharing our stories with each other. Then we started talking in small groups of three or four people. Eventually, a "faction" emerged, which included mostly female junior faculty. We were united in our anger toward the senior faculty who tried, sometimes by cruel and abusive means, to bend us to their will. We were united in our frustration at having no effective procedures available to us to intervene in the behavior. We were on our own to invent strategies through which we could respond to the bullying, and in the process of all that talking and inventing, we created a shared worldview—one in which we were victims of autocratic, morally suspect, irrational faculty who had power over us (or at least whom the institution empowered by not protecting us).

Our anger sustained a worldview that would function with "fundamentalist intensity" (Crowley 2006, 12). For my part, I would eventually come to loath one member of the other faction—the ringleader, as I saw him—and I would dismiss the others, ignoring any suggestion they made, any idea they brought to department meetings. I might "perform" interest if it served another purpose, but at a fundamental level, I believed anything they had to offer to be suspect—at best, stupid; at worst, dangerous.

As you might imagine, spending one's days dedicated to a job—a life—in which I was surrounded by perceived enemies took its toll. For starters, I never thought I'd be the sort of person to dismiss an entire group of people outright. I learned in my PhD studies that attentiveness, openness, and respect are the most fundamental practices we should participate in as rhetoric and composition scholars, teachers, and administrators, but in that space I had learned to ignore half of my colleagues. This had no small effect on my job as the director of composition.

The image that comes to mind when I think of myself in the role of director of composition is of the lone warrior who sneaks into an enemy's camp to steal their weapons before a battle. I was never that effective, I assure you. But "sneaking" became my modus operandi: writing program changes had to be planned from outside the department, or if I wanted to pursue them within the department, I had to work behind closed doors. Please know that this is no small confession for me. It's no small thing to admit that I became a shady jerk. Yet there it is. The awful truth is that by the time I left the position, I couldn't reconcile the person I felt I had to be with the person I had been trained to be. What is perhaps worse is that, in the end, my inability to navigate and our inability to change the bully culture proved an enormous failure—for me and for the department.

The writing program, last I heard, had basically collapsed: there was no formal director of composition (the chair handled whatever essential duties must be handled); the TA training was moved to an online preparatory course that ran for two or three days before the semester started; the Writing Committee didn't meet anymore. Friends still report that they are exhausted all the time, that they are not attending department meetings, that they avoid their colleagues. The administration swooped in and tasked the department with hiring an external chair (mediators were brought in several years ago; the bullied female faculty who were under greatest threat at that time either left the institution or disappeared from departmental business). As I'm writing this, the question hovering at the front of my mind is, "Did they win?"

I can only begin to answer that question here, so I won't. Instead, I want to focus on the instinct to ask about "winning." It reveals so much about how I felt in that space, how I think about it even now—and how that feeling and thinking may not be "wrong," yet it functions like a sieve for the possibilities that might have been available to us to navigate differently the bully culture in which we lived, in which my friends (and "enemies") still live. Perhaps it's commonplace now to think in terms of friends and enemies, winning and losing. Perhaps even those of us with PhDs, who spend our days examining and writing arguments, are not above those commonplaces. Perhaps, then, the most obvious solution to the problems that are enabled when we think in terms of those commonplaces is to complicate them. Crowley, for example, offers at least a few ways of complicating the polarization she identifies between liberals and fundamentalists—for example, telling our stories, describing our hopes, trying to dislodge a single belief or claim from an ideology. On the surface, these seem like good ideas, but I suspect that there's a reason why Crowley dedicates just a few pages total to them: even after writing a book about the problem of polarized, hostile (non)debate, the solution evades.

The best piece of advice I've seen on dealing with bullies is in Aaron James's *Assholes: A Theory* (2012, 125): we likely won't ever achieve "the impossible—get[ting] the asshole to listen and change."[8] But we can uphold our own rights publicly.[9] That means calling out the behavior when we see it. Too, I would suggest that if we're going to speak to each other behind closed doors about our mutual experiences of being bullied, then the focus of those conversations should not be an exercise in radical anger, but it should be about how to support each other's efforts to call out the behavior publicly—that is, how to give each other courage.

The courage to talk back, as bell hooks (1998) says, is a hard-won courage, and it certainly has been for me. I eventually learned to do it, but not consistently. Sometimes, when I was overwhelmed, I didn't have the headspace to attend carefully to my workmates' statements in department meetings, for example; I sometimes let things slide. If there had been enough people in the targeted group at each of those meetings to pick up each other's slack, then we might have succeeded in changing the culture—slowly, deliberately. A few of us spent a lot of time chatting with superiors, too, to make sure that people outside the department knew what was happening, even if there were no procedures in place for us to pursue formal complaints (or, more specifically, even if there were procedures that allowed us to complain but without any protections for us to do so safely). The point is not to cower, not to retreat into our corners and then lash out viciously when someone prods our cages; however, to respond in some other way(s) requires, I think, support—*shared* courage. That is how we care for ourselves in the face of a bully.

To sustain courage, I think it is important to remember that we live in connectivity and that forefronting that connectivity might be more productive than continuing to blindly privilege a notion of competitiveness (in an us versus them framework) that ignores connectivity, that celebrates the presumed autonomy of one person or group in relation to others. To put this in more practical terms, we must respond to bullying behaviors not as morally superior beings (who must assert our moral superiority over our opposition) but perhaps, as "joyful" ones. This no doubt seems a counterintuitive, perhaps even a vacuous and dangerous suggestion, but bear with me.

To quote folk singer and activist Ani Difranco (1997), "I do it for the joy it brings / Because I'm a joyful girl / Because the world owes me nothing / And we owe each other the world." As cheesy as that may sound on the surface, there's something profound in the "joy" that comes from "owing each other the world." In giving the world to each other in our lived, discursive, and bodily experiences, we are a sustaining part of it. Of course, what counts as "the world" in our experiences is contingent, by which I mean that my conceptions and experiences of the world, for example, are specific, temporal, situated in history, in the dynamics of race, class, gender, and so on as they work in/through me. But those conceptions and experiences, in all of their contingencies, are born of my encounters with others (e.g., the folks I work with). As such, we *owe* each other the world, as Difranco says. We are obligated, simply by the necessity of encounter, to give each other the world.

Western tradition has privileged masculine ways of being in the world, which, as Deborah Tannen (1998) famously explains, consist of being right, of winning, which would make any connectivity an exercise in competitiveness. As Krista Ratcliffe (2005, 23) suggests, though, there are other ways of participating in the logos ("the system of discourse within which a culture reasons and derives its truth"). As she explains, rhetorical listening (listening with a stance of openness) is one way to "cultivate conscious identifications in ways that promote productive communication, especially but not solely cross-culturally" (Ratcliffe 2005, 25).

Though I find the focus on identification and its variations of dis-identification and un-identification problematic in Ratcliffe's work (because I find the privileging of persuasion to be problematic, as I've explained at length in other works, such as *Beyond Argument* [Allen 2015]), I think Ratcliffe's conception of rhetorical listening connects in interesting ways to Crowley's conception of ideologics, at least in terms of how one might engage with other beliefs and values. Both seem to center on the idea that we should attend to what Ratcliffe calls "the excess" (what doesn't fit, what can't be appropriated by our "readerly [phenomenological] intent") or what Crowley might identify as values that can be dislodged from an established ideology (e.g., talking about abortion in something other than a liberal or conservative framework).

In a way, both are pointing to ways we might engage with others' beliefs and values so they don't simply get subsumed, for example, in the reader's confirmation bias or in a political ideology. As such, both of these scholars are asking us to shift away from an ethic of appropriation, which, if nothing else, is driven by competitiveness, by the desire to win in the broadest (and perhaps most dangerous) sense.

I think it's important to see the bigger picture when we're caught up in a bully culture—the key being that it is a bully *culture*, which suggests that the bullying is much bigger than any two people. Of course, in the moment, for example, in the moments I described earlier between myself and two different colleagues, it feels as though our world contracts and that it is just us alone in an exchange that is somehow unfathomable in its capriciousness, in the injustice of it. But in reality, if there is anything that history has taught us, it is that we live in a bully culture; my old department is not unique. I'm reminded of a particularly moving scene, a montage, in the documentary *13th*, which collects images of Trump supporters shoving and threatening black citizens along with black-and-white clips of images of white men shoving and threatening black activists during the Jim Crow era—"the good ol' days," as Trump calls them in a series of chilling voiceovers. Let's get real: this is a bully culture, and the problem is bigger than the university, bigger than the president of the United States.

But my point in reminding us of this fact is not to inspire despair. As the Dalai Lama explains, this suffering is not about a particular "us"; it is everywhere (Dalai Lama, Tutu, and Abrams 2016, 36). We must see beyond the shrinking rooms in which we experience the personal (and professional) wounds of bullying. The issue is bigger than professor X at University Y. And if that's true, then we must imagine change that is much more substantial—that reaches back even into the past, into a history of bullying, and confronts the ways such behavior has been normalized for us. If bully cultures seem to get their momentum from the fierce competitiveness, entitlement, and individualism of Western culture or if they are emboldened by a globally conditioned race for influence, then perhaps we need to shift our more fundamental values and attitudes as we imagine different ways of engaging with each other. If those same values shape our ideas of the successful academic (and I'd argue that they do), then we might ask ourselves: What would it mean to work, to live, in joy? If it cannot *be* within the competitive, individualized race for influence, then how can it be?

Maybe it seems a romantic idea, but in the end, working for joy is not actually cheesy. It is profound and complex, elusive and difficult. I'm not calling for a singular, kumbaya-ish vision for this experience called "joy." Rather, I'm calling for us to think about what conditions might enable the possibility of joy, and I'm suggesting that those conditions might be invented out of a different conception of connectivity—one that is rooted not in competitiveness but in an ethic of attentiveness to difference. Again, that's not to suggest that I (or anyone else) should learn to love, say, the white supremacists responsible for the violent conflict in Charlottesville, Virginia, in August 2017. But are there ways to attend to even the most dangerous positions in order to negotiate a different way of being *together* in the world?[10]

Shouldn't we all work where we don't have to spend our days sick and angry and afraid? Don't we owe each other that? What would it mean to cultivate connectivity among faculty, in which we value and attend to variation and difference instead of divisive competitiveness across categorical oppositions? Would our scholarship and teaching suffer, or would it be even stronger? I think I should have supported my peers at my prior institution by encouraging us to think not in terms of "us versus them" but in terms of a community. I should have persisted in asking the questions "what kind of community do we want" and "how can we cultivate it." I think that would have been "caring for each other" in the face of bullying. Isn't joy exactly that: in the responsibility to each other, to ourselves?

NOTES

1. Gates explains that lifting the veil equates to him revealing secrets about his family and about black culture. It is a risk—for perhaps obvious reasons—to a historically disenfranchised people. In the case of my work here, I would never suggest that academics are historically disenfranchised. There are different kinds of risks I take in revealing the secret that is the bully culture of my prior department—for example, revealing secrets that might make it easy for readers to (falsely) assume that all of our exchanges were hostile and threatening or that academics are generally bullies.

2. See Janell Ross's 2015 report for the *Washington Post*, titled "So Which Women Has Donald Trump Called 'Dogs' and 'Fat Pigs'?" on his long-standing use of pejorative descriptions of women. Kelly herself has been on the receiving end of Trump's abuse. Laura Bates (2016), founder of the Everyday Sexism Project, responds in an article for *Time* to the media's characterizations of Kelly and Trump's public interactions as "'spat' and 'drama'": "This is not a spat, a drama, a feud or a quibble. This is the relentless misogynistic abuse of a high-profile woman doing her job."

3. The recent election of Trump would suggest that bullying is not as passé as my mother has thought. See Juvonen (2017) on how Trump's bullying tactics made him popular.

4. In an effort to increase funding through tuition dollars, the university had been widening its admission-requirements window so that we saw, over the years, an increase in the number of students who didn't have the necessary preparation to succeed.

5.   The factions I'll refer to repeatedly in this chapter were divided prominently by generation—with the most senior (in terms of both age and tenure) in one group and the most junior (again, in terms of age and tenure) in the other. The most pronounced and damaging bullying behaviors, though, were carried out by a few senior male faculty against a few junior female faculty. Obviously, gender was just as important as age and tenure to the asymmetrical power relations at work in the department.

6.   Crowley (2006, 30) defines "liberalism" in a number of ways, developing the concept throughout the book, but in the first chapter she notes liberalism's "commonplaces concerning individual rights, equality before the law, and personal freedom." In terms of the exchange of ideas, which is central to democracy, liberals seek to maintain democracy by "creating consensus about contested issues [and by forwarding] reason and tolerance as means of securing agreement" (Crowley 2006, 15). In sum, liberals value debate that seeks consensus through reason and tolerance but that is guided by the values of individual rights, equality before the law, and personal freedom. I can safely say that all of my workmates at my prior institution would agree that they sought the same, at least in principle. The problems emerged when those values became essentialized in the group's fight for dominance and were thus remade into their own brand of fundamentalism.

7.   Clearly, he's not alone in this belief. One of the images that has been circulating on Facebook since Trump was elected is a parody of Verizon's coverage map in which the red portions of the map are areas where the Republican vote won. The tag line under the image is "Can you hear us now?" suggesting that Trump supporters feel they've been silenced or at least ignored in the past.

8.   James uses Trump as a key example of the "asshole" (and the text was published long before Trump was talking about running for president).

9.   See chapter 5, "Asshole Management," in James (2012) for more extensive and thoughtful advice on ways of working to diminish the asshole's destructive influence in a community.

10. I think many scholars in our discipline show us that there are ways of doing so. In fact, they do so all the time by taking up the value or assumption that we don't want to or can't see and responding to that oversight with great care (e.g., Ratcliffe's attentiveness to the field's neglect of listening; Thomas Rickert's attentiveness to rhetorical-ness as ambience; Debra Hawhee's, Diane Davis's, and many others' attentiveness to "nonhuman" [in] rhetorics, and many more).

REFERENCES

Allen, Sarah. 2015. *Beyond Argument: Essaying as a Practice of (Ex)Change*. Fort Collins, CA: AC [Writing across the Curriculum] Clearinghouse and Parlor Press.

Bates, Laura. 2016. "Donald Trump's 'Spat' with Megyn Kelly Is Sexism, and It's Abusive." *Time*, January 28.

Bruce, Steve. 2008. *Fundamentalism*, 2nd ed. Cambridge: Polity.

Crowley, Sharon. 2006. *Toward a Civil Discourse: Rhetoric and Fundamentalism*. Pittsburgh: University of Pittsburgh Press. https://doi.org/10.2307/j.ctt5hjng7.

Dalai Lama and Desmond Tutu, with Douglas Carlton Abrams. 2016. *The Book of Joy: Lasting Happiness in a Changing World*. New York: Avery.

Difranco, Ani. 1997. "Joyful Girl." *Living in Clip* (CD). Buffalo: Righteous Babes Records.

Gates, Henry Louis, Jr. 1998. "Lifting the Veil." In *Inventing the Truth: The Art and Craft of Memoir*, ed. William Zinsser, 101–18. New York: Houghton Mifflin.

hooks, bell. 1989. *Talking Back: Thinking Feminist, Thinking Black*. Boston: South End Books.

James, Aaron. 2012. *Assholes: A Theory.* New York: Anchor Books.

Juvonen, Jaana. 2017. "I Study the Psychology of Adolescent Bullies; Trump Makes Perfect Sense to Me." *Washington Post,* May 23.

Mouffe, Chantal. 2000. *The Democratic Paradox.* London: Verson.

Peters, Brad. 2003. "An Anatomy of Radical Anger in Writing Program Administration." In *A Way to Move: Rhetorics of Emotion and Composition Studies,* ed. Dale Jacobs and Laura R. Micciche, 135–46. Portsmouth, NH: Boynton/Cook.

Ratcliffe, Krista. 2005. *Rhetorical Listening: Identification, Gender, Whiteness.* Carbondale: Southern Illinois University Press.

Ross, Janell. 2015. "So Which Women Has Donald Trump Called 'Dogs' and 'Fat Pigs'?" *Washington Post,* August 8.

Tannen, Deborah. 1998. *The Argument Culture: Stopping America's War of Words.* New York: Ballentine Books.

US Department of Health and Human Services. 2016, "The Roles Kids Play." Stopbullying .gov.

Wacker, Grant. 2000. "The Rise of Fundamentalism." November. NationalHumanitiesCen ter.org.

Wajngurt, Clara. 2014. "Prevention of Bullying on Campus: Neither Collegiality nor Congeniality Are Always Present in Faculty Relations." AAUP: American Association of University Professors, May–June. https://www.aaup.org/article/prevention-bullying -campus#.W_iTjuJRc2w.

5

QUIET AS IT'S KEPT
Bullying and the Contingent Writing Center Director

Dawn Fels

I lost everything: job, insurance, income, career, savings, health,
peace of mind, friends.

—Mika

Writing center directors are writing program administrators (WPAs) whose work directly touches tens of thousands of students every semester. Yet 70 percent of today's writing center directors hold non-tenurable, contingent positions (Isaacs and Knight 2014). On its website, the American Association of University Professors (2014) describes contingent employees as those who serve in "insecure, unsupported positions with little job security and few protections for academic freedom." While some contingent writing center directors have held their positions for decades[1] and tenure affords some of them job security and certain protections, the guarantee that a seasoned, successful writing center director will remain in the position until they voluntarily leave it is no longer a given.

In recent years, the writing center field has witnessed several contingent and tenured, highly qualified writing center directors removed from their centers as a result of financial exigencies and administrators' changes to writing center programs. Often, those directors were left out of conversations that ultimately affected them, their writing center programs, their tutors, and the students who relied on their writing centers for help. Each year, others who operate off the tenure line on short-term contracts must reapply for their jobs or wait to see if their contracts will be renewed, despite having successfully run their centers. What were once full-time tenure-line writing center directorships have been converted into part-time adjunct positions. Too often it appears that administration is unaware of the absolute necessity to retain

DOI: 10.7330/9781607328162.c005

highly qualified writing center directors. Merit, training, service, and expertise—the "stuff" of good employees in any workplace but especially valued in academia—are not enough to save jobs. The current academic milieu, historically competitive, has become even more so, fueled by the silencing of faculty voices in presidential hiring decisions, the influx of senior administrators with no higher education leadership experience, the "end of tenure" wave brought on by politicians, the rise of austerity measures in the face of budget cuts, the defunding of grant programs, and the discriminatory laws that place additional burdens on those who have historically been discriminated against. Those conditions can change the culture on many campuses, increasing the struggle to hold on to funding, face, programs, power—a job. Furthermore, academia's two-tier system perpetuates the notion that some employees are more special and valuable to the institution (Harber, Donini, and Parker 2013). Those conditions create a system that devastates good old-fashioned reciprocal collegiality and support among colleagues. Bullying thrives in those conditions (Hoel, Einarsen, and Cooper 2003).

Writing center directors and their programs have already fallen victim to academe's labor and funding crises, conditions under which bullying flourishes. While it's too late to reinstate those directors who have lost their centers or their jobs, WPAs across the composition field can work harder to recognize and improve the current conditions under which many directors toil, especially those who hold contingent, short-term, precarious positions. Contingent writing center directors' institutional status makes them even more vulnerable than their tenured colleagues to workplace bullying. This chapter uses a portion of existing scholarship on bullying to contextualize the experiences of non-tenure-line writing center directors, which I've gathered through conversations at conferences, in phone calls, by email, on listservs, and through a study I'm currently conducting with Clint Gardner, Maggie Herb, and Liliana Naydan on the working conditions of contingent writing center workers. By interweaving scholarship and directors' voices, I hope to answer these questions: What does bullying look like? How does it start, and why? How does bullying damage the writing center directors' emotional, physical, and economic well-being? How should a contingent writing center director confront bullying? My hope is that by framing the realities some contingent writing center directors face with current scholarship on bullying, we can end the harm done to their programs, their tutors and students, their professional lives, and their personal well-being.

WHAT DOES BULLYING LOOK LIKE?

Bullying is a socially constructed process of intentional negative actions over a period of time (Bjørkelo 2013) taken by one or more individuals against another. Bullying is hard to define, but it tends "to threaten, to intimidate, to humiliate or to isolate members of the working university environment [and] that undermines reputation or job performance" (Farrington quoted in Wajngurt 2014). Scholars who study bullying generally agree that bullying behaviors include but are not limited to the following: verbal behaviors (e.g., gossip, rumor mongering, ridicule, mockery, name calling, hostility, false accusations of mistakes, public and private defamation, comments related to protected status); nonverbal behaviors (e.g., hostile glaring); physical harm or violence; isolation, obstruction, and exclusion; unreasonable workload or demands; withholding of necessary information, materials, or technologies relevant to doing one's job or completing a task; policing; sabotage of work and opportunities for advancement; withholding necessary information relevant to employment status; denial of due process; and challenges to academic freedom (Cowan 2011; Cowie et al. 2002; Wajngurt 2014).

Jaime Lester (2013, ix) notes that "how we define workplace bullying, and how we separate it as behavior from other organizational practices and behaviors, will determine what we consider bullying in our organizations." In the same paragraph she names the "exclusion of the contingent faculty member" as one form of bullying and points to Ståle Einarsen and colleagues' definition of bullying as a process that includes "harassing, offending, socially excluding someone or negatively affecting someone's work tasks . . . It has to occur repeatedly and regularly (e.g., weekly) and over a period of time (e.g., at least six months). Bullying is an escalating process in the course of which the person confronted ends up in an inferior position and becomes the target of systematic negative social acts" (Lester 2013, ix).

That definition, reflective of Einarsen and colleagues' (2003) work in Europe, provides a starting point from which to understand the basic characteristics of bullying. Other characteristics include intent (Bjørkelo 2013; Olweus 1993), length and frequency (Cowie et al. 2002), competence (McDaniel, Ngala, and Leonard 2015), and "imbalance of strength" (Bjørkelo 2013). Others connect characteristics of workplace bullying with whistleblowing (McDaniel, Ngala, and Leonard 2015) and workplace corruption (Vickers 2014). No matter the definition, bullying stems from an abuse of power and leads to devastating results for the bullied, their work environment, and, ultimately, the organization.

Suzy Fox and Renee L. Cowan (2015) offered a definition of bullying that builds on their work with human resources (HR) personnel. Cowan (2011) asked eighteen HR representatives to describe and share their institution's anti-bullying policies. Based on their answers and her examination of the policies her respondents provided, she found widespread inconsistencies between their interpretations and what the policies actually said. She also found that bullying was described too ambiguously, if at all, with most policies relying on the legal definitions of harassment. Legal definitions, according to Cowan (2011), do not protect victims of bullying because bullying is not considered illegal. Believing that HR professionals have ethical, legal, and professional responsibilities to sustain all employees' well-being—the bullied and the bully—Fox and Cowan (2015) sought HR professionals' help in redefining bullying so they can address it more effectively. Although I find their protection of the bully controversial, I do think their definition of bullying is a good starting point for how it invites dialogue on the basics: behaviors, time frame, and outcomes. According to Fox and Cowan (2015, 124), bullying constitutes "actions and practices that a 'reasonable person' would find abusive, [that] occur repeatedly or persistently, and [that] result in adverse economic, psychological, or physical outcomes to the target and/or a hostile work environment."

What are those actions and practices? Fox and Cowan (2015) added ten behaviors to a Workplace Bullying Checklist (WB-C) introduced by previous studies of bullying among small sample sizes in corporate, school, and university settings.[2] They then asked the HR professionals to rate each behavior as "not bullying," "subtle bullying," or "blatant bullying" (Fox and Cowan 2015, 121). Of the 204 HR personnel surveyed, 60 percent felt that twenty-two behaviors on the list constituted either subtle or blatant bullying (see table 5.1). Fox and Cowan (2015, 122) also asked respondents whether a behavior had other characteristics identified by previous studies that "differentiate bullying from other forms of uncivil, hostile, disruptive, or abusive behaviour." Those characteristics include persistence or repeated occurrence, formal power differences, informal power differences, perceived intention to harm, confirmed intention to harm, involvement of other coworkers or managers (i.e., mobbing), behavior that a reasonable person would consider abusive, and outcomes that include economic, psychological, or physical harm (Fox and Cowan 2015, 123). For instance, Fox and Cowan's (2015) respondents didn't see the presence of an informal or formal power difference as necessary to determine whether a behavior constituted bullying. This could mean that HR personnel felt that anyone, no matter their status, could be the bully or the bullied.

Although Fox and Cowan's (2015) sample did not include HR personnel from higher education, scholars who have studied bullying in higher education would agree. In their study of 1,185 university employees, Loraleigh Keashly and Joel H. Neuman (2013, 11) found that "the relevance of the actor-target relationship is strongly influenced by organizational structure." They found that "colleagues were more likely to be identified as bullies by faculty (63.4%), whereas superiors were more likely to be identified as bullies by frontline staff (52.9%)" (Keashly and Neuman 2013, 11). Neuman later studied the former phenomenon and found that "senior colleagues were more likely to be identified as bullies" (Keashly and Neuman 2013, 11). Keashly and Neuman's (2013, 11–12) work points to the reality of how one's institutional status, "as defined by occupational group and hierarchical and/or professional status, may leave specific targets vulnerable to abuse from particular actors/agents." Thus, contingent faculty are more likely to be bullied by senior colleagues, including tenured or tenure-line faculty, a fact supported by Susan Taylor's (2013) research.

Institutional rank aside, most definitions of bullying include some reference to frequency and length of action, as well as intent to harm. More than one-third of the HR respondents in Fox and Cowan's (2015) study, however, didn't feel that bullying had to take place repeatedly or over a period of time. For them and other scholars (Westhues 2006a), one incident was enough to cause concern and require action. Fox and Cowan's (2015) respondents' notions of intention to harm, however, differed from those of others. While most definitions of bullying almost always included intention to harm, Fox and Cowan's (2015, 125) respondents called for confirmed intention to harm, which the authors explained as HR professionals' "valuing of outside evidence of bullying over single target perceptions." The implication is that truly abusive behavior would be that which any "reasonable person" would see as abusive and therefore would be confirmed by others when reported by the victim. Fox and Cowan (2015, 125) noted the limitations and risks involved when applying this measure, which is typically used in legal cases regarding harassment, to bullying situations: "Here is where we can see possibly negative consequences of using this standard to label a bullying situation . . . If it is common and accepted to demean, insult, spread false rumors, etc., in a particular work environment, the reasonable person standard for bullying would likely never be met."

Another limitation comes into play in particularly toxic departments where bullying behaviors are accepted or when mobbing occurs. In either of those situations, it may be hard for an HR representative to find anyone who will confirm that bullying has taken place.

It may also be hard for employees to know when they have been bullied and for their colleagues to recognize bullying, including their own participation in it. Having had many conversations with writing center directors over the years, I have come to realize that most may be unaware that the experiences they described fit the characteristics of bullying. For instance, Riley, a writing center director, described in an interview their experiences in meetings with tenured and tenure-line colleagues: "I hate meetings because I am often shut down. In one meeting I made a suggestion, only to be told by a tenure-line colleague, 'We're not here to discuss that.' In another, I raised a concern, and a tenured colleague and another who was being groomed to take their place laughed at me. No one else said a word to address that, not even my supporters. I was humiliated. I'd been there for less than a year, had done great work, and had no idea what I'd done to deserve their dismissal or ridicule."

What Riley describes is bullying behavior perpetrated by two individuals who held a higher institutional rank than they did. It falls short of mobbing, however, because it is unclear whether the other colleagues in the room shared the two individuals' intention to silence and humiliate Riley. Being "shushed" or laughed at in a meeting may seem harmless enough, but both had a lasting effect on Riley and their relationship with colleagues. In this next scenario, Lorin describes an experience with colleagues, whom Lorin never met, who intentionally sabotaged Lorin's candidacy for another position within the department:

> Our department is huge, so I don't know a fraction of my colleagues. I was on a one-year, non-renewable contract and in my first year. I did great work. My evaluations were excellent. I worked beyond my contract expectations and volunteered to help where needed within the department. So when the opportunity to apply for a longer-term appointment came up, I applied for it. I was even asked to provide additional materials, which signaled that I was one of the top candidates. But weeks after applying, I got a heart-stopping email from the chair who said some colleagues, whom I [had] never met, expressed concerns about my performance. I quickly moved to dispel the rumors, showing the chair proof of my work over the semester, and they agreed that there must be some misunderstanding. They suggested I reach out to the colleagues to provide them with the information I shared with the chair. I did that, but no one responded to my emails. I didn't get the job, either.

While the decision not to give Lorin the position may or may not have had anything to do with the rumors and the impression they left on the chair, it is reasonable to believe that it could have. One of the easiest ways to block someone's promotion, raise, or hire is to create doubt about the person's qualifications, performance, and disposition for the job. In spreading an unfounded rumor, Lorin's colleagues sabotaged Lorin's candidacy. The fact that the colleagues worked together to do so constitutes mobbing. Spreading rumors, sabotaging opportunities, and mobbing are all bullying behaviors.

While Fox and Cowan's (2015) table of WB-C behaviors (see table 5.1) can be used to diagnose workplace bullying and train employees in how to recognize and avoid it, the authors pointed to the need for site-specific work. They called on HR professionals, scholars, employees, trainers, and anti-bullying activists to collaborate on detailed lists of abusive behaviors and specific policies to address them. I agree. I'll address that opportunity later in the chapter.

HOW DOES BULLYING START, AND WHY

> Six months into my new job, I attended a meeting for those responsible for distinct but related writing programs on campus. The meeting was described as an opportunity for each of us to share what we were working on with the goal of keeping each other in the loop, since there was a lot of overlap between our respective programs' goals. We met in a senior colleague's office, someone recognized as a leader in the field. At one point in the meeting, I made a claim about the leadership potential of writing centers that should not have surprised anyone in the room. After all, my research had focused on writing centers, and I presumed that my colleagues were familiar with it and my years of experience in the field; they were on the committee that hired me. Well, no sooner than the words "writing center" and "leadership" left my mouth, the senior colleague shifted in their chair and crossed their arms. "Well. What do you mean by 'leader,'" they asked. But it didn't sound like a question. It sounded more defensive, mocking, scolding. I don't remember my answer because I was so taken aback by the question, asked in that way, coming from that person. I felt my face flush. I do remember that the tone and purpose of the meeting shifted and [the meeting] ended shortly thereafter. The team of directors never did meet again. After that, the bullying started.

> —Emory

Emory can pinpoint when and why the senior colleague started to bully them, and they did go to their supervisor more than once to voice concerns about it, which ultimately only made matters worse. Emory left the institution. What can colleges and universities do to retain employees like Emory by identifying and addressing bullying behaviors? Although I think Fox and Cowan's (2015) work could be a helpful starting point to identify, investigate, and eradicate incidents of workplace bullying, it is not specific to bullying in higher educational institutions, whose organizational hierarchies determine the likelihood that bullying will take place, what it might look like, and what might be done to report it.

Taylor's (2013) study of 1,034 full-time faculty at a midwestern research university revealed several findings relevant to a discussion of how contingent faculty might experience workplace bullying. Of those who responded to Taylor's survey, 19 percent held non-tenure-line positions (2013, 29). Respondents were asked to complete a Negative Acts Questionnaire–Revised (NAQ-R) that listed twenty-two behaviors and asked them to note the frequency with which they experienced the behaviors.[3] Taylor (2013, 29) wrote, "The behaviors were not labeled as bullying behaviors and included items that were work-related, person-related, or constituted intimidation or abuse." Respondents were also provided with a definition of workplace bullying and asked whether they felt they were bullied at work. Taylor used answers to that question to categorize respondents as bullied or not. They were also asked questions pertaining to workplace dissatisfaction. Taylor (2013, 30) found that "approximately 12% (n = 123) of the faculty indicated they were targets of bullying behaviors." Those who identified as bullied were also more often exposed to bullying behaviors. Unsurprisingly, tenure status was "significantly related to the frequency of exposure to the specific bullying behaviors" (Taylor 2013, 30). Non-tenure-track faculty were significantly more vulnerable to bullying, followed by tenured faculty, and then tenure-line faculty. The fact that tenured faculty fall victim to bullying, Taylor (2013) surmised, has more to do with the job protection tenure affords: it's easier to bully a tenured faculty to get them to leave than to terminate them. As to why more non-tenured faculty are bullied, Taylor (2013, 30) noted that "non-tenure-track faculty may feel they have no power to address the situation" and are more likely to leave than tenured colleagues who are bullied. Pointing to Kenneth Westhues's (2006a) work on envy, Taylor (2013) suggested that envy may be a factor in the bullying of successful faculty members, no matter their institutional status. This is important to consider when identifying the reasons why outstanding writing center directors are bullied or suddenly have their centers taken away from them—or both. This happened to Emory, who was hired to direct a writing program but was later bullied by a senior colleague for asserting their expertise.

Over time, other colleagues joined the senior colleague who bullied Emory. Though Emory reported several instances to the supervisor and HR, nothing was done to address the bullying, so Emory left. Leighton describes how those alliances and mobbing form: "Bullies are power-ful and relentless. Once they get colleagues on their side, everyone abandons you. One day, you're all going out for drinks. You're invited to parties. The next day, you've found out by accident that they all went out with the new hires. Or they had a meeting without you to discuss course development for a program that you helped to develop. Or with-out informing you, they take a course you were supposed to teach out of rotation."

Bullying in higher education comes with a price tag. Talented employ-ees, like Emory and Leighton, leave. Bullies stay, and over time, alliances form. Alliances—especially with tenured and senior colleagues—may affect tenure, promotion, and contract renewal of less senior colleagues. Alliances and the threats that come with not joining them also lead to mobbing. Of the university employees Keashly and Neuman (2013) surveyed, the majority reported being bullied by two or more col-leagues. So did Emory and Leighton. They also referred to the work of Westhues (2006a, 12), who argued that "mobbing of professors by their colleagues and administrators . . . is very different from the experience (however upsetting) of being harassed by a single actor." Keashly and Neuman (2013, 12) found that "faculty members were almost twice as likely as staff to report being the victims of mobbing by three or more actors," a marked increase from Kenneth Westhues's (2006b) previous findings. Those findings should compel us to "consider the actor-target relationship, as well as the number of actors involved within the broader context of the occupational group, status differentials, and formally (and informally) defined working relationships" (quoted in Keashly and Neuman 2013, 13). They go on to refer to a study by Dieter Zapf and Claudia Gross, who "found that the longer a situation continued, the more people would join in, concluding that it may become increas-ingly difficult for bystanders to remain neutral as bullying proceeds and intensifies" (Keashly and Neuman 2013, 13). In other words, "Once bullying begins, the longer it is permitted to continue, the more likely it is that other colleagues will be drawn into the situation" (Keashly and Neuman 2013, 13).

THE DEVASTATING EFFECTS OF BULLYING

> *After I reported the bullying to my supervisor, a former supporter*
> *stopped talking to me. From that time on, I would see them in the hall,*
> *and they'd glare at me. Literally glare.*
>
> —Devyn

Reporting bullying to a supervisor or another trusted colleague doesn't always improve matters. Taylor (2013) found that faculty who were bullied felt less optimistic that anything would change, were less likely to suggest changes, and were less likely to believe leaders would work to change the conditions they endured. As a result, Taylor (2013) added, when bullied faculty stay at their institutions, they are likely to become more cynical, disengage, neglect their duties, make more mistakes, and take more sick days. Worse, they may resort to workplace violence. Any of these outcomes threatens the success of a writing center but can also severely harm the director's physical and psychological health, employment status, reputation, and economic well-being.

Even though victims of bullying can take steps to ameliorate or eradicate it, many of those actions—including those often outlined in an institution's policies and protocols—have the potential of worsening their situation (Keashly and Neuman 2013). Keashly and Neuman (2013, 14) asked employees who self-identified as targets of bullying about their attempts to improve their situations and whether the attempts "improved, worsened, or had no discernible impact on the bullying." Those who reported bullying found that their situation worsened, even when they followed standard protocols for reporting. This was true for Riley and Devyn. Among Keashly and Neuman's (2013, 14) respondents whose situations worsened were those who reported the bullying to their supervisor/chair/dean (26.7%), asked the bully to stop (38.9%), lowered their own productivity to stay out of the line of fire (29.7%), told their union representative (23.2%), told someone in HR (32.7%), had someone speak to the bully (34%), made a formal complaint (37.9%), asked for a transfer (35.3%), or threatened to tell others (28.6%). Similarly, Judith A. Richman and colleagues found that "engaging members of the organization who have the 'power' to alter the situation had a limited effect on ending bullying and when it failed, the effects on the individual were devastating" (quoted in Keashly and Neuman 2013, 15).

Although both Riley and Devyn were outstanding writing center directors, they still held contingent positions in their institutions. Two clear problems emerge, tied to the organizational structure of academia, that particularly affect contingent writing center directors' success in reporting bullying. First, as aptly described by Linda H. Harber, Patricia L. Donini, and Shernita Rochelle Parker (2013, 123), "in the education workforce, where everyone is special, some groups are just 'more special.'" Contingent writing center directors are not special enough. They may do everything right: do their jobs, publish and do research, win awards for their scholarship, create new programs, serve on and beyond their campuses, bring in grants, and work as hard as, if not harder than, their colleagues to retain students. But because they aren't considered as special as the tenured or tenure-line faculty members who bully them, they may not get the justice they deserve. It may be wiser, though certainly not healthier, to maintain quiet as kept and soldier on.

Second, a contingent writing center director on a short-term contract runs the risk of losing their job or not having their contract renewed or exacerbating the bullying if they report it. On campuses where there is no formal definition of bullying and no formal process for reporting, examining, and addressing it or where HR isn't seen as an advocate for all or where HR looks around for corroborators but can't find any because those who have witnessed the bullying are either too afraid to speak up or have become part of the mob, it's very likely that nothing will be done about what the writing center director reports, which could worsen the situation for the director. The only way a contingent writing center director has any chance of addressing any of the behaviors described in the scenarios included in this chapter is on a campus where everyone is held responsible for reporting incidents of bullying when they occur and where bullies of any rank are held accountable.

And report it we must. Bullying affects nearly every aspect of a victim's personal health and well-being. Sam describes how bullying affected them: "I knew I was stressed, but I didn't know I was sick. The experience really wrecked my health. I had to go on medication. I gained a ton of weight. I couldn't sleep. I was in constant pain. I had stomach issues. I still have issues. Still on meds, trying to make all that go away."

Sam's experience is similar to what scholars have described as the classic effects of bullying. Using twelve studies conducted outside the United States of nearly 70,500 workers, physicians Randy A. Sansone and Lori A. Sansone (2015, 34–35) note that effects of bullying range from the emotional to the economical:

- Increased stress and mental distress . . . even up to two years later
- Sleep disturbances
- Depression and anxiety; major depression; PTSD; mood, anxiety, adjustment disorders
- Fatigue
- Work-related suicide
- Increased use of hypnotics and psychotropic medications
- Greater general health complaints
    o Neck pain, musculoskeletal complaints, acute pain, fibromyalgia
    o Cardiovascular disease
    o Increased absenteeism and sick days

o   Greater likelihood of long-term absence due to sick leave
o   Greater rates of unemployment through either job loss or volun-
     tarily leave.

Other scholars note the same outcomes, which can affect a victim for years after the bullying incidents. Denise Salin and Helge Hoel's (2013, 237) study on the gendered aspects of bullying note "no clear sex differences in terms of health consequences" of bullying, but women reported a "slightly stronger relationship between exposure to negative acts and negative health consequences." They referenced Lars Glasø's work, which suggests there is no classic victim of bullying. Both bullying and interpretations of bullying are also gendered constructions. Previous studies (see Salin 2003; Escartin, Salin, and Rodriguez-Carballeira 2011) found that women were more likely to see bullying as more prevalent and negative, especially with regard to "emotional abuse, social isolation, and professional discrediting" (Salin and Hoel 2013, 237). In response to bullying, women were more likely to avoid it by taking sick leave, requesting a transfer, quitting, looking for help, doing nothing, or seeking social support. Women were also more likely to ask for help. In 2014, Emily Isaacs and Melinda Knight (2014, 49) found that 73 percent of writing center directors were female. The fact that women are more inclined to talk about being bullied may mean that more will be done to eradicate it, thereby protecting the employment, health, and economic well-being of the majority of today's writing center directors. But for those in precarious positions, asking for help comes with risks.

WHAT CAN BE DONE?

Contingency and its inherent lack of job security, support, protections, and academic freedom magnifies the potential threats of reporting bullying, especially if the bully is a supervisor, senior colleague, or a tenured or tenure-line faculty member. The two-tier system protects those members of the faculty in ways it does not protect contingent faculty. So when a tenured or tenure-line faculty member or administrator bullies a contingent writing center director and that director cannot go to other colleagues, their supervisor, HR, or their union without the threat of retaliation, what can they do? What can they do when their colleagues, who also have an ethical responsibility to report bullying, don't do so or, worse, join in? What can they do when those hired to uphold institutional policies about bullying, including those in HR, look the other way? What can they do when those who do retaliate or engage in mob bullying worsen the situation?

The director can leave. To the contingent writing center director who recognizes their situation in any of the scenarios or scholarship I share throughout this chapter, I say leave if no one helps you. Go find a new job, preferably on a unionized campus. Anyone who works with a contingent writing center director, including other WPAs, administrators, chairs, and tenure-line and senior colleagues, has an ethical responsibility to protect them from bullying, even if doing so is not explicitly part of their job description. Bullying is abuse. As with other forms of abuse, we don't want to admit that it's happening to us or how it makes us feel. So we silence ourselves. We don't want to rock the boat. We hold on to our faith that someone will do something about it or that the bullies and their allies will change. We think that perhaps dialing back our own success will stop the bully. Or maybe we think the bullying is just a test and that if we soldier on, stand up for ourselves, let our work speak for itself, we will pass that test, and the bully will stop. Quiet as kept does not work. Bullies will not stop until someone stops them.

No job, especially a short-term contingent position, is worth the devastation that comes with being bullied. You are more than your job, and you deserve one that won't wreck your identity, reputation, physical or mental health, confidence, economic well-being, or your relationships with beloved friends and family. All of those things suffer when you are bullied, and they are worth protecting. You are worth protecting. You should familiarize yourself with the bullying behaviors described in this chapter (see table 5.1) and throughout this book. If one or more people behave in those ways, document the incident and its effects on your ability to do your job, your physical and mental health, your writing center program, and your relationships with others. Realize that colleagues who support you today could easily become part of the problem tomorrow. They have to protect themselves, too. Confide in those you trust outside the organization, including a therapist. Fight the urge to stay home when things get bad. Go to work each day, and try to do your absolute best. Look for another job. When you get one, ask someone in HR for an exit interview and share your notes. And don't take another job that doesn't have a clearly defined policy for bullying and harassment. Make sure you look for the word *bullying*, as harassment pertains to legally actionable behaviors and bullying is not yet legally actionable.

First and foremost, remember that bullying is not your fault. Bullying is a process through which one or more people abuse their power in a system that allows it to happen. There are colleges and universities that have effective and systemic anti-bullying programs through which they

Table 5.1. Fox and Cowan's (2015) Workplace Bullying Checklist—List of Behaviors (122)

	Behavior	Subtle (% of respondents)	Blatant (% of respondents)
1	Made aggressive or intimidating eye contact or physical gestures (e.g., finger pointing, slamming objects, obscene gestures)	17	81
2	Situated your workspace in a physically isolated location	56	9
3	Gave you the silent treatment	70	9
4	Limited your ability to express an opinion	61	16
5	Threatened you with physical violence	1	99
6	Demeaned you in front of coworkers or clients	17	81
7	Verbal abuse (e.g., yelling, cursing, angry outburst)	1	98
8	Gave excessively harsh criticism of your performance	26	35
9	Spread false rumors about your personal life and character	42	52
10	Spread false rumors about your work performance	48	49
11	Intentionally withheld necessary information from you	63	16
12	Blamed you for errors for which you were not responsible	39	30
13	Threatened you with job loss or demotion	9	69
14	Insulted you or put you down	31	60
15	Flaunted his/her status over you in a condescending manner	52	24
16	Left you out of meetings or failed to show up for your meetings for no legitimate reason	54	10
17	Intentionally destroyed, stole, or sabotaged your work materials	6	91
18	Used email or other online media to harass, threaten, or intimidate you	2	97
19	Used email or other online media to attack your reputation or degrade you to others	10	89
20	Made unwanted physical contact such as hitting, pushing, poking, spitting	1	99
21	Told jokes or encouraged others to tell jokes about you	53	44
22	Communicated to you rudely, such as name calling or tone of voice	22	72

attempt to work with bullies and those they victimize. Find them. You want to work where your talents will be valued and rewarded and your well-being will be protected.

NOTES

1. For a look at how to create a secure contingent writing center director position, see West Virginia University's approach.
2. Fox and Cowan (2015) suggest other instruments for larger samples, such as the Negative Acts Questionnaire-Revised (NAQ-R) used by Taylor in her study of 1,034 faculty. The NAQ-R also contains a list of twenty-two behaviors.
3. Davila and Elder adapted the NAQ-R to design the survey for data that appear in chapter 1 of this collection.

REFERENCES

American Association of University Professors. 2014. "Contingent Faculty Positions." Accessed August 16, 2017. https://www.aaup.org/issues/contingency.

Bjørkelo, Brita. 2013. "Workplace Bullying after Whistleblowing: Future Research and Implications." *Journal of Managerial Psychology* 28 (3): 306–23. https://doi.org/10.1108/02683941311321178.

Cowan, Renee L. 2011. "'Yes, We Have an Anti-Bullying Policy, But . . . :' HR Professionals' Understandings and Experiences with Workplace Bullying Policy." *Communication Studies* 62 (3): 307–27. https://doi.org/10.1080/10510974.2011.553763.

Cowie, Helen, Paul Naylor, Ian Rivers, Peter K. Smith, and Beatriz Pereira. 2002. "Measuring Workplace Bullying." *Aggression and Violent Behavior* 7 (1): 33–51. https://doi.org/10.1016/S1359-1789(00)00034-3.

Einarsen, Ståle, Helge Hoel, Dieter Zapf, and Cary L. Cooper. 2003. "The Concept of Bullying at Work: The European Tradition." In *Bullying and Emotional Abuse in the Workplace: International Perspectives in Research and Practice*, ed. Ståle Einarsen, Helge Hoel, and Cary Cooper, 1–30. London: Taylor and Francis.

Escartin, Jordi, Denise Salin, and Alvaro Rodriguez-Carballeira. 2011. "Exploring Gender Differences in Conceptualizations of Workplace Bullying: Defining Bullying and Rating the Severity of Different Acts." *Journal of Personnel Psychology* 10 (4): 157–65.

Fox, Suzy, and Renee L. Cowan. 2015. "Revision of the Workplace Bullying Checklist: The Importance of Human Resource Management's Role in Defining and Addressing Workplace Bullying." *Human Resource Management Journal* 25 (1): 116–30. https://doi.org/10.1111/1748-8583.12049.

Harber, Linda H., Patricia L. Donini, and Shernita Rochelle Parker. 2013. "Higher Education Human Resources and the Workplace Bully." In *Workplace Bullying in Higher Education*, ed. Jaime Lester, 121–37. New York: Routledge.

Hoel, Hanna L., Ståle Einarsen, and Cary L. Cooper. 2003. "Organizational Effects of Bullying." In *Bullying and Emotional Abuse in the Workplace: International Perspectives in Research and Practice*, ed. Ståle Einarsen, Helge Hoel, and Cary L. Cooper, 2–30. London: Taylor and Francis.

Isaacs, Emily, and Melinda Knight. 2014. "A Bird's Eye View of Writing Centers: Institutional Infrastructure, Scope and Programmatic Issues, Reported Practices." *WPA: Writing Program Administration* 37 (2): 36–67.

Keashly, Loraleigh, and Joel H. Neuman. 2013. "Bullying in Higher Education." In *Workplace Bullying in Higher Education*, ed. Jaime Lester, 1–22. New York: Routledge.

Lester, Jaime. 2013. "Preface." In *Workplace Bullying in Higher Education*, ed. Jaime Lester, vii–xiv. New York: Routledge.

McDaniel, Karen Rogers, Florence Ngala, and Karen Moustafa Leonard. 2015. "Does Competency Matter? Competency as a Factor in Workplace Bullying." *Journal of Managerial Psychology* 30 (5): 597–609. https://doi.org/10.1108/JMP-02-2013-0046.

Olweus, Dan. 1993. *Bullying at School: What We Know and What We Can Do*. Oxford: Blackwell.

Salin, Denise. 2003. "The Significance of Gender in the Prevalence, Forms, and Perceptions of Bullying." *Nordiske Organisasjonsstudier* 5 (3): 30–53.

Salin, Denise, and Helge Hoel. 2013. "Workplace Bullying as a Gendered Phenomenon." *Journal of Managerial Psychology* 28 (3): 235–51. https://doi.org/10.1108/026839413 11321187.

Sansone, Randy A., and Lori A. Sansone. 2015. "Workplace Bullying: A Tale of Adverse Consequences." *Innovations in Clinical Neuroscience* 12 (1–2): 32–37.

Taylor, Susan. 2013. "Workplace Bullying: Does Tenure Change Anything?" In *Workplace Bullying in Higher Education*, ed. Jaime Lester, 23–40. New York: Routledge.

Vickers, Margaret. 2014. "Towards Reducing the Harm: Workplace Bullying as Workplace Corruption—a Critical Review." *Employee Responsibilities and Rights Journal* 26 (2): 95–113. https://doi.org/10.1007/s10672-013-9231-0.

Wajngurt, Clara. 2014. "Prevention of Bullying on Campus." American Association of University Professors. Accessed April 28, 2016. https://www.aaup.org/article/prevention-bullying-campus#.WZS-tjOZMUE.

Westhues, Kenneth. 2006a. *The Remedy and Prevention of Mobbing in Higher Education*. Lewiston, NY: Edwin Mellen.

Westhues, Kenneth. 2006b. "The Unkindly Art of Mobbing." *Academic Matters: The Journal of Higher Education* (Fall): 18–19.

6

BREAKING THE SILENCE OF RACISM AND BULLYING IN ACADEMIA
Leaning in to a Hard Truth

Andrea Dardello

In *Lean In: Women, Work, and the Will to Lead*, Sheryl Sandberg (2013, chapter 6) encourages women to do what we would if we were not afraid, what she calls "leaning in," so that we might "seek—and speak—our truth." But I am skeptical. And to be honest, I am afraid. I know all too well the severe penalties that come when those of us born without status or privilege speak "our truth." As an African American woman in academia, my truth is quite different from that of the chief operating officer of Facebook. While she has defied the glass ceiling that eludes millions of women, I wonder if anyone will listen to me, a community college educator speaking about academia's bastard child, bullying, as it is manifested through racist practices.

Speaking one's truth often comes with a cost for African American women. Rochelle Garner (2005, 1267) quotes Patricia Bell-Scott who writes that a "flat-footed" truth occurs for African American women when one "[offers] a story or statement that is straightforward, unshakable, and unembellished." Bell-Scott goes on to say, "This kind of truth-telling by and about Black women can be risky business because [the lives of black women] are often devalued and [their] voices periodically silenced" (quoted in Garner 2005, 1267). Hence, the act of truth telling for African American women may result in that very same truth and the speaker of it being neglected, disrespected, and even rejected. And while I am not suggesting that the act of speaking the truth is easy for any of us, my purpose is to demonstrate that when speaking the truth about difficult topics such as bullying and racism as an African American woman, the cost can be great. This is clearly borne out in the introduction to this book when editors Cristyn L. Elder and Bethany Davila reveal that when the call went out for contributors for an anthology that would address bullying in the WPA workplace, many supported their efforts

DOI: 10.7330/9781607328162.c006

and thanked them privately but felt they could not share their stories publicly because of the risks. As one who has an intimate understanding of what those risks entail, I am keenly aware of the reasons some would hesitate to tell their story. I acknowledge that what makes it easier for me to write now is that I am in a much better place than I was four years ago, both physically and emotionally. I was able to walk away from the site of my oppression and now enjoy the privilege of working at an institution where I am supported by faculty and administrators, including the president, to continue the work of social justice, which includes my contribution to this important collection.

I choose narrative as the primary form with which to examine racism as manifested through bullying because as Richard Delgado and Jean Stefancic (2012, 45, 49) point out, stories not only help members of the dominant group to understand what it is like to be a member of a marginalized group, but stories also "name a type of discrimination, [and,] once named, it can be combated." To this extent, stories can offer a different version of the truth, giving voice to those who have been silenced. I write to challenge the perception that racism must be overt, male, violent, involve the police, and take place in the streets. I write to bring attention to the covert nature of racism in an unsuspected space, the academy, among those who are rarely implicated: women. I tell my story to offer a version of the truth told not merely from the perspective of someone who has witnessed it but from the soul of one who has lived through it.

To understand my truth is to understand that it is not simply a racialized truth or a gendered truth; it is a truth that is inextricably tied to race, gender, class, and culture. As many other African American feminist scholars have pointed out, "Racism, sexism, and other interlocking oppressions create troubling obstacles for Black women at all levels in academia" (Wilder, Jones, and Osborne-Lampkin 2013, 27–28). Intersectionality helps us to understand that racism and other forms of oppression do not occur in isolation; rather, intersectionality is a result of multiple systems of oppression operating simultaneously (Crenshaw 2015). This chapter demonstrates how bullying—another form of oppression—operated alongside racism and classism to disempower me as an African American woman in an academic setting. Though I do not claim to speak for all African American women or people of color, it is my hope that my experience resonates with all who have witnessed or experienced oppression of any form. Equally important, I hope my story might clarify for those who have ever doubted or been unable to see the ways racism is endemic to academic culture and the subtle forms oppression might take and move them not only to acknowledge its existence but to do something about it.

While the act of speaking the truth arouses many legitimate fears for me even now, I write to free myself from the excruciating pain, if not the memory, of the experience. I write in the same vein as others who have written before me and in the shared spirit of contributors to this anthology, knowing that if I give power to shame with my silence, it erases this horrendous act—and others like it—and I forfeit the change that can happen if I but dare to speak (Onwuachi-Willig 2012). I write to become a part of a conversation, believing as Sandberg (2013, 148) does that "talking can transform minds, which can transform behaviors, which can transform institutions."

WOMEN OF COLOR IN THE ACADEMY

Patricia Hill Collins (1986) argues that African American women in the academy often perceive themselves as outsiders because of the vastly different beliefs, values, assumptions, and worldviews they bring. Shaping their perception are the interlocking oppressions of racism, sexism, and classism. Nevertheless, this position as outsider, she argues, can be a powerful space African American academics use to creatively address injustice both inside and outside of the academy (Collins 1986, S15). To address oppression as an outsider, the African American female intellectual must first redefine the academy and her role in it. As an outsider empowered to question commonly held assumptions (Collins 1986, S17), the African American female intellectual is able to transform the academy from a space that accommodates Western, patriarchal values of individualism, colonialism, objectivity, and exclusivity (Benjamin 1997, 3) to an inclusive space that values "cooperation, collectivity, harmony, and interdependence with the environment" as well as "subjectivity [as] *a* way of knowing" (Benjamin 1997, 3, emphasis in original). This freedom to re-envision the academy as well as her role in it allows the African American female scholar to preserve that part of her identity shaped by communal ties stemming from her home culture. However, at the same time this reappropriation empowers her, it also naturally creates tension with those invested in keeping the patriarchal, hegemonic view of the academy firmly intact.

The tension created when African American women exist as outsiders within the academy is clearly demonstrated in two essential texts, written more than a decade apart. Each is a compilation of essays written by women of color within the academy detailing their experiences as well as the experiences of others like them. Both powerfully demonstrate the range of choices women of color often make while navigating the space of outsider within.

The first text, *Black Women in the Academy: Promises and Perils*, edited by Lois Benjamin (1997), provides thirty different accounts of what African American female faculty members and administrators experienced in academia. The book, according to Benjamin (1997, 1), was the result of a historic meeting of African American women scholars who convened at the Massachusetts Institute of Technology in January 1994 for a conference titled "Black Women in the Academy: Defending Our Name, 1894–1994." The fact that the conference title focused on a century's worth of need for African American women in academia to defend their name—and that more than 2,000 showed up in their defense—demonstrates their pervasive struggle. In their overview of black women in the academy, scholars Nellie McKay and Yolanda T. Moses, in separate chapters, describe the kinds of injustices women of color faced in the academy between the 1960s and 1980s, including racially insensitive comments (McKay 1997, 14; Moses 1997, 25), stereotypes (Moses 1997, 23), racial and group isolation (McKay 1997, 11; Moses 1997, 23, 31), over-scrutiny and underappreciation (McKay 1997, 21), pressure to perform (McKay 1997, 21), being passed over for promotion by those who were less qualified (Moses 1997, 26), being the token who must speak for all black people (Moses 1997, 26; McKay 1997, 12), and lack of mentors or sponsorship (Moses 1997, 26). While McKay and Moses outline the challenges women of color faced in the academy, other contributors relayed their struggles and provided solutions.

The creative responses to oppression take on many forms. Some scholars recommended conducting one's own self-analysis to explore the ways the academy has contributed to negative self-perception for people of color (John 1997, 61); others recommended placing the experiences of those who are oppressed at the center of classroom discussions to better understand how race, class, and gender both empower and disempower certain groups (Brewer 1997, 78); others suggested bringing the need for diverse faculty before the administration and making students aware of the contributions people of color have made to various academic fields (Cox 1997, 113). Still others had students take the work of social justice to the streets by getting them involved in community causes and projects (Guy-Sheftall 1997, 118). In terms of their own self-care, some suggested that faculty of color should join support groups on and off campus (Daniel 1997, 176). When none of these strategies works, faculty of color may find it helpful to "move on, move out, or move over" (Green 1997, 156).

While Benjamin's (1997) collection captures the unique experiences of African American women, a more recent collection of essays, *Presumed Incompetent: The Intersections of Race and Class for Women in Academia*, consists of thirty chapters that detail accounts not only of African American women but also of women who represent a variety of racial and ethnic groups (Gutiérrez y Muhs et al. 2012). As the title suggests, the text also includes stories about how class intersects with race and gender to create sites of oppression.

It is not surprising that many of the same themes of alienation, isolation, tokenism, and the like persist. What is different is that this anthology invokes new language that is used to describe old problems. For example, subtle forms of racism are now called microaggressions (a term I explain in depth later), and the draining effect of devising coping mechanisms for dealing with the outsider-within status is referred to as "racial battle fatigue" (Wilson 2012, 70). *Presumed Incompetent* is a valuable contribution to the literature about women of color in academia because it demonstrates that many of the experiences of African American women in the academy are also shared by women of other racial and ethnic identities. While the stories provide evidence that the same issues and survival strategies have persisted over time, the repetition of themes also leads us to ask, "Who is listening?"

Although contributions were made by community college professors in *Presumed Incompetent* (Flores Niemann 2012a, 446), missing from both texts are faculty of color who share their experience of teaching within the context of the community college. While many perceive research institutions to be more prestigious than community colleges (Harris and González 2012, 3; Locke 1997, 341), the stories of faculty of color at two-year schools are no less important. According to the National Center for Education Statistics, in 2013, African American women accounted for 3 percent (24,283) of all faculty (791,391) in postsecondary schools (IES and NCES 2014), with the overwhelming majority—51 percent—teaching at community colleges (Moffit, Harris, and Berthoud 2012, 79). Because of their significant representation in two-year schools, it is important to give voice to, as well as bring attention to, the ways African American women navigate being outsiders within the community college and the result of their choices. An absence of these stories may lead one to believe that racism, sexism, classism, and other forms of oppression do not exist in community colleges, but as my story will bear witness, nothing could be further from the truth.

BULLYING IN ACADEMIA

In *Faculty Incivility: The Rise of the Academic Bully Culture and What to Do about It*, Darla J. Twale and Barbara M. De Luca (2008, 14) cite attorney Ann Franke as saying that bullying in the form of retaliation would "surpass discrimination as the most severe employment problem in higher education." Perhaps more troubling is the claim by Margaret W. Sallee and Crystal R. Diaz (2013, 42) that "the marginalization of particular social identity groups . . . is a reason for higher rates of bullying among gender, racial and ethnic, and sexual identity minorities in academe." It is ironic that academia, the emblem of ideas and freedom, is a potentially toxic place to work for those who are ethnically, racially, and sexually different. Soko S. Starobin and Warren J. Blumenfeld (2013) argue that a reason for this is that educational institutions often reflect the same attitudes about race as those held by the larger society. If this is true, ethnic minorities have much to be concerned about in the academic workplace, given the nation's current racial climate. Giving greater weight to this problem is the difficulty of defining workplace bullying. Because of its subtlety and because it is based in part on perception, it is difficult to develop a hard-and-fast definition. What a target might view as bullying, an organization, out of fear of tarnishing its reputation, might view as a personal problem (Lewis 2006, 120). Because bullying is defined differently by different institutions, coming up with a comprehensive statement about bullying in academia is challenging (Keashly and Neuman 2013).

Psychiatrist and anthropologist Carroll Brodsky defines what we now refer to as bullying as "repeated and persistent attempts by one person to torment, wear down, frustrate, or get a reaction from another. It is treatment which persistently provokes, pressures, frightens, intimidates or otherwise discomforts another person" (quoted in Keashly and Neuman 2013, 2). While this definition emphasizes the perpetrator acting alone, other definitions emphasize bullying as involving numerous participants targeting one individual, otherwise known as mobbing. A particularly vivid definition of mobbing given by Heinz Leymann reads like a gang rape: the victim is "pushed into a helpless and defenseless position, [and is] held there by means of continuing mobbing activities" that occur anywhere from weekly to six months (quoted in Keashly and Neuman 2013, 2). This definition becomes incredibly impactful when it is understood that women target other women 80 percent of the time (Sallee and Diaz 2013) and suffer more psychologically than men when they have been targeted (Lewis 2006, 121).

Stereotypes of African American women as "dangerous, sexually promiscuous, and violent" make them prime targets for discriminatory practices (Perry, Pullen, and Oser 2012, 335) that can be a manifestation of bullying behavior. Ethnic minorities become especially vulnerable when they defy the standards established by the "White, heterosexual male" (Sallee and Diaz 2013). Yolanda Flores Niemann (2012b, 343) notes that those who choose specialty interests and topics, such as race and gender studies, find themselves isolated and confronted by those who maintain patriarchal hegemonic views regarding pedagogy. The academy then becomes a place where one finds not happiness and fulfillment but a battleground. Faculty who choose specialty interests outside the mainstream may endure incendiary comments about the nature of their work, may not have their work taken seriously, may jeopardize opportunities for promotion, and may experience isolation and lack of faculty support (Flores Niemann 2012b, 342–50). It is this discomfort with the ways women of color choose to navigate their status as outsiders within that leads to both unconscious and deliberate forms of racism that manifest as bullying in academia.

Although it is difficult to determine if bullying experienced by non-whites can always be linked to race, what is clear is that supervisors are more likely to target ethnic minorities by "assigning demeaning work tasks, belittling their subordinates, offering unnecessary and continued criticism, and spreading rumors" (Sallee and Diaz 2013, 46). What is also clear is that racial minorities are more likely than their white counterparts to report being targets of bullying (Sallee and Diaz 2013). According to a 2012 study conducted by the Workplace Bullying Institute, 40 percent of Latinos, 38.6 percent of African Americans, and 13.5 percent of Asian Americans reported having experienced bullying on their jobs at some point (Sallee and Diaz 2013). An earlier study, in 2001, conducted by researchers Hoel and Cooper indicated even higher rates of reported bullying by Asian Americans, at 20 percent (Sallee and Diaz 2013). In contrast, two separate studies indicated that only about 10 percent of whites reported having been bullied (Sallee and Diaz 2013). These statistics make it difficult to ignore the possible connection between bullying and race.

BULLYING AND RACISM

Racism has been defined as "the institutionalized emotional, cognitive, behavioral, and social policy practices that assume and/or promote the cultural, biological, and socioeconomic superiority of people of European descent" (Watts-Jones 2002, 592). Because racism is embedded in American culture (Constantine and Sue 2007, 142), we are not always aware of its occurrence. While the all too frequent incidences of brutality and deaths of African Americans at the hands of police officers point to blatant forms of present-day racism that many reject and condemn, the more common-place expressions of racism elude even those who mean well.

Derald Wing Sue and colleagues (2007) note that racism in America is prevalent and has taken on a more covert nature. Microaggressions are defined as "subtle, and at times, unconscious forms of racism" that can be expressed in the form of stereotyping another's racial group (micro-insults), diminishing or making light of accounts of racism (micro-invalidation), or displaying culturally demeaning symbols, such as a swastika (macro-assaults) (Sue et al. 2007, 273–74). While a single offense might not be significant in the life of a recipient, the repeated occurrence in various forms can have a tremendous effect on both sender and receiver (Fox and Stallworth 2005, 440). If unchecked, microaggressions can result in "increased levels of racial anger, mistrust, and loss of self-esteem for persons of color; prevent White people from perceiving a different racial reality; and create impediments to harmonious race-relations" (Sue et al. 2007, 275). Because of their subtlety, microaggressions can be devastating tools in the hands of a bully.

By its very definition, bullying is about maintaining power at the expense of another. Twale and De Luca (2008) give specific examples of bullying that, when used against minorities, could also be interpreted as microaggressions. I include the list in its entirety to bring attention to the range of bullying behavior that can occur:

- Manipulating and intimidating the seemingly powerless
- Divulging confidential information
- Insulating and protecting negative behaviors while ignoring positive contributions
- Assigning overloads coupled with unrealistic expectations
- Using public humiliation, insults, innuendo, rumor, slander, libel, sarcasm, backstabbing, talking down to, and lies
- Excluding, alienating, marginalizing, ostracizing, silencing, patronizing, and scapegoating others
- Unfairly treating, hounding, micromanaging, undermining, and unfairly criticizing [others]
- Distributing resources unequally by supervisors
- Withholding resources and information from colleagues and subordinates or failing to render a decision
- Belittling or dismissing others' valid opinions and ideas
- Deceiving, using passive-aggressive behaviors, and flaunting power and authority

- Eroding another's self-confidence and self-esteem
- Not correcting false information
- Involving others as allies who become complicit in these behaviors
- Shunning, denying someone's existence, questioning one's judgment of decisions, and continually and consistently interrupting. (Twale and De Luca 2008, 19)

Whether targets suffer bullying in general or race-based bullying, the effects on the target can be severe and traumatic. The psychological effects of workplace bullying include stress, anxiety, feelings of helplessness, and burnout (Lewis 2006, 119). More severe symptoms include post-traumatic stress, depression, alcohol abuse, and suicide (Martin and LaVan 2010, 179). Targets who suffer bullying based on race could feel a range of trauma-induced emotions, including "anxiety, anger, rage, depression, low self-esteem, shame, and guilt" (Carter 2006). Yet because targets of bullying are not protected by the law (Vega and Comer 2005, 101), they are often left vulnerable to attack with little recourse for help or protection.

Unlike sexual harassment cases, when a charge can be made based on a "reasonable" person's determination of inappropriate behavior (Vega and Comer 2005, 101), targets who complain of race-based bullying must demonstrate intent to harm (Carter 2006). Without the force of the law to protect them, targets of bullying who call out the act are less likely to be considered brave truth-tellers fighting for their humanity but rather "hyper-sensitive . . . trouble maker[s] . . . unable to take a joke" (Vega and Comer 2005, 103). It is no wonder that the majority of those who experience bullying in the workplace avoid the institutional channels designated for handling employee complaints, such as faculty unions or human resources (Keashly and Neuman 2013). Perhaps they understand all too well what I discovered the hard way: when it comes to protecting the individual or the institution, most administrators will choose the latter (Twale and De Luca 2008, 81).

MY STORY, MY TRUTH

The following is a cautionary tale of what can happen when one dares to speak her truth. I am intentional about describing what follows as "my truth," since I recognize there are many truths to any story. But this is my recollection, to the best of my ability. No doubt, my telling of it is biased by my being on the receiving end of what is still in some ways a painful experience. It is my story nonetheless, and it is necessary. It is not a full recounting of events, since space will not allow me to tell all that transpired, but what I've included here is an examination of what can happen when one brings attention to microaggressions committed by another protected by gender, race, and class privilege.

For more than a decade, coaching had been a popular trend at my institution. Coaching strategies and techniques were used in leadership training and were implemented as an integral component of a mentoring program for students. An opportunity arose for me to develop a new course for the college's writing program. I wrote a proposal to create the course using coaching as its primary methodology. The proposal was accepted, and I began conducting a three-year study that would influence the way writing classes at the institution were taught. The prospect was huge.

The coach-based curriculum I developed emphasized the student as subject and incorporated narrative as a way of knowing—a practice advocated by black feminists, culturally responsive educators, and critical race theorists. Angela P. Harris and Carmen G. González (2012, 3) in particular argue the need for marginalized voices to provide a more complete history from the perspective of those who have been left out of traditional accounts. Sherri L. Wallace and colleagues (2012, 427) argue that allowing stories to be told by those who have been silenced in the past is a way to empower them. Furthermore, culturally responsive educators, such as Geneva Gay (2010), use stories to help students understand who they are and how they have come to think and believe as they do, as well as to form connection with others. Though many in my department had steered away from narratives, arguing that their use lacked intellectual rigor, the practice of storytelling in academic settings is used by those who embrace a nontraditional (i.e., a non-Western), non-patriarchal approach.

Just as narratives are used to give voice to underrepresented groups, I wanted to use narratives to create a space to learn from underserved students in the classroom. Since "it is well documented that community colleges serve a large proportion of minority, first-generation, low-income, and adult students" (Ma and Baum 2016, 5), I allowed students to share their stories as a way to help them find their voices, to validate them, and to give them a sense of belonging. By its very nature, the course challenged the Western patriarchal view that reinforces objectivity, the teacher as sole knower, and the divorce of emotion from the subject being taught. For these reasons, I received pushback from faculty. Some faculty made it known that they were not comfortable with the course design. Some expressed concerns about sharing the authoritative space with students and turning the writing classroom into a "feel-good" therapy session. Although some were open to the coaching concept, others preferred to resort to what they knew and were comfortable with. According to them, the job of the instructor was to teach writing. Period.

I imagine that there must have been whisperings and murmurings about the new course I was developing. It was one thing to develop a course based on coaching for my students; it was another to develop such a course for the entire department. Increasingly, the meetings I had with my supervisor became more tense. She suggested I scrap the project during its pilot phase to go with a more traditional approach. The initial run did not demonstrate a clear connection between students' writing and applied coaching skills. However, I was able to convince her to allow the project to continue as it was, since the pilot was only in its first year. I would make necessary changes based on the research findings.

Although the supervisor agreed to continue the project as planned, she undermined both me and the program's success by making a series of decisions unilaterally. She assigned new faculty to the project, faculty who did not buy into the coaching philosophy. Without discussing it with me, she had even given a faculty member permission to co-direct the course. Because this faculty member often publicly challenged the coaching methodology I was using, it made it difficult for me to confidently lead the project when it was time to bring other faculty members onboard. Even after I made modifications to the course to more clearly show that students' success was positively influenced by the coaching method, she continually found reasons to suggest that the project would not work on a grand scale. The pairing could not have been more devastating. Rather than promoting the efforts of the original vision of the project, the new co-director labored against it. The work that had exhilarated me soon began to drain me. I went to my supervisor and asked to be removed as head of the course, especially if no one could trust my vision and direction. Although she assured me this was not the case, things would get far worse before they got better.

My last private meeting with the supervisor was riddled with bullying behavior in the form of insults, innuendo, unreasonable expectations, and threats. She began with complaints about my tendency to ask questions in meetings, which embarrassed her; to my proposing to explore the politics of power between basic writing and college-level writing courses at a local conference, which would make the college look bad; to my refusal to walk into a meeting at a minute's notice and speak on issues on which I was unprepared. When I tightly gripped both sides of my chair when she reprimanded me for asking for a room in which to hold a meeting, she described my behavior as "hostile." I cringed at the characterization, since the term conjured up images of an "angry, black woman" capable of invoking fear rather than being heard or understood. A more accurate description could have been *determined* or *persistent*, but the term *hostile* indicated that I was a threat. Had I known what I know now, I would have walked away when the conversation between us got heated.

But hindsight is 20/20. Rather than walking away, I suggested that perhaps it was her perception of me as "hostile" that was the problem.

Derald Wing Sue (2015, chapter 2) suggests that "talking back" is what occurs when those without race privilege or power offer a counternarrative or story that challenges the views of those who hold power. At the same time, "talking back" for me was an attempt to bring attention to and correct her mischaracterization of me as a "hostile" person. Talking back was a form of resistance intended to preserve my identity and character by correctly naming who I was and who I am.

In *Talking Back: Thinking Feminist, Thinking Black*, bell hooks (1989, 9) writes: "Moving from silence to speech is for the oppressed, the colonized, the exploited, and those who stand and struggle side by side a gesture of defiance that heals, that makes new life and new growth possible. It is that act of speech, of 'talking back,' that is no mere gesture of empty words, that is the expression of our movement from object to subject—the liberated voice." While I had "found" my voice, so to speak, by choosing no longer to apologize for actions that were an expression of my identity and by challenging the supervisor's perception as "truth," this act of defiance and freedom came with a price. hooks warns that those who find their voices through talking back do so at great risk. I discovered that she is right. While I had determined that I was done apologizing before leaving her office that day, the supervisor assured me that I was just "done."

Initially, I was not required to be at the assignment norming session; participation for most faculty was optional. Two days after the confrontation with my supervisor, however, my attendance status changed from "optional" to "required." Complicating the matter was a fifteen-year friendship that extended beyond the supervisor's administrative appointment. I had regarded her as a dear friend, one in whom I could confide in difficult times and could depend on for sound advice. But as time wore on and my confidence began to grow, I depended on her less as an adviser and saw her as an equal. Grace Chang (2012, 204) explains how this type of assertiveness can create conflict for white women who feel empowered when they are in a position of "saving" women of color. This type of friendship is sustained by a constant feeling of superiority by one party, expressed by the need to always be in the position to provide help. It is understandable, then, how the lack of a need for help could threaten the relationship by upsetting the power imbalance.

When I arrived at the meeting, the supervisor, other writing administrators, and part-time faculty—some of whom I mentored—were present. A sample of instructors' essay assignments was distributed. I found two assignments I had used with students. No one had asked my permission to use them, but I thought nothing of it since I figured they would be used as models. I soon realized, though, that I had not been called to the meeting to serve as anyone's role model; it was quite the opposite. Granted, the overall tone of the meeting was negative, with far too much emphasis on the faults of the assignments rather than the good in them, but by the time my colleagues got to my assignments, the criticism was merciless. Most of the comments were not directed at the assignment itself but at my character. In an attempt to have students write about a topic that was relevant to them, I gave them an article about a teenager who had committed suicide over sexting. Since numerous parties were involved, the assignment asked them to argue who was responsible for her death. In my instructions I told the students to "have fun" exploring a relevant and current issue. The supervisor called the comment "insensitive." How inappropriate, she argued, to ask the students to have fun dealing with such a serious and somber topic. The writing administrators at the table agreed: any instructor who would tell her students to have fun writing about sexting and suicide was inherently flawed. One indicated that of all the assignments in the pile, this one was by far the worst. Perhaps the critique of the assignment was justifiable, and had it been done privately, I could have received it, but it was done publicly not only in front of my peers but in front of those I supervised. The mere presence of the number of administrators at the table publicly critiquing my work was not only intimidating but its impact was powerful in that my confidence as a leader was shaken.

What else became clear was that I had been called into the meeting to be taught a lesson. The supervisor had far more power and influence than I and, if need be, could marshal others to work alongside her to do her bidding. This expression of power was palpable. What was most painful was that other faculty, whom I had considered friends, agreed to go along with publicly criticizing my work, work with which many at the meeting were familiar. Because the supervisor was able to solicit the help of peers to obtain my assignments and publicly disparage my work, it was the first time I was made keenly aware of the imbalance of power between us. It was also the first time I felt fear on the job. I was not convinced that a conversation between us would resolve our differences, so I requested a meeting with the chief academic administrator to mediate between us to help come to some resolution. While they ignored any possible merits of the assignment, the invitation to students to have fun with it was blown out of proportion to shift focus to my character rather than to the assignment itself. The specific nature of the critique purposely discredited my expertise and experience as a full professor, with a PhD, who had served the college for nineteen years.

In my letter to the chief academic administrator, I recounted the supervisor's reference to me as "hostile" in our private meting. I pointed out that the word *hostile* is a pejorative used by whites to speak negatively of African Americans and that the supervisor had used this term to describe my actions in a private meeting. While I perceived this as a mere detail to describe the events that led up to my work being publicly excoriated, this single point became the focus of the letter of reprimand I received when I met collectively with the supervisor, the chief academic administrator, and a representative from human resources (HR). While the major issue for me was having my work obtained without my permission and then having it critiqued harshly in front of my peers, the major offense for the supervisor was my calling the issue of race into question and bringing the matter to the chief academic administrator.

In my letter to the chief academic administrator as well as in subsequent communications, I made it clear that I did not desire to make any formal complaint with human resources against my supervisor or other administrators. What I desired was a conversation. Initially, the chief academic administrator, after hearing my description of events, appeared to empathize with me. She assured me that under her watch, bullying or anything like it would not occur at the institution. Consequently, she agreed to serve as a mediator between myself and all others involved. However, when the crucial moment came, the tables had turned. When I walked into the chief academic administrator's office, she, the supervisor, and the HR representative were already present. I was informed that I would no longer head the writing course I had developed. Ironically, the person about whom I had made the complaint was now the one who needed protecting. The charge was that because I had gone to the chief academic administrator to report my concerns, I had violated the Employee Code of Conduct. With the chief academic administrator and the HR representative looking on, the supervisor handed me a letter of reprimand, labeling my account of events "inaccurate and unfounded" and my decision to speak with the chief academic administrator an act of insubordination that was also "unprofessional." Implicit in the letter was that I had also been uncivil and disrespectful.

Neither the chief academic administrator nor the HR representative acknowledged that the same employee conduct code guaranteed the protection of any employee who reported unethical treatment of employees or coworkers. They were equally silent about my right to work in an environment "free of harassment, threats, [or] intimidation." Even if raising race as an issue was my primary offense, my rights under Title VII, which protects employees against retaliation for making a complaint based on discrimination (Sallee and Diaz 2013), were completely disregarded. When I reminded the chief academic administrator of our previous conversation, of her promise to mediate between myself and those who were involved in the bullying, she informed me that she and the HR representative had conducted their own private investigation and found no evidence of wrongdoing on the supervisor's part. It was I who had overreacted. It was at this moment that the supervisor's promise had been fulfilled. I knew I was done. Even though I walked into the meeting confident, I left feeling small, unimportant, and defenseless. What began as a fight for my dignity ended in yet another apology for my "bad" behavior.

I could not have imagined the turn of events at that meeting in my wildest dreams. On the slow walk back to my office, I felt my entire world collapse around me. I began to question everything, particularly the faith I had placed in the ideals of nurture, innovation, and integrity that the institution touted. More significant, I questioned my choice to speak out. At the very least, I could have kept my position and some measure of respect among my colleagues. But it was too late. Alone, I would have to suffer the fallout. If I had remained silent or agreed with the supervisor that I was fundamentally flawed rather than challenge the claim, I would have been rewarded with maintaining my job and my status, but it would have also meant losing something far greater. For me, it was a matter of choosing between my dignity or accepting the role of complicit mammy who saw no evil, heard no evil, and spoke no evil being imposed on me. To accept this role would have been to accept the mantle of shame on which a racist institution depends. I opted for my dignity. Speaking out was a type of self-preservation, although from the look of things, I had lost a great deal.

The institution's decision to acknowledge and validate only the supervisor's interpretation of events is steeped in a Eurocentric ideal that protects the image of white women as pure, innocent, and vulnerable (Harris-Perry 2011, 55) and reinforces the image of black women as "animalistic" and "aggressive" (Harris-Perry 2011, 56). While the institution felt it was unacceptable for me to suspect the supervisor of racist behavior, it was not at all far-fetched for the supervisor to view my defending my character against her accusations as an act of insubordination. To add insult to injury, the letter of reprimand included a "strong" recommendation that I contact business health services, the Employee Assistance Program (EAP). Although "employee assistance" sounds friendly enough, it is common knowledge that those issued an EAP at work have been perceived as troublemakers. The goal of the EAP is remediation, to fix what is perceived as broken. Melissa V. Harris-Perry (2011, 57) writes that black women's anger is often thought to be "irrational." Such was the case when the chief academic administrator turned to me during the aforementioned meeting and asked, "Don't you think you're just making too much of this?" Rather than even begin to consider the conversation, albeit a difficult one, around race and bullying, it was easier to trivialize—and with the issuance of an EAP counselor, to pathologize—my complaint. In her write-up, the supervisor warned me that any similar actions on my part "could lead to my dismissal." With the institution clearly on her side and with the threat of losing my job hanging like death before me, the deed had been done. I was officially silenced.

The indignity I suffered at the hands of the supervisor and my colleagues at the assignment norming meeting that led to my complaint would pale in comparison to the humiliation that would soon follow. My removal as coordinator for the program was quite public, as the position involved numerous constituency groups across campus. What I feared most was not losing the position but being viewed as an incompetent failure by my peers. Faculty and administrators were told that I was no longer heading the course because it was not clear that the curriculum I had developed met college-level standards. Students had experienced success because I had "dumbed down" standards for college writing. Once silenced, I was never given the opportunity to explain my research or to elaborate on the pedagogy that guided it.

An even more crushing blow occurred when the results of the three-year study I had conducted were completely obliterated, and the course was rebuilt from scratch with no trace of my research or its findings to guide or inform it. Consequently, I was forced to participate in meetings with the new program director and dismantle the program's guiding philosophy and methodology piece by piece. I was forced to watch everything I had created be discredited and destroyed.

In meeting after meeting, I was constantly reminded of my demotion as I sat alongside others whom I had once been entrusted to guide. Each day became more stressful, and I eventually became grateful for the EAP counseling in which I had been "strongly advised" to participate because I would soon find that I needed it.

After losing my position, going to work became emotionally draining. My hair fell out, and the ten pounds I had struggled with for years after childbirth came off in two weeks because I had lost my desire to eat. For months, I cried during my hour-long commute and once at work, I barricaded myself in my office, coming out only to teach classes and attend required meetings. It took me a year to build up the courage to walk across campus to the school cafeteria, when before doing so had been a mundane activity. Some of the faculty started to distance themselves. One even told me she had been warned not to get too close. Increasingly, I felt isolated and helpless.

Having found no justice at my institution, I turned to the legal system. I spoke with three lawyers about my experience, and none of them would take me on as a client. A five-year study of litigated cases regarding workplace abuse reveals that employers prevailed nearly 75 percent of the time, and even when litigants won, no monetary retribution was awarded (Martin and LaVan 2010, 175). Add the emotional stress of litigation to that already suffered by targets, along with legal fees, and one will find that the cost for targets rarely outweighs any potential benefits. While businesses can pay anywhere from $30,000 to $100,000 per bullying incident, targets suffer a higher emotional and psychological toll (Meglich-Sespico, Faley, and Knapp 2007, 31). Increasingly, I felt trapped. My private thoughts of suicide led me to seek additional therapy beyond the EAP counselor to whom I was initially assigned.

HOW I SURVIVED

Clinical psychologist Dee Watts-Jones (2002) talks about the importance of finding sanctuary for survivors of racism, those places where we can discuss the pain of our lived experiences freely, without fear of retribution. As is the case for many African Americans, the church became such a place for me (Watts-Jones 2002, 594). When I felt my spiritual energy, my sense of purpose, dignity, importance, and meaning being drained from me at work, I turned to the church to help restore them. The ability to use my gifts and talents helped me cope with the pain. I conducted workshops, sang in the choir, and spoke at women's events. In my church's women's group, I found connection with those who had endured similar hardships of shame and had survived abuses that seemed far greater than mine. I drew strength from their stories of survival and faith.

In addition to the church, I sought sanctuary in other groups. I reactivated membership with my sorority and became active in an organization for African American mothers. At times, issues of race would come up, and we would find comfort in talking about them. These conversations assured me that I was not alone and that the way I had interpreted my experience was justified. Most important, these sister circles reassured me of my sanity. What most found unbelievable was how I had survived at any job as long as I had without any prior experience of racism. For many, racism, whether covert or defined, had become an expectation, a rite of passage that certified one's identity as a bona fide African American. While it was comforting to be validated by those who endured similar experiences, I am troubled by the notion that racism should be an expectation for any of us, particularly in the workplace where a great deal of our energy and time are spent. This reality troubles me and propels me to write.

It has been years since that fateful meeting in the chief academic administrator's office, and I am finally starting to feel more like myself. I have left the institution where I experienced the bullying and am now working in an environment that is welcoming and embraces conversations about race. I am a member of a professional development team that facilitates racial dialogues with faculty. This work has been especially fulfilling for me, as I get the opportunity to help other instructors take on the challenging and necessary topic of race. My days are filled with deep gratitude and are infused with a much larger purpose. I survived, and I get to walk with others through the process of sharing their truth and bear witness to its telling.

RECOMMENDATIONS

Those of us who have survived bullying must look for places of sanctuary where we are free to tell our stories without fear of judgment or retribution. While researchers have found that the most "passive, indirect, and informal strategies" make life easier for targets of bullying (Keashly and Neuman 2013), psychologists warn that silence is one of the most harmful responses to trauma, since it only exacerbates the shame (Watts-Jones 2002, 593). And while many find safety in sharing their stories outside the walls of academia, it is important that we are allowed the freedom to tell our stories in the places in which the violence has occurred, even if it means causing discomfort for those who have sheltered these acts in silence. It is equally important that survivors are given a space to tell their stories in academic journals and that we expand our research on the issue so those who wield power may listen more readily and begin to implement institutional changes.

Beverly Guy-Sheftall (1997, 116) asks if the university can be a site of activism for social justice: "Are we [educators] willing to endure the anger and frustration and even hostility, at times, of students and other faculty when we challenge their most cherished ways of seeing the world and themselves?" Indeed, hers is a powerful question; and the fact that we are still engaging issues about race, gender, and class in the academy twenty years after the question was initially raised means it is also still relevant. However, the weight of responsibility for change cannot rest on the shoulders of faculty alone. If change is to happen, all stakeholders must be involved, including administrators and other decision-makers. We must be open to "courageous conversations," even the ones that most frighten us.

Some of these difficult conversations are already being conducted at America's most successful corporations. Sheryl Sandberg (2013), for example, points out how Ken Chenault, CEO of American Express, immediately brings it to his employees' attention when a woman's ideas are overlooked or are credited to a male. In other words, Sandberg (2013) is suggesting that the workplace become a sanctuary, a safe place to address the subtle and not-so-subtle messages that maintain the status quo. What she also suggests is that these conversations must be initiated by our leaders. But that means having the courage to acknowledge the problem and get the conversation started in the first place.

And while it is commendable that both four-year and two-year institutions recognize the importance of increasing the number of faculty of color at their institutions, it is equally important that they allow those faculty to express the unique perspectives that make us who we are rather than pressuring us to compromise our values and truths by conforming. It is important that everyone in academia strive toward cultural competence, which includes, but is not limited to, knowing how to engage in difficult conversations about race (Sanchez-Hucles and Jones 2005, 548).

I understand that what I am asking might mean creating discomfort for some, but we cannot afford to ignore the issue of bullying in an institution that is ideally meant to be a repository for ideas that lead to the advancement of society as a whole. The benefits of conversation, understanding, and transformation far outweigh the price we are paying for evading what frightens us. In that space awaits a larger vision of what can be if we arch forward and lean in.

REFERENCES

Benjamin, Lois. 1997. "Introduction." In *Black Women in the Academy: Promises and Perils*, ed. Lois Benjamin, 1–7. Gainesville: University Press of Florida.

Brewer, Rose M. 1997. "Giving Name and Voice: Black Women Scholars, Research, and Knowledge Transformation." In *Black Women in the Academy: Promises and Perils*, ed. Lois Benjamin, 68–80. Gainesville: University Press of Florida.

Carter, Robert T. 2006. "Race-Based Traumatic Stress." *Psychiatric Times*, December 1. http://www.psychiatrictimes.com/articles/race-based-traumatic-stress.

Chang, Grace. 2012. "Where's the Violence? The Promise and Perils of Teaching Women of Color Studies." In *Presumed Incompetent: The Intersections of Race and Class for Women in Academia*, ed. Gabriela Gutiérrez y Muhs, Yolanda Flores Niemann, Carmen G. González, and Angela P. Harris, 198–218. Logan: Utah State University Press. https://doi.org/10.2307/j.ctt4cgr3k.21.

Collins, Patricia Hill. 1986. "Learning from the Outsider Within: The Sociological Significance of Black Feminist Thought." *Social Problems* 33 (6): S14–S32. https://doi.org/10.2307/800672.

Constantine, Madonna G., and Derald Wing Sue. 2007. "Perceptions of Racial Microaggressions among Black Supervisees in Cross-Racial Dyads." *Journal of Counseling Psychology* 54 (2): 142–53. https://doi.org/10.1037/0022-0167.54.2.142.

Cox, Donna M. 1997. "Eurocentric Hegemony in the College Music Curriculum: The African American Woman Professor Singing the Blues." In *Black Women in the Academy: Promises and Perils*, ed. Lois Benjamin, 103–14. Gainesville: University Press of Florida.

Crenshaw, Kimberlé. 2015. "Why Intersectionality Can't Wait." *Washington Post*, September 24. https://www.washingtonpost.com/news/in-theory/wp/2015/09/24/why-intersectionality-cant-wait/?utm_term=.9cca6465ed67.

Daniel, Elnora D. 1997. "African American Nursing Administrators in the Academy: Breaking the Glass Ceiling." In *Black Women in the Academy: Promises and Perils*, ed. Lois Benjamin, 168–78. Gainesville: University Press of Florida.

Delgado, Richard, and Jean Stefancic. 2012. *Critical Race Theory: An Introduction*, 2nd ed. New York: New York University Press.

Flores Niemann, Yolanda. 2012a. "Lessons from the Experiences of Women of Color Working in Academia." In *Presumed Incompetent: The Intersections of Race and Class for Women in Academia*, ed. Gabriella Gutiérrez y Muhs, Yolanda Flores Niemann, Carmen G. González, and Angela P. Harris, 446–500. Logan: Utah State University Press. https://doi.org/10.2307/j.ctt4cgr3k.40.

Flores Niemann, Yolanda, 2012b. "The Making of a Token: A Case Study of Stereotype, Threat, Stigma, Racism, and Tokenism in Academe." In *Presumed Incompetent: The Intersections of Race and Class for Women in Academia*, ed. Gabriella Gutiérrez y Muhs, Yolanda Flores Niemann, Carmen G. González, and Angela P. Harris, 336–55. Logan: Utah State University Press.

Fox, Suzy, and Lamont Stallworth. 2005. "Racial/Ethnic Bullying: Exploring Links between Bullying and Racism in the US Workplace." *Journal of Vocational Behavior* 66 (3): 438–56. https://doi.org/10.1016/j.jvb.2004.01.002.

Garner, Rochelle. 2005. *Contesting the Terrain of the Ivory Tower: Spiritual Leadership of African-American Women in the Academy*. New York: Routledge. Kindle edition.

Gay, Geneva. 2010. *Culturally Responsive Teaching: Theory, Research, and Practice*, 2nd ed. New York: Teachers College Press. Kindle edition.

Green, Phyllis S. 1997. "Rites of Passage and Rights of Way: A Woman's Chief Academic Administrator's Experiences." In *Black Women in the Academy: Promises and Perils*, ed. Lois Benjamin, 147–57. Gainesville: University Press of Florida.

Gutiérrez y Muhs, Gabriella, Yolanda Flores Niemann, Carmen G. González, and Angela P. Harris, eds. 2012. *Presumed Incompetent: The Intersections of Race and Class for Women in Academia*. Logan: Utah State University Press.

Guy-Sheftall, Beverly. 1997. "Transforming the Academy: A Black Feminist Perspective." In *Black Women in the Academy: Promises and Perils*, ed. Lois Benjamin, 115–23. Gainesville: University Press of Florida.

Harris, Angela P., and Carmen G. González. 2012. "Introduction." In *Presumed Incompetent: The Intersections of Race and Class for Women in Academia*, ed. Gabriella Gutiérrez y Muhs, Yolanda Flores Niemann, Carmen G. González, and Angela P. Harris, 1–14. Logan: Utah State University Press. https://doi.org/10.2307/j.ctt4cgr3k.5.

Harris-Perry, Melissa V. 2011. *Sister Citizen: Shame, Stereotypes, and Black Women in America.* New Haven, CT: Yale University Press.

hooks, bell. 1989. *Talking Back: Thinking Feminist, Thinking Black.* Boston: South End.

IES (Institute of Education Sciences) and NCES (National Center for Education Statistics). 2014. "Table 315.20. Full-time faculty in degree-granting postsecondary institutions, by race/ethnicity, sex, and academic rank: Fall 2009, fall 2011, and fall 2013." https://nces.ed.gov/programs/digest/d14/tables/dt14_315.20.asp.

John, Beverly M. 1997. "The African American Female Ontology: Implications for Academe." In *Black Women in the Academy: Promises and Perils*, ed. Lois Benjamin, 53–63. Gainesville: University Press of Florida.

Keashly, Loraleigh, and Joel H. Neuman. 2013. "Bullying in Higher Education: What Current Research, Theorizing, and Practice Tell Us." In *Workplace Bullying in Higher Education*, ed. Jaime Lester, 1–22. New York: Routledge. Kindle edition.

Lewis, Sian E. 2006. "Recognition of Workplace Bullying: A Qualitative Study of Women Targets in the Public Sector." *Journal of Community and Applied Social Psychology* 16 (2): 119–35. https://doi.org/10.1002/casp.850.

Locke, Mamie E. 1997. "Striking the Delicate Balances: The Future of African American Women in the Academy." In *Black Women in the Academy: Promises and Perils*, ed. Lois Benjamin, 340–46. Gainesville: University Press of Florida.

Martin, William, and Helen LaVan. 2010. "Workplace Bullying: A Review of Litigated Cases." *Employee Responsibilities and Rights Journal* 22 (3): 175–94. https://doi.org/10.1007/s10672-009-9140-4.

Ma, Jennifer, and Sandy Baum, 2016. *Trends in Community Colleges: Enrollment, Prices, Student Debt, and Completion.* Research Brief. College Board Research, 1–23. https://trends.collegeboard.org/sites/default/files/trends-in-community-colleges-research-brief.pdf. PDF.

McKay, Nellie. 1997. "A Troubled Peace: Black Women in the Halls of the White Academy." In *Black Women in the Academy: Promises and Perils*, ed. Lois Benjamin, 11–22. Gainesville: University Press of Florida.

Meglich-Sespico, Patricia, Robert H. Faley, and Debra Erdos Knapp. 2007. "Relief and Redress for Targets of Workplace Bullying." *Employee Responsibility Rights Journal* 19 (1): 31–43. https://doi.org/10.1007/s10672-006-9030-y.

Moffit, Kimberly R., Heather Harris, and Diane A. Berthoud. 2012. "Present and Unequal: A Third-Wave Approach to Voice Parallel Experiences in Managing Oppression and Bias in the Academy." In *Presumed Incompetent: The Intersections of Race and Class for Women in Academia*, ed. Gabriella Gutiérrez y Muhs, Yolanda Flores Niemann, Carmen G. González, and Angela P. Harris, 78–92. Logan: Utah State University Press. https://doi.org/10.2307/j.ctt4cgr3k.12.

Moses, Yolanda T. 1997. "Black Women in Academe: Issues and Strategies." In *Black Women in the Academy: Promises and Perils*, ed. Lois Benjamin, 23–37. Gainesville: University Press of Florida.

Onwuachi-Willig, Angela. 2012. "Silence of the Lambs." In *Presumed Incompetent: The Intersections of Race and Class for Women in Academia*, ed. Gabriella Gutiérrez y Muhs, Yolanda Flores Niemann, Carmen G. González, and Angela P. Harris, 142–51. Logan: Utah State University Press.

Perry, Brea, Erin L. Pullen, and Carrie B. Oser. 2012. "Too Much of a Good Thing? Psychosocial Resources, Gendered Racism, and Suicidal Ideation among Low Socio-economic Status African American Women." *Social Psychology Quarterly* 75 (4): 334–59. https://doi.org/10.1177/0190272512455932.

Sallee, Margaret W., and Crystal R. Diaz. 2013. "Sexual Harassment, Racist Jokes, and Homophobic Slurs: When Bullies Target Identity Groups." In *Workplace Bullying in Higher Education*, ed. Jaime Lester, 41–59. New York: Routledge. Kindle edition.

Sanchez-Hucles, Janis, and Nneka Jones. 2005. "Breaking the Silence around Race in Training, Practice, and Research." *Counseling Psychologist* 33 (4): 547–58. https://doi .org/10.1177/0011000005276462.

Sandberg, Sheryl. 2013. *Lean In: Women, Work, and the Will to Lead*. New York: Knopf. Kindle edition.

Starobin, Soko S., and Warren J. Blumenfeld. 2013. "A Model of Social Ecology of Bullying in Community Colleges." In *Workplace Bullying in Higher Education*, ed. Jaime Lester, 74–86. New York: Routledge. Kindle edition.

Sue, Derald Wing. 2015. *Race Talk and the Conspiracy of Silence: Understanding and Facilitating Difficult Dialogues on Race*. Hoboken, NJ: Wiley. Kindle edition.

Sue, Derald Wing, Christina M. Capodilupo, Gina C. Torino, Jennifer M. Bucceri, Aisha M.B. Holder, Kevin L. Nadal, and Marta Esquilin. 2007. "Racial Microaggressions in Everyday Life: Implications for Clinical Practice." *American Psychologist* 62 (4): 271–86. https://doi.org/10.1037/0003-066X.62.4.271.

Twale, Darla J., and Barbara M. De Luca. 2008. *Faculty Incivility: The Rise of the Academic Bully Culture and What to Do about It*. San Francisco: Jossey-Bass.

Vega, Gina, and Debra Comer. 2005. "Sticks and Stones Can Break Your Bones, but Words Can Break Your Spirit: Bullying in the Workplace." *Journal of Business Ethics* 58 (1–3): 101–9. https://doi.org/10.1007/s10551-005-1422-7.

Wallace, Sherri L., Sharon E. Moore, Linda L. Wilson, and Brenda G. Hart. 2012. "African American Women in the Academy: Quelling the Myth of Presumed Incompetence." In *Presumed Incompetent: The Intersections of Race and Class for Women in Academia*, ed. Gabriella Gutiérrez y Muhs, Yolanda Flores Niemann, Carmen G. González, and Angela P. Harris, 421–38. Logan: Utah State University Press. https://doi.org/10.2307/j.ctt4cgr3k.38.

Watts-Jones, Dee. 2002. "Healing Internalized Racism: The Role of Within-Group Sanctuary among People of African Descent." *Family Process* 41 (4): 591–601. https://doi.org /10.1111/j.1545-5300.2002.00591.x.

Wilder, JeffriAnne, Tamara B. Bertrand Jones, and La'Tara Osborne-Lampkin. 2013. "A Profile of Black Women in the 21st Century Academy: Still Learning from the 'Outsider-Within.'" *Journal of Research Initiatives* 1 (1): 27–38. https://digitalcommons .uncfsu.edu/cgi/viewcontent.cgi?article=1013&context=jri.

Wilson, Sherrée. 2012. "They Forgot Mammy Had a Brain." In *Presumed Incompetent: The Intersections of Race and Class for Women in Academia*, ed. Gabriella Gutiérrez y Muhs, Yolanda Flores Niemann, Carmen G. González, and Angela P. Harris, 65–77. Logan: Utah State University Press.

7

RACE, TEACHING ASSISTANTS, AND WORKPLACE BULLYING
Confessions from an African American Pre-Tenured WPA

Staci Perryman-Clark

According to Denise Salin (2003), workplace bullying has been defined as "*repeated* and *persistent negative acts* towards one or more *individual(s)*, which involve *a perceived power imbalance* and create a *hostile work environment* (cf. Einarsen 1996; Hoel and Cooper 2000; Zapf, Kornz, and Kulla et al. 1996). Bullying is thus a form of interpersonal aggression or hostile, anti-social behaviour in the workplace" (Salin 2003, 1214–15, italics in original). Salin (2003, 1215) distinguishes workplace bullying from normal workplace conflict by stating that the "major difference . . . is not necessarily what and how it is done, but rather the frequency and longevity of what is done." For Salin, it is also interesting that the relationship between bullying and power is not as simple as the perpetrators having direct control, as they can target victims when they have no direct supervisor duties over them, when they are peers, and when they are subordinates.

The notion of workplace bullying—though often not named as such—is no stranger to writing program administration (WPA) scholarship. In many cases, sources that address WPA working conditions reveal the ways writing program administrators (WPAs) have been accused of bullying instructors into teaching composition, adopting the WPAs' pedagogy, or counteracting bullying by lobbying for better working conditions for composition faculty (Sutton 2007). Other WPA scholarship identifies examples of political pressure by key legislative figures who use "bully pulpits" to enact policies that often conflict with WPA best practices (Cambridge 2011, 136).

Furthermore, additional scholarship addresses the sociopolitical implications associated with WPAs and faculty who are bullied based on their social, cultural, political, and gendered identities. Specifically, Harry Denny's (2014, 2) essay, "Of Sticks and Stones, Words That

DOI: 10.7330/9781607328162.c007

Wound, and Actions Speaking Louder: Academic Bullying Becomes Everyday Oppression," reprinted in this collection, serves as "a cautionary tale not just for queer people in academe, for junior faculty, or for those who find themselves in WPA positions." Denny (2014, 3) argues that in relation to academic bullying, "resistance also can be about people oppressing one another, whether out of some misguided notion of leveraging for power [or] a move to gain greater control over conditions not entirely within one's purview." What distinguishes Denny's narratives from many WPA conversations about workplace bullying is the emphasis on oppression in relation to power dynamics and authority. Denny's own experiences with workplace bullying as a writing center director were deeply tied to instances of harassment based on sexuality. But Denny's (2014, 5) experience with workplace bullying was also impacted by his status as a pre-tenured WPA, where certain faculty attempted to capitalize on his pre-tenure status to bolster and improve their own chances for tenure. Put simply, one of the most compelling points about Denny's experiences in relation to workplace bullying is how in many cases the bully achieves minimal benefit: The bully does not achieve upward professional advancement and experiences minimal gains. In short, the bully does not achieve any significant positive consequences as perpetrator.

While the subject of bullying is one that college-level instructors and scholars are now willing to address, the relationships that exist among workplace bullying, race, gender, and the varying levels of privilege associated with faculty negotiating these multiple and often competing subject positions remain under-explored, although significant WPA scholarship has consistently acknowledged the vicarious and competing roles pre-tenured WPAs have in the teaching and administration of campus-wide writing programs. When speaking of working conditions, much WPA scholarship takes the form of professional advice for WPAs who wish to situate their professional identities in relation to administrative work as demonstrated opportunities for intellectual and productive work (Rose and Weiser 1999). Other scholarship offers recommendations for WPA faculty at various stages of their careers, ranging from senior to junior levels in the profession (Enos 2002; Rose and Weiser 1999; Dew and Horning 2007). More specifically, Debra Frank Dew and Alice Horning (2007) question the perils of pre-tenured WPAs, which they identify as jWPAs. Horning (2007, 6) writes that "WPAs nationwide know that jWPA appointments are both widespread and problematic—professionally risky and rife with conflict . . . On the one hand, the Council of Writing Program Administrators . . . discourages junior appointments . . . At the same time, more and more graduate programs are offering WPA seminars to train their doctoral students for administrative positions."

While Dew and Horning's collection (2007) addresses the politics and the double-edged sword that come along with taking a jWPA/pre-tenured WPA position, the role of race in relation to WPA identity politics is given consideration in only one chapter, in relationship to Asian American identity politics (Eng 2007). As Collin Lamont Craig and the author of this chapter (2011) remind us, both race and gender play integral roles in the way WPA bodies are read, especially at the institutional sites where WPAs work. More precisely, these sites "challenge the status quo of representation in writing program administration and within the academy at large" (Craig and Perryman-Clark 2011, 39). Craig and I then further share experiences of how race and gender were read in problematic ways that created very hostile working environments.

As Craig and I (2011, 45) also assert, "Power dynamics determine who gets to say and do what to whom in our institutional and disciplinary spaces." Specifically, in institutional spaces, power dynamics, which pertain to who gets to say and do what to whom, are often abused by those with greater positions of power and authority. This authority often creates hostile working conditions when those in positions of power attempt to exercise control by using their authority to inflict punishment on those with less authority. These dynamics then play out significantly in the working conditions of WPAs who don't yet have tenure. The work of pre-tenured WPAs at times requires that they make decisions about their programs with potential consequences for their own employment and job security, especially when tenured faculty challenge such decisions and threaten pre-tenured WPAs' job security.

Power dynamics between tenured faculty and pre-tenured WPAs also become complicated when race and gender are added to the equation. What happens when the pre-tenured WPA is also a female faculty member of color who must consider the ways her subject positions as both female and racial minority reflect the historical legacy of limited systemic forms of power? Craig and I (2011, 45) argue that "race, gender, and power dynamics . . . parallel societal roles in relationship to power." Thus, building on a discussion of race and hostile work environments, this chapter aims to discuss the role of racialized and gendered bodies as WPA practitioners who must confront racism from tenured faculty advisers and graduate teaching assistants.

In the subsequent sections of this chapter, I share my experiences as a pre-tenured WPA that reflect workplace bullying instances that (1) "involve a perceived power imbalance and create a hostile work environment" extending beyond the traditional supervisor/subordinate relationships, (2) identify workplace bullying "as repeated and persistent negative acts," and (3) identify occasions where the end results of bullying and harassment lead to no significant gain and power for the perpetrators (Denny 2014, 5). In short, experiences such as these point to the need to address bullying not only of tenured faculty against pre-tenured faculty but also of WPAs of color in the workplace. This chapter concludes by proposing suggestions for faculty in positions of authority and privilege to serve as stronger allies to support pre-tenured WPAs of color.

BEYOND SUPERVISION: FACULTY ADVISERS, WHITE PRIVILEGE, AND RACIAL OPPRESSION

As previously stated, workplace bullies need not be supervisors of victims; they may simply be department colleagues. That said, from my experience, while such bullies may not directly supervise or evaluate my work, they may use their white privilege and status as tenured faculty in ways that create vulnerable positions for pre-tenured WPAs of color. My experiences with being bullied by a tenured white female faculty member began after a particular department meeting three or four years ago. At this meeting, my department's undergraduate committee presented a proposal to revise its curriculum for English majors and proposed eliminating an introductory literature course and shifting its graduate teaching assistants (GTAs) over to sections of first-year writing (ENGL 1050) without discussing these changes with me, the WPA. The proposal also stated that ENGL 1050 simply taught "the basics of rhetoric and writing," while the proposal areas that pertained to the creative writing and literature courses included carefully crafted and thoroughly detailed course descriptions. Both of these instances infuriated me because no one from the committee took the time to discuss with me how these changes would impact the writing program or to find out exactly what happens in our first-year writing courses. In fact, the only times several colleagues outside of rhetoric and writing studies expressed any interest in first-year writing were when they were trying to advocate for a tenure-track hire in English, to receive department funds from tuition revenue from online sections and textbook royalties from our first-year writing program's custom reader that I edited, or to request summer teaching when their literature classes weren't offered because of low enrollments. Having sat quietly for roughly two and a half years at that point, I decided to tell the committee that "slapping [in] a sentence about 'the basics of rhetoric and writing'" was irresponsible; I also asked that when any changes that would affect my program were proposed, they should be discussed with me.

The meeting ended with several female committee members crying visibly and loudly, even though I never reprimanded them personally or directly. The conversation became so heated that a break was requested after one female faculty member—Lauren—chastised me[1] for being uncivil. As reported in "When White Women Cry," Mamta Motwani Accapadi (2007) conducted a case study of the interactions and conflicts that can arise when white women and women of color engage in dialogue. She argues that when race and gender collide, white women's emotional reactions involving crying were often "aligned with the 'standard of humanity' which is rooted in White norms . . . [The white female participant] received consolation, absolution of guilt, and ultimately, validation of her position, without a critical inquiry of the situation," while the woman of color "was held accountable for causing the whole situation" (Accapadi 2007, 213). In other words, the crying worked to absolve white women of responsibility for their role in the conflict. While Lauren may or may not have been consciously aware of the privilege she attempted to afford herself by crying, I was aware of how my verbal performance might be targeted in an act of oppression that characterizes me as an Angry Black Woman who defies social norms associated with department meeting discourses. From that moment on, Lauren refused to attend future department meetings for a significant period of time after this encounter.

POWER STRUGGLES AND ABUSE: BULLYING WPAS OF COLOR WITH THE ASSISTANCE OF SUBORDINATES

On some occasions, workplace bullies unite with the target's subordinates to rebel against the target being bullied. In December 2013 I found myself in the middle of a dispute between an African American ENGL 1050 student and a white female first-time teaching assistant (TA); the TA's faculty adviser, Lauren, was among those who had cried at a previous department meeting. The TA claimed the African American male student had been intimidating and disrespectful toward her during several meetings outside of class. I agreed to meet one on one with both the student and the instructor. While I observed disrespect and resistance in the student's attitude, I heard no evidence of him being threatening or intimidating in the meeting or in the details provided by the TA. The TA nonetheless requested that he be removed from her class because of her fears. Because we weren't confident that the TA would grade the student fairly, my department chair (a white male) and I agreed to remove the student from her class so my chair (with my support) could work with the student one on one. The student's work improved considerably over the course of my chair's five weeks of work with him, and all was well until the TA said she expected to assign the student's final grade, assuming that the student remained on her course enrollment despite the fact that the department chair had removed him from her course. She determined that because the student had been failing prior to being removed from the class, he should receive a D at best. Based on our assessment of the student's portfolio, we believed he should earn a C. In addition, the student needed a C or higher in the course to declare a major, or he risked dismissal from the university for maintaining a GPA lower than a 2.0.

When my department chair and I raised concerns about whether the TA's cultural biases and negative experiences with the student had clouded her judgment, the TA refused to meet formally with me, refused to accept my phone calls to discuss the incident, refused to return voice messages from me, threatened to leave the graduate program, and threatened to file a formal grievance with the Teaching Assistants Union (TAU). She then called on her faculty adviser, Lauren, to plead the case on her behalf. When the TA refused to discuss the matter with me and refused to return my voice messages, I attempted to discuss the matter with Lauren, who assured me that she understood my vulnerable position as a pre-tenured faculty member who had to negotiate conflict between the TA and my department chair. From her perspective, Lauren acknowledged that I had done nothing wrong, and she sought to move forward with our working relationship.

At that point, I sincerely believed that Lauren and I had resolved any negative feelings, thinking we had moved on from our conflict in the faculty meeting, until I received notice that she and the TA had challenged our grading of the student and consulted the TAU about filing a grievance. Lauren also went to the dean of our college and sought to contact our provost with the request that my department chair and I be removed from our administrative positions. I was shocked and angry at what Lauren had done after admitting to me privately that I had done nothing wrong. But more important, I was angry that I had not seen this coming; I was angry that I had trusted and believed her. After finding out about Lauren's betrayal, I experienced a year-long depression and also began to experience physical side effects, including hair loss. From that moment on, I knew there was no chance of reconciliation and her vendetta with me would continue. Fortunately, the administration sided with the department chair and me, and we remained in our positions with no formal grievances filed. Our assessment of the student's work, in addition to our experiences with teaching many years of college composition against the TA's one semester of teaching, made their decision easy.

REPEATED ACTS OF NEGATIVITY: SUBORDINATES AS AGENTS FOR RETALIATION

As noted earlier, workplace bullying functions "as *repeated* and *persistent negative acts* towards one or more *individual(s)*" (Salin, 2003, 1215, emphasis in original). In addition to department colleagues who capitalize on white privilege and their tenure status to bully despite having no direct supervision or authority to evaluate faculty members' performances, subordinates whom the faculty member of color supervises may also use white privilege to bully. Several repeated instances involve Lauren encouraging graduate students, whom she advises and whom I supervise, to resist first-year writing teaching requirements concerning required professional development meetings and curriculum materials. Lauren scheduled an off-campus forum, which my then department chair tried to stop, inviting all the TAs in her program who were teaching first-year writing to discuss problems and concerns about the ENGL 1050 curriculum, program, and requirements. I later received word that Lauren held an informal forum despite the efforts of the chair to stop it.

After this forum was held, I began to notice that several of the TAs in Lauren's graduate program were not fulfilling ENGL 1050 instructor requirements. They refused to submit required course syllabi for the classes they were teaching and also stopped attending required professional development training sessions. Seeing that this resistance was becoming endemic, I met with the department chair and graduate program director to document that these TAs were not fulfilling their contractual agreements. After numerous attempts and reminders from me, my department chair, and the graduate program director, several of these students continued to rebel against their teaching requirements, especially since many would graduate at the end of spring semester. Others of Lauren's students attempted to argue that ENGL 6690: Methods in Teaching College Writing, the graduate seminar required of all new ENGL 1050 instructors, violated the TAU because they claimed the course was not required for any graduate program in English and therefore unjustly increased time spent in pursuit of the graduate degree. TAs from this group also attempted to negotiate the 2014–15 collective bargaining agreement to eliminate ENGL 6690 as a required course for teaching ENGL 1050. This attempt failed, and the administration determined that because ENGL 6690 is one of many courses that fulfill a graduate student's pedagogical distribution requirement, it does not inhibit progress toward the degree. Thus, nothing significant was gained by these forms of resistance in terms of undermining my status, although significant forms of interference disrupted my ability to manage a teaching staff on certain occasions.

WORKPLACE BULLYING BY SUBORDINATES AND COLLEAGUES: FOR WHAT GAIN?

In the final instance of repeated resistance and bullying I share, I draw on Denny's (2014, 5) assertion that perpetrators often benefit minimally from workplace bullying. During the spring of 2015, the year my tenure and promotion case would be decided, I received resistance and harassment from one of Lauren's students. During that semester, the student requested a medical leave of absence and needed her ENGL 1050 course to be assigned to another instructor for the remainder of the semester. The TA informed my department chair, who directed the student to send her syllabus, remaining teaching materials, and grade records to me so I could transfer them to a new instructor. The TA refused to transfer any materials to me, even after several requests from both my department chair and me. We informed her that doing so was necessary so the new instructor would be prepared for the class and the students would not be put at a disadvantage. After she failed to submit any materials, my department chair added me to her assigned course as the instructor of record until we could find a replacement. Once I accessed the course, I observed that no grades had been recorded, only one assignment had been given, classes had been canceled on at least nine occasions per the TA's documented email notifications, none of her students had purchased the required textbooks and course materials because the instructor told them not to bother with them (according to reports from students enrolled in the course), and the TA had taught the class as a literature and creative writing workshop, using flash fiction and graphic novels.

Eventually, the TA was removed from accessing this course, since her employment at the university had ended. Upon learning that she no longer had eLearning access to her course, the TA wrote a scathing email to the department chair (copying me on the exchange) accusing me of locking her out, discriminating against her medical illness, and evading questions about teaching a different course instead of ENGL 1050 (a course for which I have no authority and therefore chose to defer those requests to the undergraduate director, graduate program director, and department chair). The only thing I had ever asked of the TA was that she send her materials, which she had initially agreed to do before the department chair deferred those instructions to me. In the same thread of email exchanges to the department chair, she copied both me and Lauren so I would be fully aware of her accusations. The TA addressed the department chair, saying she thought he was doing a great job of covering for me and my incompetence as the WPA. She also accused me of discriminating against a disability she had not disclosed to me and said I was petty because I avoid eye contact with her when we encountered one another in our faculty workspaces.

In response to the email and accusations, I requested that the TA not contact me unless she is assigned to teach ENGL 1050 in the future. Fortunately, upper administration again sided with me, as the TA did not fulfill any of the ENGL 1050 requirements. Since this exchange, the TA has been assigned non-teaching-related duties and is no longer permitted to teach any course in the English department. What is disconcerting, however, is the fact that the TA chose to copy Lauren on all ENGL 1050 exchanges unrelated to the faculty member's duties as her graduate thesis adviser, perhaps because she wanted an advocate in a position of authority to offer her protection. It is not clear whether Lauren had asked for or granted consent for the TA to copy her on email exchanges related to ENGL 1050. However, given past patterns of Lauren's attempts to undermine my authority, it seems that both she and the TA share opposition to my leadership as the WPA. From my perspective, it seems as though the TA is fighting a battle on behalf of her thesis adviser. Under no circumstances should a graduate student become involved in workplace disagreements between faculty members, and under no circumstances should a faculty member condone such disrespectful and unprofessional behavior. It is interesting that Lauren never emailed me directly or replied concerning the student's accusations; the fact that she chose to remain silent in the aftermath while I was continually harassed in several exchanges with the TA speaks volumes to the ways tenured faculty can treat pre-tenured faculty members, especially tenured faculty members who possess white privilege.

From this whole exchange, neither the TA nor the faculty member gained anything significant. In fact, since this exchange occurred, both have experienced negative outcomes. The TA is no longer permitted to teach in our department, yet she has expressed a desire to pursue a PhD and a teaching position. For the adviser, it is public knowledge that she is dissatisfied with the upper administrative and departmental leadership at our institution and is actively searching for academic positions elsewhere. On social media, she often writes about her dissatisfaction with the institution and how unhappy she is with her current position. She makes accusations about denied requests for sabbatical and gender inequity in the department, and on at least one occasion she petitioned her Facebook friends for advice as to whether she should resign her position even if she did not have another position lined up. After 100-plus comments that ranged from offering support to advising her to either keep or quit her position, she removed the posting, but her dissatisfaction with her position and her disdain for upper administrative leadership has manifested itself publicly. Clearly, the bullying in which she participated carried no extrinsic value: At this point in her career, the toxicity and negativity she inflicted have garnered no significant gain and, in contrast, have negatively affected her career and status at my institution.

For me, however, my career and status in the profession were viewed favorably by upper administrative officials. Just two short weeks after these emails were sent to my chair, I received, first, a college-wide institutional award for research and scholarship; second, I was promoted to associate professor of English. My rank within the university also continued to rise. The following year I was granted a 50 percent appointment as the associate director of my campus's office of faculty development. Part of my position includes facilitating teaching, learning, and academic leadership programs and workshops for graduate students and faculty members. With this role, I was granted the opportunity to develop new programs and am thus interested in developing additional support through the office of faculty development for women of color. I am thrilled to embark upon a new opportunity, and I'm also pleased that this opportunity has taken me to a place to think about larger-scale support for faculty of color, including a stronger need for allies.

One of the reasons I began to pursue opportunities beyond my department and writing program was because when I was being bullied, I needed stronger allies in higher-ranked spaces, with those who possessed the agency and authority to effect change on a level that was less local. While I do not intend to suggest that department chairs do not possess this agency, that agency often becomes limited to conflict mediation between faculty members. While this form of mediation can be helpful, it often does not do much to change the system and cultural conditions that allow workplace bullying to continue beyond a single department. Many studies acknowledge that the "academic department is an important location of faculty work" and that scholars "have called for studies that improve our understanding of academics' relationships within their departments (Tight 2003), suggesting that such relationships are sources of faculty support, knowledge generation and dissemination, and collaboration" (Pifer, Baker, and Lunsford 2015, 181). However, a recent study that examined the relationships between university departments and faculty development centers revealed nine frequently identified challenges associated with one's ability to improve working conditions beyond the department level: general challenges with colleagues, isolation/lack of fit/lack of colleagues, rank-based challenges, poor behavior, discrimination, mentoring-related challenges, strained relationships, and faculty turnover/attrition (Pifer, Baker, and Lunsford 2015, 187).

For me, then, I believed that the change I wanted to help create needed university-wide campus attention outside of a single department unit, where multiple colleges, units, and departments were collaborating to improve working conditions on behalf of those who often do not possess the power and agency to speak for themselves. In other words, moving part of my appointment outside a college and a department created campus-wide attention to attend to pressing working conditions, including bullying, that affect faculty and women of color. I needed a new space to fight systemic workplace bullying; in contrast, dealing with these disputes solely at the department level permitted me to focus only on colleague-to-colleague personal interactions, which did not lead to progress toward institutional change.

More recently, during the revision stages of this chapter, Lauren signed up to attend a two-day workshop on diversity and inclusion I was facilitating as associate director of the office of faculty development. To my surprise, Lauren was eager to participate and attended both of the session topics I presented. She sincerely engaged with the materials and topics and sent a very pleasant note thanking me for facilitating.

When participants shared their reasons for attending the workshop, Lauren stated that she wanted to learn how to be more inclusive and to advocate, especially for students of color. She further explained that she had advocated for doctoral admission for an African American female a graduate director and recent department chair intended to reject. According to Lauren, both administrators justified this decision based on "fit"—despite the candidate's outstanding admission materials—because there were no faculty specializing in African American women writers. While I am admittedly hesitant about forging a closer relationship with her and trusting her as a colleague, I did want to acknowledge her willingness to reach out and take responsibility for learning how to support students of color.

CONCLUDING REMARKS: THE NEED FOR ALLIES
TO COMBAT WORKPLACE BULLYING

I recognize how fortunate I was to escape removal from my position and to obtain job security as a tenured faculty member given my experiences as an African American female pre-tenured WPA. Critical to understanding my success is the fact that I had allies in greater positions of power and authority who were willing to advocate on my behalf. In this space, I discussed the role of my department chair. It is essential to point out his position as an ally here because he chose to provide protection and advocacy despite the fact that his position as an administrator is more vulnerable to removal because that appointment is outside the collective bargaining contractual agreements surrounding tenure and promotion. In addition to my department chair, several tenured white female faculty members in my department were willing to defend and advocate for me. There are too many to name in this space; however, it is important to emphasize that advocacy, unit support, and emotional support go a long way in helping a pre-tenured faculty member of color feel a sense of belonging and welcoming in a department in which she is the only African American female faculty member.

As I have discussed elsewhere, the need for white ally-ship is essential for the retention of faculty of color (Perryman-Clark 2016; Craig and Perryman-Clark 2016). As Craig and I argue (2016, 25), beyond the institutional unit, "WPA faculty of color still need stronger advocacy and broader institutional (white) allies in building administrative support." Put simply, providing ally-ship and advocacy at the department level is a start toward effecting larger-scale social change. The extension of that support to our disciplinary organizations, such as the Council of Writing Program Administrators (CWPA), provides further potential for ally-ship. For instance, writing external letters of support and participating in external review cases for the tenure and promotion of faculty of color provides another space for those in positions of power and authority to advocate for those of us who do not occupy those same positions. In short, ally-ship is one immediate and doable solution to supporting pre-tenured WPAs of color.

Finally, I recognize that the question of how faculty members can serve as stronger allies is easier asked than answered. In an earlier publication I (2016, 206–7) ask: "While no WPA is immune to resistance from graduate students and writing instructors, the questions raised in this space require us to consider what roles might college deans, department chairs, and white allies in our organization fulfill to support WPAs of color." I further assert (Perryman-Clark 2016, 206–7), however, that to foster stronger senses of ally-ship, those "of us in composition who are in positions of power and authority must work more actively to become stronger allies of WPAs of color and WPAs charged with doing writing assessment on/with racially and linguistically diverse students. This includes finding department chairs and deans who are willing to share the responsibility and support the work of WPAs of color."

In our profession, there is no shortage of scholars who have become department chairs and deans. Some of us have even achieved status as provosts and presidents. What I suggest in this space is that while many administrative positions, including WPA positions, are often discouraged or seen as less desirable, more of us in composition need to pursue larger-scale university administrative positions with the purposeful intent to use such positions to transform and effect institutional change for the collective good of our faculty and our students. When we understand our institutional administrative roles as ones of social justice, we must consider these roles as our moral and ethical obligation to advocate on behalf of those who are disenfranchised. Taking this role seriously, then, suggests that we are permitting faculty and students to place their trust in our ability to lead ethically and morally, so disenfranchised faculty do not constantly have to question whether we have their best interests at heart or whether we intend to betray them: "In essence, this is what social justice is about: it is about using our power to effect institutional change in ways that foster equality and fairness in the classroom" (Perryman-Clark 2016, 211). Supporting faculty of color and those who experience workplace bullying can then become another agent for effecting social change.

NOTE

1.   Lauren is a pseudonym for the TA's faculty adviser.

REFERENCES

Accapadi, Mamta Motwani. 2007. "When White Women Cry: How White Women's Tears Oppress Women of Color." *College Student Affairs Journal* 26 (2): 208–15.

Cambridge, Barbara. 2011. "Research and Policy: Antithetical or Complementary?" *WPA: Writing Program Administration* 35 (1): 135–47.

Craig, Collin Lamont, and Staci Maree Perryman-Clark. 2011. "Troubling the Boundaries: (De)Constructing WPA Identities at the Intersections of Race and Gender." *WPA: Writing Program Administration* 34 (2): 37–58.

Craig, Collin Lamont, and Staci M. Perryman-Clark. 2016. "Troubling the Boundaries Revisited: Moving Towards Change as Things Stay the Same." *WPA: Writing Program Administration* 39 (2): 20–25.

Denny, Harry. 2014. "Of Sticks and Stones, Words That Wound, and Actions Speaking Louder: When Academic Bullying Becomes Everyday Oppression." *Workplace: A Journal for Academic Labor* 24: 1–8.

Dew, Debra Frank, and Alice Horning, eds. 2007. *Untenured Faculty as Writing Program Administrators: Institutional Practices and Politics*. West Lafayette, IN: Parlor.

Einarsen, Ståle. 1996. "Bullying and Harassment at Work: Epidemiological and Psychological Aspects." PhD dissertation, Department of Psychosocial Science, University of Bergen, Norway.

Eng, Joseph. 2007. "Demystifying the Asian-American WPA: Locations in Writing, Teaching, and Program Administration." In *Untenured Faculty as Writing Program Administrators: Institutional Practices and Politics*, ed. Debra Frank Dew and Alice Horning, 153–71. West Lafayette, IN: Parlor.

Enos, Theresa. 2002. "Reflexive Professional Development: Getting Disciplined in Writing Program Administration." In *The Writing Program Administrator's Resource: A Guide to Reflective Institutional Practice*, ed. Stuart C. Brown and Theresa Enos, 59–70. Mahwah, NJ: Lawrence Erlbaum Associates.

Hoel, Helge, and Cary Cooper. 2000. *Destructive Conflict and Bullying at Work*. Manchester, UK: Manchester School of Management, Institute of Science and Technology, University of Manchester, UK. https://sites.google.com/site/qmcmonitor/Destructiveconflict andbullyingatwork.pdf?attredirects=0.

Horning, Alice. 2007. "Introduction: What Is Wrong with THIS Picture?" In *Untenured Faculty as Writing Program Administrators: Institutional Practices and Politics*, ed. Debra Frank Dew and Alice Horning, 3–12. West Lafayette, IN: Parlor Press.

Perryman-Clark, Staci M. 2016. "Who We Are(n't) Assessing: Racializing Language and Writing Assessment in Writing Program Administration." *College English* 79 (2): 206–11.

Pifer, Meghan J., Vicki L. Baker, and Laura G. Lunsford. 2015. "Academic Departments as Networks of Informal Learning: Faculty Development at Liberal Arts Colleges." *International Journal for Academic Development* 20 (2): 178–92. https://doi.org/10.1080 /1360144X.2015.1028065.

Rose, Shirley, and Irwin Weiser, eds. 1999. *The Writing Program Administrator as Researcher*. Portsmouth, NH: Boynton/Cook.

Salin, Denise. 2003. "Ways of Explaining Workplace Bullying: A Review of Enabling, Motivating, and Precipitating Structures and Processes in the Work Environment." *Human Relations* 56 (10): 1213–32. https://doi.org/10.1177/00187267035610003.

Sutton, Brian. 2007. "That Kind of Person." *Writing on the Edge* 18 (1): 77–85.

Tight, Malcolm. 2003. *Researching Higher Education*. Maidenhead, UK: Open University Press.

Zapf, Dieter, Carmen Knorz, and Matthias Kulla. 1996. "On the Relationship between Mobbing Factors and Job Content, Social Work Environment, and Health Outcomes." *European Journal of Work and Organizational Psychology* 5 (2): 215–37.

8

A BARBARIAN WITHIN THE GATE
The Detriments of Insularity at a Small Liberal Arts College

Erec Smith

Arguably, the terms "diversity worker" and "writing center director" describe two of the most thankless jobs in academia. I have been both simultaneously and liken the aftermath to a kind of PTSD. This trauma resulted from being an African American male promoting diversity and running a writing center at a small, predominantly white liberal arts college with no writing program and no real respect—or knowledge—of the field of rhetoric and composition. Double-marginalized by my institution, both culturally and disciplinarily, I felt an onslaught of aggressions and "microaggressions" that was difficult to navigate. In synthesizing personal experience with theoretical work, I've noticed that insularity is the main source from which racial and disciplinary supremacy derive. This insularity caused a multifaceted xenophobia that thwarted my attempt to fabricate a subject position that was comfortable in such a context. Although the collection to which this chapter belongs focuses on the bullying of writing program administrators (WPAs), I feel my status as a WPA of color is an important detail. Also, because of my status as a black male at a predominately white school, my work as a promoter of diversity was part of my identity as an academic. Thus, I mention my work on diversity initiatives as well as an aspect of my blackness. Based on a synthesis of my experience with theories of race relations, bullying, and rhetorical context, I have concluded that my experience of being "othered," a more specific category of bullying because of my harboring of what Mark Anthony Neal (2006, 28) calls "meta-identities," is ultimately a result of academic insularity.

Although my definition of bullying matches the definition articulated in this book's introduction, for this chapter I abide by the definition articulated by Ståle Einarsen and colleagues (2003, 15):

> Bullying at work means harassing, offending, socially excluding someone or negatively affecting someone's work tasks. In order for the label

DOI: 10.7330/9781607328162.c008

bullying (or mobbing) to be applied to a particular activity, interaction or process it has to occur repeatedly and regularly (e.g., weekly) and over a period of time (e.g., about six months). Bullying is an escalating process in the course of which the person confronted ends up in an inferior position and becomes the target of systematic negative social acts. A conflict cannot be called bullying if the incident is an isolated event or if two parties of approximately equal "strength" are in conflict.

This definition distinguishes between more general definitions of bullying and the form of workplace bullying known as "mobbing," the central aspect of this chapter. Note that this kind of bullying, unlike more general definitions, often involves a group of bullies attacking a single target.

FROM COLLEAGUE TO TARGET

Of course, the intersectionality of my experience makes it theoretically fecund. In my roles in diversity matters (throughout my time at this institution I either sat on or chaired the diversity committee, which was charged with promoting difference and educating the campus on matters of race and ethnicity) and writing administration, I was a threatening Other. The only way I fit was through what Roland Barthes (1972, 152) called "eroticism," or the interpellation of the Other in a way that makes sense within hegemony's status quo: "The Other becomes a pure object, a spectacle, a clown. Relegated to the confines of humanity, he no longer threatens the security of the home." My work in both diversity matters and rhet/comp were novel sideshows to my colleagues' more "serious" academic work.

I was consistently "locked out" of this environment. I was dismissed and spoken over in meetings, not invited to social faculty events, and often treated like a child. I often fought to get words in edgewise and was smiled at like a precocious child when I was finally "heard." A need to infantilize me or, as Athena Mutua (2006, 720) would suggest, emasculate me seemed ubiquitous. Mutua's theory is salient if one considers her take on "hegemonic masculinity," which, by definition, requires the domination of "women, children, and, yes, other subordinate, or 'weaker' men." As a black man whose upbringing instilled in me what some would call "Anglo-conformity," I still did not fit into the meta-narrative of a predominately white and very conservative liberal arts college.[1]

My only respect came when people were discussing sports or popular culture. I was allowed to be a funny guy, but once I began to talk like an academic, I was a problem. Some people's faces would squirm with disgust when I'd speak as if I knew what I was talking about. Some would challenge me in rude ways when they would engage others with a more civil demeanor. An air of "how dare you think you know something" was present like a debilitating miasma.

The debilitation I speak of often results in what Claude Steele (2010) calls "stereotype threat." Steele (2010, 145–53) defines stereotype threat as the psychological and often physical effects of "identity contingencies": "the things you have to deal with in a situation because you have a given social identity, because you are old, young, gay, a white male, a woman, black, Latino . . . Other people in the situation didn't have to deal with them, just the people who had the same identity [you] had." My experience is testimony to the legitimacy of this concept.[2]

Although stereotype threat was an issue, I experienced more observable modes of silencing as well. I simply was not acknowledged as a colleague or an academic in general. People would ignore direct statements I made to them as if I was not present. A member of my own department called me by the wrong name for over four years, only getting it right during my final semester at the institution. I recall one incident during a meeting to revamp a first-year great books course. Taken aback by the dismissal of literature on the Holocaust and of the "never forget" mantra, I implored that we not jettison the entire section. I used what I thought would be recognized as a rhetorical statement and not taken literally: "Can we at least do a little bit of this?" A professor who had talked down to me on a regular basis mocked me by asking a rhetorical question of his own: "A little bit of the Holocaust?" This induced an eruption of laughter. I bring this up because it is quite telling of the benefit of the doubt given to more hegemonic, that is, white, faculty. If I were white, my statement may have been taken as the rhetorical trope it was. However, as a black man, I was not afforded this assumption; I was taken literally. (Apparently, a black man can't use figurative language.) When I expressed my indignation with a sarcastic "sorry, I had no idea that statement was so funny," another colleague responded "that's okay, Erec," in a condescending tone one might use with a precocious child.

The behavior of my "colleagues" is not a theoretical novelty. Such bullying is common in the workplace when the setting is threatened with a change agent of some sort (Coyne 2011, 167–68). But more specifically, in what some capriciously deem a post-race society or, more accurately, what Touré (2011) has dubbed a "post-black" society, black men in positions of power suffer from "gendered racism" (Mutua 2006, 720). Behavior deemed normal in white males may be deemed intimidating, aggressive, and pathological in black men (Touré 2011, 182). Thus, my infantilization/emasculation is no surprise. According to Helan E. Page (1997, 102), to be accepted and embraceable, a black man must be a comedian, a musician, or an athlete. Exuding power in any other way is threatening. This sad fact seemed apparent during my time at this institution.

And why wouldn't it? Barack Obama, the former erstwhile leader of the free world, also suffered from gendered racism (Smith 2016). In fact, as I point out in "Obama's Feminine Discourse: A Rhetorical Necessity of Black Male Leadership," exertion of authority by a black male in any way would threaten too many people (Smith 2016). Exuding any kind of masculinity, whether stereotypically "white" masculinity or stereotypically "black" masculinity, is anathema for black men in positions of power (Smith 2016, 482). As a professor, administrator, and chair of a committee that promoted the existence and fair treatment of others who looked like me, I made it clear that this flagship of Anglo-centricity—the small liberal arts college—had been boarded by the enemy. Exuding anything other than submissiveness was a problem.

In addition to embodying marginalization, my position as a scholar of rhetoric and composition induced further dismissal. As a writing center director at a school with no writing program and as a junior faculty member, my calls for meetings to discuss writing pedagogy were ignored. I was unsupported in my work, even though I rebranded the center, created a new mission statement that melded nicely with the college's mission statement, and provided as many workshops as possible. No one cared about any of this. I recall one moment when a supportive dean allowed me to speak to a group of department chairs about academic discourse and how we may do well to break down writing expectations per discipline. I was met with silence, except for one professor who claimed that his discipline doesn't have a discourse; he "just writes." My discipline was not merely dismissed, it was completely unacknowledged.[3]

Clearly, "rhet/comp scholar" and "misfit" were synonymous terms in this context. I was often treated as if I was telling a tall tale about academics who teach process pedagogy, non-directive tutoring, and distinctions in speech genres and discourse communities. I was blamed for student writing issues by faculty who refused to work with me. I was asked to fix writing at a school with no writing program and whose definition of writing intensive—another conversation I tried to start, to no avail—was shabby. I was given no support other than a small budget and a limited number of writing fellows for a Common Intellectual Experience (CIE) course adopted in lieu of a first-year writing course. (CIE was a great books course with some contemporary "alternative" writings thrown in that would change every year or two. All instructors shared the same syllabus, with no room for revision.)

Efforts to change minds seemed fruitless. Large events I scheduled and ran by myself were met with little to no acknowledgment. In an effort to both educate my colleagues about the field of rhetoric and composition and claim that this field was indeed taken seriously in academia, I organized two major events. The first was a two-day presentation/workshop on academic discourse and writing-intensive pedagogy. I spoke for three hours the first day and ninety minutes the next (on rhet/comp, discourse, creating assignments, grading, teaching the thesis statement) before having people break into groups to discuss approaches to grading based on my presentations. I don't know how seriously I was taken, especially because one professor, the aforementioned discourse denier, entered the room, raised a beholding hand toward me, and declared "our savior" in a sarcastic way.

I also organized a one-day conference with the regional affiliate for the Council of Writing Program Administrators that featured presentations from various surrounding schools, from Ivy League to community college, with Gerald Graff and Cathy Birkenstein as keynote speakers. The day went rather well, including some heated debate about what constitutes the fundamentals of academic discourse. The regional attendees gave abundant and positive feedback. However, I heard nothing from my institutional colleagues, including those who attended. They acted as if the event had never happened.

My writing fellows were often usurped without my knowledge. The main culprit was a man who told me in so many words that he did not respect my field, and he tried to spread his beliefs to my writing fellows. This figure, the man who spearheaded the CIE program and gave me the most pushback during my job interview because he did not believe in rhetoric as a viable academic genre (but at least he acknowledged its existence), decided without discussing it with me to usurp my writing fellows for a special CIE project in which classmates shared the same dorm hallways (thus creating a discourse community, a concept denied by some of his colleagues). When I expressed the fact that he had not discussed the project with me to my department colleagues during a meeting, I was met with silence and a few shrugs. The students he usurped returned to me arrogantly dismissing the entire concept of writing centers and rhetoric and composition during staff meetings. I would push back, but I did not want to create a spectacle of debate to digress from the important tasks of the meeting. This job was officially a nightmare.

Again, I was an Other who needed to be present but defused. As I (2015, 533) articulate in "Cultural Logics, Impact, and the State of 'Scholarship in Composition,'" rhetoric and composition has an inherently interdisciplinary and pragmatic impact that flies in the face of what some call the conception of liberal arts as values, habits, and dispositions—an education meant to create a certain kind of person indicative of an ideological status quo. Thus, in presenting myself as something other than a grammar checker, my field was "Othered" as representing pedestrianism or dilettantism without giving me much opportunity to explain my discipline otherwise.

I recall a meeting with a college administrator to discuss criteria for my evaluation—a meeting that took me three years to set up. I had emailed him a copy of the Council of Writing Program Administrators' (1998) "Evaluating the Intellectual Work of Writing Administration" to preface the meeting in hopes of giving him an idea of the best practices of writing program administration. During the meeting, I noticed a printout of the article on the table next to him. After I asked if he had read it, he picked up the essay, rolled his eyes, stated an exasperated "yeah," tossed the essay back on the table, and proceeded with the meeting as if I had never asked the question. As an apparent representative of traditional academic values and particular definitions of erudition, he seemed to see writing program administration as decidedly nonacademic and therefore unworthy of his consideration, let alone his respect. He directly represented the attitudes and beliefs of my colleagues as well. The support I thought I had from the dean fizzled out at the very next level; from this administrator downward, I was on my own.

As Muriel Harris (2001, 427) points out, a writing center at an institution with no writing program must have top-down support, ubiquitous and systemic throughout the institution. This was not the case; august support at the executive level fizzled out when it reached lower administration, faculty, and staff. Calls to work together with each department were seen as calls to "overwork" (teach writing), attempts to spy on a department's utter lack of a writing pedagogy, or attempts to undermine the fundamental concepts of "the life of the mind." I was at best a veritable "fool on the hill" announcing the existence of a strange concept called rhetoric and composition that dealt with both writing *and* meaning. At worst, I was the junior faculty member coercing everyone to work harder to teach something they did not want to teach and to question the rhetorical nature of tried, true, and strongly embraced institutional ideology.

Altogether, I was a black sophist troublemaker whose words and mere presence were irrelevant, anathema, or threatening. Much of this can be gleaned from Stanley Fish's take on academia and the crisis in the humanities. Fish would like to preserve the low-stakes, life of the mind culture of the English discipline, a culture that reduces rhetoric to style and belletristic interests, a culture bound by Anglo-centric, upper-class sensibilities (Zwagerman 2015). Many small liberal arts colleges, these "schools of Fish," as it were, will fight for this way of life.

THE CRISIS OF INSULARITY

My dual experiences—bullying based on my embodiment of otherness and my representation of rhet/comp—exposed a singular problem in academia: insularity. This insularity incubated a xenophobia that made me a threat. (I was the ultimate barbarian at the gate who somehow infiltrated the ivory tower.) Thus, to remedy bully culture, one must eliminate this insularity. To do so, a paradigm shift is in order.

The "crisis in the humanities" may really be a crisis in academic insularity; the impending death of traditional notions of the humanities may be the birth of a more modern, diverse, and far less insular academy. Civic engagement initiatives that encourage public interactions—such as urban humanities and community outreach—may raze the barriers that harbor an isolating ideology of "knowledge for its own sake" as well as an exclusionary mind-set against social/racial others. That is, civic engagement, by definition, necessitates reaching beyond the (safe) confines of academia. If academics already scoff at outsiders within, the thought of engaging them elsewhere could hardly be entertained.

As I have conveyed, this insularity manifests as both racial (my status as black man and diversity worker) and disciplinary discrimination. Both conflate when it comes to the protection of academic hegemony. The field of rhetoric and composition is inherently editorial in its mission to critique discourse—especially hegemonic discourse—and opens academia to the non-academic world in a way that may also legitimize the experiences and standpoints of "Others." So the presence of minorities, too, revises the perception of Anglo-centric superiority and the norms and mores that come with it. Discussing each individually is imperative to understand their confluence.

The marginalization of civic engagement and public intellectualism is, unsurprisingly, illustrated by a personal experience. For three years I included civic engagement—the tutoring of inner-city middle and high school students—in my writing center teaching and tutoring course. I partnered with high schools, community centers, and public writing centers (these writing centers were comparable to entities like 826

Valencia, a community-based writing center that has spread to several cities) to give my tutors experience in the critique and transfer of discourse and provide needed resources to the extra-academic community. As many professors who take on the challenge of civic engagement will tell you, it is messy work that does not always work out as planned: students do not show up, outside institutions do not uphold their end of the bargain, and so forth. I was willing and able to take these risks and to have my institution—one ignorant of rhet/comp and its subfields, let alone their common relationship with pedagogical outreach—ask questions and critique my projects. However, this didn't happen. No one cared that I was taking it upon myself to secure a campus van to drive my students forty minutes into the city and back for weeks at a time. It was not important work. No one knew why I was doing it (despite my telling them), and no one cared that I was doing it. No one.

My colleagues' collective disinterest resulted substantially from the hierarchical viewpoint that goals pursued within academia were more erudite and important than those that took place outside its confines. That is, to work with non-academics was to do non-academic work and thus unimportant work. Despite the fact that, according to the Conference on College Composition and Communication (2015), rhetoric and composition as a field proudly and explicitly deals with a variety of texts and contexts, such endeavors provided no scholarly ethos. This is not a new story; rhetoric and composition's history overflows with stories of shunning and dismissal from more traditional academic colleagues.

However, what I do find interesting is the denial that the civic interests of rhetoric and composition can enhance academia and remedy a perceived crisis in the humanities. I believe this to be a dangerous and habitual allegiance to ideology. This institution, like many others, strives to preserve a moment in higher education when academic insularity did not perpetuate a crisis. This institution, like many others, strives to preserve a time when outreach would distract from the more favored pursuits of discipline-specific and often esoteric works of scholars. Interdisciplinarity and civic engagement—now a logical (and ethical) next step in English departments and other humanistic disciplines—were seen as the actions of those who simply did not belong. Thus, to acknowledge my outreach to surrounding institutions and organizations was to take part in exercises of inferiority. Of course, many know that civic engagement and highly intellectual work are not mutually exclusive, and I believe some of those who share sentiments with my aforementioned colleagues would agree. However, insularity breeds a kind of introversion that steers clear of outreach and anything else that would necessitate extroversion and an immersion in a "foreign" discourse.

Rhetoric has always been about a wider public sphere. As James Dubinsky (2010, 259) writes, civic engagement "prepares students for the workplace in a more comprehensive way than many other peda-gogical strategies because students apply what they have learned by working with real audiences." My erstwhile colleagues, even those in the humanities—even those in the English department—did not have such faith in the efficacy of "real audiences" and surely did not share this alle-giance to the "back woods" of popular culture. In fact, they seemed to pride themselves on their status as an "unreal audience," preferring the perceived haughtiness of a sheltered academe. Sean Zwagerman (2015), when discussing the insularity of the humanities, speaks of the cognitive, ideological, and rhetorical dissonance felt when juxtaposing academia and non-academic realms. He writes that "there can be no common vocabulary for identification [among academics and non-academics], since to appeal for the humanities by speaking the other person's lan-guage would be a betrayal of the humanities" (Zwagerman 2015, 477). My experiences strongly support this claim. Like royalty who get nervous and uncomfortable around less fortunate townsfolk, many academics avoid the alien context of non-academics. Academic insularity gives way to a cultural homogeneity that feels threatened outside of its own comfort zone. To those within such a comfort zone—a quarantine of sorts—civic engagement is inherently unpleasant. Perhaps to my col-leagues, acknowledging my work felt akin to flirting with disaster—the contagion of the masses.

Of course, the insularity that creates a disdain for rhetoric and com-position also creates a xenophobia that discourages cultural diversity within academia. As a black man—one carrying a torch for diversifica-tion to boot—I was a reminder of the outside world that was always threatening. In fact, my presence suggested that the outside world had infiltrated and might begin to change the comfort zone many had enjoyed for so long. I was a harbinger of a slippery slope that would introduce a diversity inimical to the insular "club" model of academia. More than once, I heard colleagues call the faculty "a family" and state that tenure was about making sure someone fit into that family. Apparently, in that family, people needed to know their places. In my time at this institution, two tenured black males and one tenure-track female were let go, the former two under suspicious circumstances. In the five years I worked there, the black faculty had been reduced to one person who was never on a tenure track but who was, as explained

during a faculty meeting, eventually given tenure because of her duration at the institution. Perhaps in some way she had proven herself a
palatable member of the family.

One can glean from all of this a desire to create a certain kind of
citizen. This molding of citizens, what A. Anthony Appiah (2005) calls
"soul making," naturally reflects a particular ideology. At this institution, that ideology promoted a certain kind of citizen, one steeped in
Anglo-centricity who saw any attempt at progressiveness as a departure
from such citizenry. This citizen could not be enhanced, only changed
for the worse.

This sentiment fully displayed itself during my final faculty meeting
at this institution. As fate would have it, the diversity committee, which
had been taken over by a junior faculty member who had my trust and
admiration, was on the docket to discuss a new diversity statement for
the college. After my colleague presented the statement, one typically in
favor of multicultural "tolerance" and openness to a diversity of cultural
viewpoints, faculty members stood up one by one to challenge the statement. Each—white men all—insisted that the definition of diversity had
only to do with a diversity of ideas; the institution should not be charged
to advocate for the viewpoints of marginalized peoples. (Regarding the
diversity of ideas, the irony that the "idea" of rhetorical theory was not
included may not have occurred to them.) My colleague, a progressive
white woman, seemed floored by the responses to the idea of multicultural acceptance. I was not. This incident was just the latest to illustrate an
ever-more-popular maxim: some people have been privileged for so long
that to them, equality feels like oppression.[4] I believe my colleagues would
not have been so opposed to diversity if they were not afraid of change
and the loss of a comfortable, familiar, and safe insularity. I believe this
insularity was both an addiction and a blindfold to the benefits of cos-
mopolitanism. I believe the degree of aggression my colleagues leveled
against me was caused by their collective belief that I was a threat to that
insularity, a harbinger of inevitable change. I believe my colleagues were
analogous to bees at summer's end who are more aggressive because they
know the end is near. To be clear, I believe that bullying at this institution
was a result of a staunch insularity that closes off cultures, ideologies, and
disciplines from participation. To be an African American rhetorician in
such a community is to agitate, inherently.

Thus, the citizen this institution wanted to make was a citizen of a
"world" in which minority concerns and sensibilities were of no concern
at all—a world where "the life of the mind" was lauded over "a life of
civic duty." The resemblance to the confrontation in Plato's *Gorgias* is not

lost on me. I played a collective Gorgias, Polus, and Callicles to my institution's Socrates. I was not a rhetorician but a sophist there to weaken virtue. Worse yet, I was a black sophist charged with worsening virtue and pulling refined sensibilities into base, anti-intellectual savagery. Of course, contemporary rhetoricians believe the study and practice of rhetoric is more than just a "knack," as it is labeled in *Gorgias*. Even Plato came around to this idea in his later work on rhetoric, the *Phaedrus*. However, through either ignorance or subterfuge, I was presented as the less-than-worthy non-academic whose minority status, focus on diversity of culture and discourse, and desire to reach out beyond the college walls solidified my designation as "Other."

Generally, this dismissal of rhetoric and composition as a field and issues of xenophobia in academia are connected. I believe they both stem from a deep-seated insularity that has helped define certain institutions. This insularity, then, is a form of identity politics. Accepting me, an African American rhet/comp scholar, created a cognitive dissonance that could only be alleviated through various degrees of bullying. Thus, like most incidents of insularity, the kind that permeated this institution may be a fear of irrelevancy or a lack of "groundedness." Perhaps they saw me as a signpost at the edge of a slippery slope of devolution toward something other than a place of comfort and humiliation. Such devolution had to be staved off. Thus, I *had* to be disrespected. I had to be bullied away.

Perhaps the most depressing aspect of this story is that the institution of which I speak was my alma mater. As an undergraduate, I learned the value and beauty of critical thinking, literary critique, and intellectuality. Although I had various race-based issues with other students, I had always thought of my faculty with fondness. After all, they were the ones who helped me cultivate a desire to spend my life in academe. Unfortunately, I was never intended to enjoy that life if I was among them. I was never meant to be an equal. That is one lesson they waited to teach me after graduation. When the environment that nurtured in one's youth bullies in one's adulthood, what is one to do? Write about it, I suppose.

NOTES

1.   And why didn't I fit in? Yes, I did have dreadlocks for the first couple of years—very long dreadlocks. I eventually altered my look by completely shaving my head. In essence, I went from the most feared hairstyle on black males to perhaps the second-most feared hairstyle (Mannes 2012). Who I was as a person, an academic, and an educator seemed to have no bearing on my reception.

2. Steele (2010) elaborates on the debilitating effects of stereotype threat. Because one may spend so much time thinking about the stereotype threat and all that goes with it, the phenomenon "induces rumination, which takes up mental capacity, distracting us from the task at hand—from the questions on the standardized test we're taking or from the conversation we're having with persons of a different race. So beyond the physiological reactions that identity threat causes, it also impairs performance and other actions by interfering with our thinking" (Steele 2010, 1786–95). After a while, the bullying had me doubting myself when doing routine tasks I had taken for granted for years. I developed chest pains that caused me to wear a heart monitor. (The pains turned out to be a result of stress, which the colleagues who caused the stress had predicted.) My experience surely illustrates the power of stereotype threat.

3. Also, rhetoric and composition is inherently critical of hegemony by breaking it down into a convention-laden discourse that is constructed and not "natural." My colleague's insistence that he abided by no discourse but "just wrote" strongly suggests that the field of rhetoric and composition itself questioned conceptions of normality with which my colleagues identified. Postmodernism, deconstructionism, poststructuralism were in essence games, ideologies and methodologies that were fine as curious topics of conversation but deplorable as lenses through which to analyze and critique the world—well, *their* world, anyway.

4. Although the anecdotal aspect of this chapter ends here, many incidents of bullying are not included herein. A complete telling of these incidents may be too extensive or digressive for the purpose of this chapter. Issues of stereotype threat abound, but they would serve better in a separate work.

REFERENCES

Appiah, A. Anthony. 2005. *The Ethics of Identity*. Princeton, NJ: Princeton University Press.

Barthes, Roland. 1972. *Mythologies*. New York: Hill and Wang.

Conference on College Composition and Communication. 2015. "Statement of Professional Guidance." http://cccc.ncte.org/cccc/resources/positions/professionalguidance.

Council of Writing Program Administrators. 1998. "Evaluating the Intellectual Work of Writing Administration." http://wpacouncil.org/positions/intellectualwork.html.

Coyne, Iain. 2011. "Bullying in the Workplace." In *Bullying in Different Contexts*, ed. Claire P. Monks and Iain Coyne, 157–84. New York: Cambridge University Press. https://doi.org/10.1017/CBO9780511921018.008.

Dubinsky, James. 2010. "Service-Learning as a Path to Virtue: The Ideal Orator in Professional Communication." In *Writing and Community Engagement: A Critical Sourcebook*, ed. Thomas Dean, Barbara Roswell, and Adrian J. Wurr, 61–74. New York: Bedford/St. Martin's.

Einarsen, Ståle, Helge Hoel, Dieter Zapf, and Cary L. Cooper. 2003. "The Concept of Bullying at Work: European Tradition." In *Bullying and Emotional Abuse in the Workplace: International Perspectives in Research and Practice*, ed. Ståle Einarsen, Helge Hoel, and Cary Cooper, 3–30. London: Taylor and Francis.

Harris, Muriel. 2001. "A Writing Center without a WAC Program: The De Facto WAC Center/Writing Center." In *The Allyn and Bacon Guide to Writing Center Theory and Practice*, ed. Robert W. Barnett and Jacob S. Blumner, 426–41. Boston: Allyn and Bacon.

Mannes, Albert E. 2012. "Shorn Scalps and Perceptions of Male Dominance." *Social Psychology and Personality Science* 00 (0): 198–205. http://opim.wharton.upenn.edu/DPlab/papers/publishedPapers/Mannes_2012_%20Shorn%20scalps%20and%20perceptions%20of%20male%20dominance.pdf.

Mutua, Athena D. 2006. *Progressive Black Masculinities.* New York: Routledge. E-book.

Neal, Mark Anthony. 2006. *New Black Man.* New York: Routledge.

Page, Helan E. 1997. "'Black Male' Imagery and Media Containment of African American Men." *American Anthropologist* 99 (1): 99–111. https://doi.org/10.1525/aa.1997.99.1.99.

Smith, Erec. 2015. "Cultural Logics, Impact, and the State of 'Scholarship in Composition.'" *College Composition and Communication* 66 (3): 531–36.

Smith, Erec. 2016. "Obama's Feminine Discourse: A Rhetorical Necessity of Black Male Leadership." *College Composition and Communication* 67 (3): 478–83.

Steele, Claude. 2010. *Whistling Vivaldi: How Stereotypes Affect Us and What We Can Do about It.* New York: W. W. Norton. E-book.

Touré. 2011. *Who's Afraid of Post-Blackness? What It Means to Be Black Now.* New York: Free Press. E-book.

Zwagerman, Sean. 2015. "Local Examples and Master Narratives: Stanley Fish and the Public Appeal of Current-Traditionalism." *College Composition and Communication* 66 (3): 458–82.

9

THE PROFESSIONAL *IS* PERSONAL
Institutional Bullying and the WPA

Amy Heckathorn

In 1999, my dissertation documented the historical evolution of the writing program administrator (WPA) position from its nascent beginnings to that moment. I described what I labeled an "Early Era," a time during which WPAs were not trained in the discipline, lacked institutional power, and were not professionally respected. By most accounts, WPAs were academics trained in fields other than rhetoric and composition who, often grudgingly, took on the administrative tasks of running a writing program as service to their department or university. However, by the end of my research, the late 1990s stood out as a "Professional Era" in which WPAs were highly trained, wielded significant institutional power, and had fully established professional identities. While the literature was clear that program development and management was an evolving and challenging endeavor, it was presented as academically focused work in an acknowledged field. As an aspiring WPA myself and one who had served as an associate WPA as a graduate student, I felt not only prepared to take on the intellectual work of the position after graduation but grateful to be entering an established disciplinary field. Little did I realize that almost twenty years into my career as a "Professional Era" WPA, I would experience the lack of power and professional respect I had associated with an era in the distant past.

This chapter will explore how the bullying of WPAs, and more specifically the mobbing of writing programs, reflects disciplinary divisions that prevent our field from achieving professional status. I trace a pattern of bullying in my department that began as programmatic questioning and pushback, escalated to faculty disenfranchisement and isolation, and ended in the complete dismantling of the writing program and its faculty. Begun by individuals, the bully majority grew to include most of the department, some college administrators, and then some upper

DOI: 10.7330/9781607328162.c009

administration who either participated in the bullying or refused to address and prevent it.

CHANGING CONTEXT

Paul Ranieri and Jackie Grutsch McKinney (2007) note that as professionals engaged in rhetorical action, WPAs should be well equipped to analyze and understand the importance of context in any particular situation. When exploring their own decisions to take on WPA positions as junior faculty, they noted, "Understanding context is important for deciding whether to assume an administrative position, and even more critical for succeeding in a position" (Ranieri and McKinney 2007, 250). This assessment, however, is not a onetime situation. I would extend their idea to suggest that context cannot be understood as a fixed situation. Indeed, my experience would indicate that context can change significantly, and because of its volatility, WPAs—particularly those housed in English departments—can find their circumstances greatly evolved over time. This precariousness of context is largely what can lay the foundation for bullying and mobbing.

In 1999, the English department at California State University, Sacramento provided what I thought was a unique and ideal working context for a WPA. The department was large, boasting forty tenure-line faculty (all tenured and nearly all full professors) and almost sixty adjunct faculty, making it a sizable force within not only the college but the university as a whole. Most faculty members had been in the department for a long time, weathering changing institutional priorities, cyclical budgets, and one another. The department chair was the epitome of leadership by example: he arrived before anyone else on campus to work on his publications and excellent teaching, his door was always open to listen to whatever joys or sorrows needed to be shared, and he encouraged a collegial comradery with Friday-evening trips to the local bar for beer and friendship. Although none of the faculty had PhDs in rhetoric and composition specifically, many had developed the programs and taught the classes that comprised the writing program—it was a shared responsibility. The adjunct lecturers were a respected part of the department, the writing classes were taught by most faculty, and the department as a whole was growing and thriving as it was moving out of the recession of the early 1990s. While most of the faculty were not intellectually invested in the writing program, they recognized that it accounted for nearly 75 percent of the department's course offerings and student enrollments. It was the sizable foundation on which the department largesse was built.

Hired fresh out of graduate school with a PhD in rhetoric and composition and a dissertation in program administration, I moved straight into the WPA position. They were happy to hire someone in the discipline (even though a few suspected I might "out" myself at any moment as a closet literature specialist because they did not honestly believe there really were people whose professional and academic interests were in composition and its administration). The faculty who had been running the program and teaching in it were ready to move back into their various areas of expertise. The department and the university were still very supportive of writing, but, with a new "specialist" at the helm, they encouraged me to take on leadership responsibility for as much as I was interested in and capable of doing. As most WPAs can attest, given the opportunity to take on work and challenges, I jumped in with both feet. By fall 2004 there were five rhet/comp faculty in the department who oversaw all of the department and university writing requirements and resources. We had developed a WAC position, expanded the writing center and various tutorial programs, and begun updating all of the writing courses—both required and elective—at the undergraduate and graduate levels. Although it was hard work and not without the requisite challenges we all face when creating, running, and revising such large undertakings, it was incredibly rewarding. These experiences allowed me many opportunities to develop alliances within the department, the university, and beyond. I felt professionally fulfilled—I was using my disciplinary knowledge and training in conjunction with many others to accomplish many writing-related endeavors—and this continued for several more years.

Fast forward almost twenty years from my hiring, and what I once described as my "dream job" has morphed into a nightmare. In dissertation terms, the department regressed from a "Professional Era" environment to an "Early Era" fiasco. Most of the faculty who hired and supported me are retired, and the four other rhet/comp specialists have either retired early or taken jobs elsewhere. Within the last three years, it seems our program has gone from a place that embraced diverse ideas, programmatic change, and disciplinary expertise to a place that has alienated its people and actively demeaned disciplinary expertise. In terms of rhetorical context, it is a completely new environment.

In keeping with trends across the country, since approximately 2012, funding for our public institution has been on the decline. Senior faculty were retiring, and many were not replaced. A tenure-line faculty of forty was cut in half, and junior faculty felt increasing research pressure in spite of a university mission focused on teaching effectiveness.

Class sizes began to grow, and competition for resources increased. New emphases on assessment did not easily fit into traditional literary studies, and the push toward an open major made hiring justifications complex. Meanwhile, the writing program used the opportunity to streamline and eliminate dated remedial practices and expand interdisciplinary writing collaborations. Within this climate, the university undertook an internal review process to rank majors and programs in an effort to explore how resources should be allocated. The English major was ranked in the third quartile and the Teaching Composition Certificate in the first. The stage was set for general anxiety and internal strife. I argue that the department was disposed toward a mobbing environment in great part because of its demographics. The writing program, with only 9 percent of the tenure-line faculty, offered approximately 75 percent of the classes in the department. This imbalance places composition faculty in the difficult position of running a significant program subject to the approval of 91 percent of the faculty who do not share a similar disciplinary perspective.

FROM BULLYING TO MOBBING—AN ORGANIZATIONAL CONSTRUCT

We are all familiar with the popular image of the bully—the brute on the playground inflicting his will, physically and emotionally, on the diminutive social outcast. This is not the kind of behavior one would expect in higher education, as it seems to stand in contrast to everything we represent—intellectual insight and the pursuit of understanding with others. It is precisely this disconnect that makes bullying in the academic workplace such a complex issue. When those dedicated to the search for enlightenment feel ignorant or threatened, they often have ample intellectual resources to bring to the table in their defense. As Kenneth Westhues (2005, x) notes, "The flight from truth and reason that mobbing represents harms workers, wastes resources, and impedes productivity in all workplaces, but in universities most of all. Here is an organization whose defining purpose is to seek and share true knowledge."

Noreen Tehrani (2012, 4) defines bullying as having four main features: "(a) the behaviours need to be perceived as negative and unwelcome; (b) they have to be persistent and long-term; (c) they need to involve an imbalance in power; (d) they do not have to be intentional to cause bullying to have taken place." She notes that bullying often comes to the fore in situations "when there is an inequality in the balance of power and this is used by the more powerful individual or group to undermine or subjugate another individual" (Tehrani 2012, 5). And this power imbalance comes in many forms, two of which seem pertinent to this situation: "positional power" and "resources power" (Tehrani 2012, 5). Once a person with positional power begins to exert bullying behaviors, it can become the model by which others judge their behavior—developing into mobbing. Westhues acknowledges that the original conception of *workplace mobbing* comes from Swedish psychologist Heinz Leymann, who coined the term when reading a study about aggression in birds and animals—the phenomenon that occurs when a group of animals works together to terrorize and often kill an outlier. Westhues then picks up this term to look at the practice as seen in academe: "It occurs most often in public-sector bureaucracies where, on account of collective agreements, policies, contracts or traditions, workers cannot be fired without cause. It thus involves months or years of often subtle and secretive maneuvers to isolate, marginalize, and devalue the target, make the target's life generally miserable, to the point that he or she commits suicide, dies of stress-related illness, becomes physically or psychologically disabled, quits voluntarily, takes early retirement, or does something that can be construed or misconstrued as legitimate cause for dismissal" (Westhues 2005, x).

While this is an acceleration of violence, the infractions need not be dramatic to cause significant damage: "As mobbing is group behavior, the bad behavior from a single member of the mobbing group need not be particularly bad or frequent for the impact of the group behavior to have a major impact on the target" (Tehrani 2012, 10). The consequences of this mobbing behavior can be devastating. Sarah Vaughan (2012, 51) explains, "Work is central to our lives and is essential in the building and shaping of our identity and search for daily meaning and recognition. Bullying can be a traumatic and overwhelming experience which violates the target's core values, challenging and impacting on their expectations of the world in general and their professional world in particular."

With these concepts in mind, I argue that there are three underlying reasons that often combine to foster a unique environment for the bullying of WPAs and writing programs: (1) ignorance of the field, (2) unwillingness to accept disciplinary expertise, and (3) fear of growing disciplinary prominence as resulting in the diminishing of other fields. These motivations prompt not only personal, individual bullying but also mobbing at a disciplinary and institutional level. When our subject matter is seen as something anyone can teach, faculty are often relegated to second-class citizen status. Adding to this mix, the concept of the WPA as administrator rather than disciplinary expert only compounds the problems. So once one's personnel and profession are downgraded, it becomes easier to use a bully majority to assert a counter-agenda. In addition, as the place and purview of writing programs grow, it can plant a seed of concern among other faculty and programs. So a chair's positional power and resources power (having personal privilege as well as access to upper administration, budgets, and greater disciplinary numbers) puts that person in a unique position to set and encourage (or discourage) bullying and mobbing.

What follows is far from an exhaustive accounting of the bullying and mobbing behavior we experienced in my department. It is a representative sampling to provide insight, as there is not room for an extended accounting, and personnel rules do not allow divulging evaluation and hiring details—another protection afforded the bully mob. In addition, names and administrative titles have been modified to mask individual identities, but as I worked my way through the bureaucratic channels to address these challenges, I followed standard university chain-of-command protocols.

In bullying and mobbing situations, it is not surprising that the most vulnerable faculty, non-tenure-line writing lecturers, are targeted first. The practices do not begin in an organized, full-on assault but develop after problematic behavior goes unchecked. First, there needs to be an undermining and devaluing of people and their professional expertise. We are well aware that these slights can happen every day, but one tangible example was when the writing program asked for increased computer resources for lecturer faculty, as they needed regular online access to perform their jobs and few multi-person offices had even one working computer. The Writing Programs Committee noted that unused machines were being recycled out of the department that could easily fulfill this need. (These recycled machines were generated as all tenure-line faculty received regular computer updates.) The response from a department administrator was to decline our request, noting, "I'm frankly not sure that it is the university's responsibility to provide hardware for adjunct faculty since there is no way to ensure that the hardware is being used solely for official university business and since lecturer faculty are 'temporary' not 'permanent' employees. As temporary employees, I think the assumption is that they will have ready and prepared the necessary resources to perform their jobs when they enter into the position" (Lewis, departmental email, October 9, 2013).

When left unchecked, prevailing classist/discipline-based attitudes like this can develop into direct bullying actions. I argue that a clear example of this disciplinary bullying born out of concern about growing influence occurred when another department administrator used scheduling/staffing power to disenfranchise a lecturer with growing institutional power. As one of only two lecturers holding a reassigned time position to supervise a tutorial program, the department administrator violated written staffing procedures by scheduling lecturers ranked below her first. She was denied the classes and teaching times she was entitled to teach. When one's livelihood is in the hands of one person whose bullying remains unchecked, it is not surprising that the person would leave the institution out of a sense of self-preservation. Her departure from our program was the first of what would become a mass exodus of some of our best and brightest faculty. Finally, as complaints about these kinds of individual harassment and bullying go unchecked, the larger department understands that it is okay to mistreat those in positions of lesser power—the shift to mobbing.

This shift was most clearly seen in our department when revisions were being made to the Lecturers Policies and Procedures document. Historically, our department has, without exception, voted to enfranchise lecturers as voting members in department meetings when we are discussing/deciding anything that directly impacts lecturer faculty. As the department mobbing was gaining momentum, the policy document was coming to the department for ratification. In a standard move, my opening motion at the department meeting was to enfranchise the lecturers present to vote on the relevant policy document. There was immediately a motion to make the vote a "secret ballot," and by overwhelming majority the motion to allow lecturers the vote was denied. The bully majority had sent a very clear message: you have no voice, and we are hiding behind procedure so as not to have to be publicly responsible for our position. Once it was clear that the majority could enforce its will on writing program lecturers, it was not long before this treatment extended to the entire faculty and program.

Within the larger writing program, the bullying began through what we considered ignorance of our field/discipline. Our MA concentration in composition originally required a culminating thesis. When the writing faculty proposed changing the thesis to a culminating portfolio, the proposal was met with confusion and derision. One faculty member noted that she found it impossible to imagine how one could judge the quality of such an undertaking and likened portfolios to something "fit for a Ricky Lake show." After the proposal was passed, this same faculty member went out of her way to attend the college-level review to speak against the proposal again. Other faculty, when complaining about the workloads of those outside of literature, criticized the "assigned time and boutique classes" of non-literature faculty as not requiring nearly as much work as their own teaching duties. Similarly, programmatic changes that materially affected lecturers were arbitrarily postponed, noting, for example, that the change to the new Lecturers Policies and Procedures document would need to be delayed because the work involved would be inconvenient for vice chairs who wanted to apply for sabbaticals. Finally, disciplinary ignorance was clearest when one colleague teaching our graduate seminar on the theory and practice of composition quit mid-semester. Instead of consulting composition faculty about how to address the loss, a department administrator who is a literature specialist simply presumed that the administrator could take over the course.

This ignorance of the field laid a bullying foundation that escalated into an active unwillingness to accept composition faculty members' disciplinary expertise. It began with small decisions; for example, when we were establishing teaching rotations for courses, writing faculty were not given precedence to teach the advanced composition requirement. This quickly mushroomed into much larger and more consequential decisions. As we moved to make more programmatic changes, our disciplinary expertise and research were met with a lack of belief and unjustified resistance. When moving the campus from a high-stakes placement test to directed self-placement, we presented the department and the university with substantial data about the process, tests of our materials, and nationwide research supporting the process. While the University Faculty Senate passed the proposal unanimously, the department refused to accept the research and, without any counter-evidence, consistently voted to retain the status quo. When the pressure of university acceptance forced them into an approving vote, faculty members continued to attend college- and university-level meetings to speak against the change. The same was true for our shift to a first-year stretch composition program. In spite of overwhelming research attesting to the failures of our remedial sequence and the proven benefits of a stretch offering, the rest of the department used its bully majority to stall the program out of fear of how it might impact other areas of the department. This leads me to my final sense of how the situation elevated to departmental mobbing.

The mobbing seemed to center on a fear of our growing disciplinary prominence and perceptions about how this might negatively impact other faculty members' programs. The directed self-placement and stretch changes seemed to bring these issues to a head. Rather than acknowledge any of the positive research or even understand that the changes streamlined the writing footprint in the department and the university, faculty focused on concerns that the stretch course would "take over." They complained that if given a choice, overwhelming numbers of students would self-place into the longer course, which would require more resources and necessarily diminish literary offerings. In spite of contrary research and assurances from the associate dean that any overages would be made up through other means, this was a constant critique of the program.

Nowhere was our growing presence more keenly felt than in the area of hiring. In the middle of one academic year, the acting provost called for proposals for emergency hires. The call required significant paperwork and rationale, and the writing program was the only group in the department to complete the work. The proposal was acknowledged as an area of great need, but the writing program position was unable to be filled at mid-year. So as the department entered its end-of-year hiring priorities phase, it seemed clear that the composition hire would be ranked highly. As the faculty met, every program submitted a hiring request—far more limited in scope than our emergency hire justification. After all was said and done, the top three positions would be forwarded to the dean for consideration. After a secret ballot vote, a unanimous—exclusive of the composition faculty—first ranking was given to a British literature hire. Our department employed five British literature faculty and had no British literature requirement. By the end of the vote counting, the composition hire did not rank high enough to be forwarded to the dean.

After we approached the dean directly about the voting bloc that was strategically working against the writing program, he forwarded our hiring request as a separate line item. This, however, was not the end of the story. Once the composition hire was approved, writing faculty were concerned about the viability of hiring anyone into the toxic work environment that now existed in the department. We asked a college administrator for help in addressing the situation so we could inform future candidates that our problems would be dealt with. Instead, a department administrator, with approval from the college administrator, rewrote the job description to include two new sub-specialties, linguistics and English education, so the department could reconstitute the hiring committee. If the position had gone forward as a straight composition hire, composition faculty would have had the voting majority and final say in the hire. With the newly listed sub-specialties, the hiring committee now contained only one composition faculty member, and the other four voting members were in other fields—effectively re-inscribing the tyranny of the voting majority. It was clear that positional and resource power and numbers would always win.

"RESOLUTION"

I have always found it curious that the word *resolution* has two ironically different meanings: either to resolve/solve a point of contention or problem—implying that change must happen—or to be resolved/firm in one's belief, knowing that change will not happen. My initial hope in moving beyond the department for help was that resolution in the form of change would take place. In the end, however, it was clear that there was far greater resolution to maintain the mobbing status quo.

When faced with mobbing, one must move beyond the immediate environment for help; change cannot come from within. At a certain point, there are no devices for working or reasoning with a bully majority that has seen the power of its numbers. This is when, as a WPA and a person, one often must appeal to a larger group or higher authority. As writing faculty who have collaborated significantly with the larger university community, it was natural for us to turn to these quarters for support. The Faculty Senate Subcommittee on Reading and Writing was sympathetic to the deteriorating situation and began drafting a proposal to create a separate writing department. And the larger university community often did what it could in terms of supporting and passing proposals over which it had jurisdiction. Ultimately, however, these outsider groups are relatively powerless to affect any kind of change at the department level. When going through regular channels, the last appearance of hope came in the form of our regularly scheduled departmental review. Internal and external reviewers met with faculty when evaluating the department and its programs, and it was clear that faculty strife and disciplinary division were key areas of concern. This formal channel was unable to make any headway, however, as external reviews were never released to the department and the internal review was never written, thus leaving the department unaccountable for its state of affairs.[1] Having exhausted these internal resources, the only place for faculty to appeal is up the chain of command.

Bullying and mobbing situations are particularly challenging to address within workplace cultures for a variety of reasons—most often because the behavior, while creating an inhospitable work environment, is not easily articulated and managed in workplace codes of conduct. One of the more common responses is to attempt mediation.

Psychologist and mediation specialist Moira Jenkins (2013, 182) notes that "mediation is one of the most common strategies used to address discrimination and harassment." When unable to broker a détente in the department turmoil, the college dean agreed to bring in an outside mediator to address the situation. After an initial meeting with some of the involved parties, writing faculty were informed that the mediator would not be returning because, as stated to those of us present, "there was no common ground on which to build." Indeed, Jenkins (2013, 183) notes that mediation is not always possible, and "mediation is NOT recommended for serious complaints." Two of her four categories of seriousness include when "the alleged perpetrator is a senior manager and the complainant is a base grade employee" and when the "alleged bullying has gone on for a long time" (Jenkins 2013, 183). Both of these categories seem relevant in this situation, with department administrators having significant positional and resource power and with the growing bullying and mobbing developing over several years. Her only suggestion in these cases is an "occupational health and safety" approach to mediation that goes much more in depth into the "background risks that may have contributed to the dispute . . . to explore the sources of the conflict" (Jenkins 2013, 183). This more time- and work-intensive mediation was not offered as an option, and any external resources for conflict resolution were abandoned.

The lack of investment in purposeful, proactive mediation left the situation to fester and devolve: without some path forward, the writing program was left to flounder at the discretion of the voting majority. It was at this point that a wider institutional failure exacerbated the situation. With no forthcoming mediation planned, a college administrator noted that they would use "administrative tools to restrain behavior." The first decree was to separate the different factions. Whether intended as protection or punishment, the division further alienated writing program's faculty and added to the toxic work environment. In an email, the administrator said, "I think it has been and continues to be evidence [*sic*] that tensions between Composition and the rest of the department have continued. Therefore, I asked [name redacted] to separate the two groups and, to . . . administer the two groups separately . . . [name redacted] will work to diminish contact (particularly with meetings) to the best of [their] ability" (Ingram, email to author, November 3, 2013). Writing faculty were asked to hold separate meetings with department administration and to provide input to this faculty member rather than attend committee meetings. If writing faculty needed to attend faculty meetings based on disciplinary business, they could attend only the portion of the meeting that pertained to their subject-matter area. The result of this decree was to silence what little voice the writing faculty had left (a decree of separation and segregation that has never been officially rescinded).

The final blow from this administrative level came when the faculty hire in rhetoric and composition was approved by the university provost. As detailed earlier, this hire was co-opted by administrators who rewrote the job description and reconfigured the hiring committee so as to re-inscribe the bully majority. As the WPA, I publicly challenged this move in a departmental email:

> So . . . [title redacted] has decided to craft his own job description (ignor-ing the one that the Rhetoric/Composition faculty submitted when the job was approved). [Title redacted] decided to send the draft to the "Department" for "feedback," but . . . [the only remaining composition specialists] were not included in this message and were informed in another, separate message. Evidently we are not supposed to be a part of this department or included in its feedback . . . When the Dean supported this hire he noted several times in a meeting that he was looking for a strong Composition person who could step right into a position of leader-ship because of our great need. Now we have a call which is not only NOT a strong Composition person . . . it doesn't even have to BE a composition person. (Heckathorn, email to [name redacted], October 28, 2014)

This response was met with a college administrator using his posi-tional and resource power to join the bully majority. The response to my email noted, "I believe your email of October 28, 2014, constitutes a violation of University policy related to Collegiality, Professional Ethics, and Harassment. Before I submit my report, I want to make sure I accurately convey your point of view and if I am missing something or misunderstand what you wrote, please let me know" (Ingram, email to author, October 28, 2014). The email goes on to detail the administra-tor's reading of policies and procedures, the assertion that I was trying to "harass colleagues" and "attempt to prevent or inhibit a colleague from moving forward with his duties," and the accusation that the "tone and demeanor of the e-mail [w]as fostering a climate of intimidation" (Ingram, email to author, October 28, 2014). Bullying literature often discusses the further victimization of the targets by accusing *them* of being the ones responsible for creating the hostile environment—blaming the victim. By trying to put me on the defensive for calling the offending behavior into question, the college administrator violated something Jenkins (2013, 210) cautions is critical to the resolution process: "It is important that a complainant will not be treated unfairly or unreason-ably by the organization for lodging a complaint in good faith." Upon investigation of the specific policies referenced in the email, it became clear that the threats were groundless. Language had been taken completely out of context, obscure footnotes manipulated, and intentional meanings clearly ignored. My union representative noted that it was clearly an attempt to silence and intimidate me—the college administrator had become part of the mob.

My final institutional resource was the Office of Human Resources. In a long meeting with a key representative, I laid out the bullying and mobbing behaviors and the lack of resolution. I noted specific violations of university staffing and hiring policies as well as the day-to-day actions that had driven off significant numbers of lecturers and other tenure-line rhet/comp faculty. At the end of the interview, the representative asked if she could ask me one question: "Why are *you* still here?" It was at this point that my hope for any resolution was completely shattered. The representative promised three times to follow up with me on these allegations. When the person had not contacted me three weeks later, I sent an email asking for information. The curt reply was, "Thanks for following up. I have spoken with [Ingram] and with [title redacted] about the issues you raised and some of the possible approaches for resolution that we discussed. As you might expect, they each have a somewhat different perspective than you do about what the issues are and how they might be resolved. I am continuing to discuss these issues with them and if I find any opportunities for movement on any of them I will let you know" (George, email to author, March 27, 2015). I was never contacted again—the bully majority was complete. Jenkins (2013, 211) observes, "Workplace bullying and sexual harassment can result in psychological injury. A misguided investigation or mishandling of a complaint can exacerbate an injury and can alienate a vulnerable worker, contributing to further psychological harm." This situation illustrates how investigations of complaints often have the effect of further silencing those being bullied. In this case, the voices of those in positional power were seen as the last word on the situation. The lack of meaningful follow-up left those reporting the bullying not only ostracized from the academic workings of the program but also outside the bureaucratic means of resolution.

SOME POSSIBLE SOLUTIONS

Our WPA literature is replete with stories of rhetorical positioning and coalition building in the face of great challenges. As a field and as a people, we know we have undertaken a task that, because of its constant change in constantly changing contexts, requires savvy vigilance. But this is *not* one of those stories. Similarly, there is a lot of research on bullying and, increasingly, mobbing. There are human resources and psychological strategies for dealing with outlier people and problems to make one's personal well-being and professional working environment as protected as possible. But this is *not* one of those stories. It would be nice if there were tidy answers to these kinds of complex problems. Indeed, the editors of this collection, when accepting my chapter proposal, suggested in an email, "As you draft your chapter, please consider how this framing will help other WPAs develop agentive responses to these destructive behaviors and structures" (Cristyn L. Elder and Bethany Davila, December 11, 2015). We would like to believe, as agents of change, that there are concrete steps we can take to prevent or resolve these fractious situations. Having experienced a situation that was far beyond my ability to control, having borne witness to the devolution of a work environment that I could never have anticipated, leaves me with three insights—two short-term solutions and the only long-term remedy I can imagine.

First, we can take solace in sharing our stories with others—knowing we are not alone in these toxic environments can give us the courage to fight on or move on. This kind of communication is as critical to our work and well-being as almost any other kind of disciplinary training. At the 2016 Conference on College Composition and Communication (CCCC), I was placed on a panel discussing program administration. The first speaker, Amy Nichols of Louisville, Kentucky, gave a lovely talk on her intellectual and scholastic preparation for a WPA position—illustrating the enormous advances that have been made in our discipline. I think it is fair to say that all of us in attendance were impressed with her depth of knowledge and readiness for this complex task. I followed with a preliminary version of this chapter—sharing my incredible lack of preparation for the ostracizing and bullying I eventually encountered. This same group nodded knowingly as I shared one destructive example after the next. Following the talk, I was greeted by many who shared similar stories and had no idea that the problems were much more pervasive than they had imagined.

This collection of chapters on bullying is a good start toward a more fulsome discussion of the disciplinary and psychological challenges we face as WPAs. It seems important that we no longer limit our discussions of challenges to budgetary negotiations or curricular wrangling. The very rise of our discipline has brought many professional advances, but many of these steps forward for us are often perceived as stepping on the toes of others who have historically enjoyed greater institutional power.

The more we share these stories and examples, the more we are both personally buoyed and professionally prepared for what comes our way. Wendy Bishop reflects on whether she should have been more proactive in considering departmental independence. After reading reports from many programs sharing their departmental trials, she notes, "I've been encouraged to speak up—and plan to do so regularly and forcefully, hoping to shake off an encroaching sense of weariness. Such a reaction is evidence in the power of shared knowledge . . . The problems don't go away, but can be better digested" (Bishop 2002, 246).

The act of sharing our stories, while empowering and beneficial, may not be enough of a short-term solution for some bullied and beleaguered WPAs. Thus, my second short-term solution is to consider leaving our work behind. Our literature is full of research that talks about how to build disciplinary respect and what actions we can take in the face of disciplinary disrespect. What we rarely document and discuss, however, is a situation when disciplinary disrespect is so vast and deep that action is no longer possible and we must stop our work—removing ourselves from the local context, the final action of leaving. WPAs are increasingly prepared to consider how to enter the field, but scant attention is devoted to our departure—I know this was definitely the case for me.

My experience suggests that WPAs must consider leaving in the face of bullying and mobbing when (1) they have exhausted internal and external resources. WPAs are not institutional lightweights. Even in healthy, productive departments and campuses, there are regular challenges that fuel our work. It is not to say that once the going gets tough or there is a setback we should throw up our hands and walk away. But if there are no supporters within or without the department willing or able to take a stand, then working against a department is merely spinning one's wheels—and often this spinning leads to my next reason to leave: (2) when staying compromises your mental/physical health. Here I rely on my mother's folk wisdom, "No job is more important than your health." One can only withstand the constant and powerful resistance of a bully majority for so long. The daily norm of people ignoring your input at best and directly working against your input at worst takes a mental and physical toll. You cannot defend a people, a program, or a discipline against daily and long-term onslaughts. These onslaughts affect one's outlook, professionally and personally. Stories of breakdowns and cancers and other physical and mental problems appear in our literature, but these are not badges of courage; they are manifestations of severely compromised working environments—bullying and mobbing—that need to be acknowledged and addressed head-on.

Finally, (3) WPAs must consider leaving when it is right for them. I outline this choice because I think it is something scholars can objectively consider and should be prepared to consider as they move into a profession that might require that they leave. That said, each person and place is unique and must be assessed by us as individuals. No one could have told me to walk away from the WPA position until I decided it for myself. In fact, many encouraged me to walk away sooner, and some still do not understand how I walked away at all, but I finally had to come to the self-realization that no matter how much my personal and professional identity was wrapped up in my work, I would need to revise and re-create a new sense of identity in which I could productively operate.

At first I stayed to protect the programs we had developed. When that was no longer possible, I stayed to protect the people working in those programs who were more vulnerable than I. When I was no longer able to protect them, I finally had to consider what I was staying for—and other than "the principle of the matter," I was accomplishing very little at great personal expense. I ultimately decided that I could no longer serve as the WPA. I stepped down from the administrative position and went back to being a full-time professor teaching in the composition program. Hindsight has taught me that it was the right choice for me, but it continues to be a struggle. I must watch as others, many hand-picked by those who bullied the program and drove off the composition specialists, now run most facets of the writing program. It is difficult to see, but I also know that I would have no power to change it even if I were in what has become a token figurehead position. So I struggle to keep completely away from the "business" of the program and focus entirely on my work as a faculty member in the discipline—teaching, reading, and writing in my field. It is a bittersweet landing for me, and just when I think I have reconciled myself to my new role, the flood of loss overwhelms me. The decision to leave was not easy for me, but it was absolutely necessary.

If we make the decision to remove ourselves from these situations, I argue that how we leave should be an outgrowth of how we stay. Linda Adler-Kassner (2013) notes that as WPAs we need to seriously consider the "principles" that will govern our actions, programs, and interactions. These principles are the foundations that drive our work (Adler-Kassner 2013, 395). As WPAs, then, I would argue that these same principles need to inform our walking away. If our principles embrace our public building of alliances through diplomacy and education, that is how we should leave—publicly, diplomatically, but with the educational force of specific details that could enable others to understand and learn from and work with our experiences. So I am doing that very thing. I went before various university-wide committees I served on related to my writing expertise and shared my reasons for leaving, I am presenting some of these details at conferences, and I am writing about my experiences, planting the seed for what I now see as the only long-term solution for our field: autonomy and independence.

As long as we are subject to the department-level approval of others, we will never be free of the potential for disciplinary disregard and mobbing. Separation is not a new idea. Maxine Hairston proposed this very possibility in her CCCC chair address in 1985. Her words, spoken more than thirty years ago, ring true today: "A major reason we get discouraged is that our worst problems originate close to home: in our own departments and within the discipline of English studies itself . . . the people who so frequently are our adversaries in our efforts to make the writing programs in our departments as good as they should be and can be" (Hairston 1985, 273). She called for us to establish ourselves as a legitimate discipline—clarifying who we are and what we do, publishing and setting high expectations for our research, and extending our reach beyond the academic community (Hairston 1985, 278–80). The momentum to build the discipline and disciplinary autonomy was so palpable that it filtered into other disciplinary areas.

Francis Lide uses the rhet/comp model as a paradigm to inspire changes in the study of foreign languages. Lide (1988, 42) argues, "The past quarter century has witnessed a movement in English departments to constitute the study and teaching of written discourse as a discipline and to define writing teachers who profess that discipline as its practitioners. Rhetoricians have made impressive achievements in professionalizing themselves and institutionalizing their discipline." However, twenty years later, Susan H. McLeod (2006, 532) reflected on our progress: "We have made a start in the past twenty years by developing PhD programs and becoming identified with research as well as service. If we are to be truly independent, a major is the next logical step. Such independence is material as well as intellectual." Perhaps the best starting place to connect with the disciplinary progress in this area is through the Independent Writing Departments and Programs Association. Begun as a special interest group (SIG) at the annual CCCC conventions in the mid-1990s, it "functioned as an informal gathering at which CCCC members in independent units and those seeking freestanding status outside English departments could meet to discuss the implications of separation" ("History of the IWDPA" 2016). It has since grown into a full-scale organization that includes formal leadership, a constitution and bylaws, a website and listserve, and a large membership. In addition to this resource there are numerous publications—including a book-length collection (*A Field of Dreams* [2002])—that explore the reasons for considering, processes of enacting, and joys and challenges of implementing an independent writing program.

When considering the appropriateness of one's departmental home, Chris M. Anson (2002, 161) notes: "Clearly, the question of 'why not English' must always remain local, answered in the context of how receptive literary specialists may be to the principles of contemporary composition theory and instruction or how freely and equitably composition leaders feel they can work within a department populated by colleagues who do not share their expertise or particular values. Every composition leader making such a judgment brings to the task not only an analysis of the local political scene but a rich assortment of prior experiences that help to inform that analysis."

Clearly, the local context of my situation would support the necessity of a move. Not only were our English colleagues unreceptive to our disciplinary theories and actions, but the work environment became openly hostile toward writing program faculty and ideas. We laid out many documented reasons for separating into an independent department—we were concerned with budgetary oversight, curriculum and program development, personnel management (hiring, evaluation, staffing), and general operations—all boiling down to a core need for disciplinary respect and autonomy. Although no department is without challenges, perhaps even in all of these areas, negotiating across disciplinary boundaries when one is in a minority voting position would always leave us at the mercy of an othered majority. Within an independent writing department, there would be no disciplinary majority/minority split.

Let me be clear that disciplinary autonomy is not a panacea for departmental strife. The literature of independent writing programs is careful to acknowledge some of the potential pitfalls of striking out on one's own. Wendy Bishop (2002, 240–42) touched on several significant concerns that have been raised by independent departments/programs: loss of potential "English studies" collaborations, concern that writing departments be thought of as service-only disciplines, the vulnerability of any new academic unit (as well as the students and faculty who inhabit it), potential territoriality that might arise among other department/programs, the question of what areas reside within a writing department, the possibility that one is merely moving departmental strife to a new location, and similar factors. Even long-established departments will tell us that they must still battle many people and places to accomplish their goals. I would argue, however, that *these* are the battles WPAs are educated to face: how to manage people and programs within the discipline of rhetoric and composition. And these purposeful battles can bring about the many benefits of independence—innovative, coherent programs.

Selfishly, I must say that the thought of sitting in a hiring committee and not having to explain to three literature specialists why a potential composition hire is strong or weak is appealing. Even more appealing, having supported my opinion with decades of disciplinary research, is the thought of not being outvoted by these same colleagues. Such are some of the most basic benefits of independence. In larger scope, independence provides writing programs with greater budgetary control, curricular options, disciplinary focus, and the like. Beyond this, Bishop (2002, 238–40) suggests many other potential upsides to disciplinary autonomy: "improved program morale," more just treatment of faculty of all types, increased sense of professional identity, smoother hiring and evaluation processes, and other factors. There is not necessarily one right way for this to be accomplished, so I am not suggesting a one-size-fits-all model. The literature is filled with examples of departments and programs that have worked through and discussed the challenges and benefits of independence. Many articles detail some of the larger and more public transitions: Syracuse University, the University of Arkansas at Little Rock, San Diego State University, the University of Texas, and others. Bishop's (2002, 238) article alone lists ten different real-life options for designing one's own program/center/department based on the work and stories of others. Thus, not unlike the work of WPAs themselves, the idea of disciplinary independence is no longer a fledgling concept. We do not have to fly by the seat of our pants, and we can and should point to the work of our colleagues when understanding how and why we should create a home that privileges our voices first before moving into the interdisciplinary arena in which we often work.

Several decades into this enterprise, however, most of us still work in departments where we are minority voices running majority programs. And I understand that in many places, this seems to be working—I know that my first ten years or so went remarkably well. Chris M. Anson (2002, 165) notes, "Across the United States, many outstanding composition programs operate smoothly and equitably within English departments," and this is likely true. But he later notes what seem to be the determining factors in their successes:

They *feel* that the role and legitimacy of their discipline are respected and honored by their colleagues and by their administration;

    they *are granted* intellectual authority for making or helping to make decisions about the nature and delivery of instruction in composition; and

    they *are allowed* some degree of administrative autonomy. (Anson 2002, 165, emphases added)

Telling in this insight is how much writing programs' successes are at the mercy of other actors—we must "feel" legitimate and be "granted" and "allowed" to do our work by others who are not trained in our area. While I do agree that a significant part of our work is the rhetorical and communicative necessity of sharing our ideas with others and convincing them of the validity and importance of the work we do, I argue that it is not our primary *departmental* work. That is the interdisciplinary, university work that writing professors and WPAs have been trained to undertake—to share our disciplinary knowledge with others. As a department, however, we must be able to move beyond these missionary positions so we are able to develop, evaluate, and revise what we offer students and faculty as rhet/comp specialists. We must mobilize as a field to develop our own programs and disciplinary homes, or we will always be potentially subject to the kinds of abuse I have experienced. Ultimately, we need disciplinary autonomy or the departments that now benevolently support small numbers of rhet/comp people may one day become the departments that are either threatened by them or no longer see their value.

NOTE

1.   As an update, after the drafting of this chapter, the departmental review was finally sent to the department in fall 2016—many semesters after its deadline. By the time it was received, the department had already hired non-composition specialists to run the writing programs.

REFERENCES

Adler-Kassner, Linda. 2013. "What Is Principle?" In *Writing Program Administration: Rhetoric for Writing Program Administrators*, ed. Rita Malenczyk, 394–406. Anderson, SC: Parlor.

Anson, Chris M. 2002. "Who Wants Composition? Reflections on the Rise and Fall of an Independent Program." In *A Field of Dreams: Independent Writing Programs and the Future of Composition Studies*, ed. Peggy O'Neill, Angela Crow, and Larry W. Burton, 153–69. Logan: Utah State University Press.

Bishop, Wendy. 2002. "A Rose by Every Other Name." In *A Field of Dreams: Independent Writing Programs and the Future of Composition Studies*, ed. Peggy O'Neill, Angela Crow, and Larry W. Burton, 233–46. Logan: Utah State University Press.

Hairston, Maxine. 1985. "Breaking Our Bonds and Reaffirming Our Connections." *College Composition and Communication* 36 (3): 272–82. https://doi.org/10.2307/357971.

"History of the IWDPA." n.d. Independent Writing Departments and Programs Association. Accessed July 1, 2016. http://independentwriting.org.

Jenkins, Moira. 2013. *Preventing and Managing Workplace Bullying and Harassment: A Risk Management Approach.* Toowong, Australia: Australian Academic Press.

Lide, Francis. 1988. "On Constituting and Institutionalizing a Foreign Language Discipline: The Example of Rhetoric and Composition in Departments of English." *Modern Language Journal* 72 (1): 42–51. https://doi.org/10.1111/j.1540-4781.1988.tb04169.x.

McLeod, Susan H. 2006. "'Breaking Our Bonds and Reaffirming Our Connections,' Twenty Years Later." *College Composition and Communication* 57 (3): 525–34.

Ranieri, Paul, and Jackie Grutsch McKinney. 2007. "Fitness for the Occasion: How Context Matters for jWAPs." In *Untenured Faculty as Writing Program Administrators: Institutional Practices and Politics,* ed. Debra Frank Dew and Alice Horning, 249–78. West Lafayette, IN: Parlor.

Tehrani, Noreen. 2012. "Introduction to Workplace Bullying." In *Workplace Bullying: Symptoms and Solutions,* ed. Noreen Tehrani, 1–17. New York: Routledge.

Vaughan, Sarah. 2012. "Ya'makasi or the Art of Displacement in the Corporate World: A Target's Perspective on the Impact of Workplace Bullying." In *Workplace Bullying: Symptoms and Solutions,* ed. Noreen Tehrani, 51–66. New York: Routledge.

Westhues, Kenneth. 2005. "Editor's Introduction." In *Winning, Losing, Moving On: How Professionals Deal with Workplace Harassment and Mobbing,* ed. Kenneth Westhues, ix–xvi. Lewiston, NY: Edwin Mellen.

10

REMEDIATION VIA MANDATE
The California State University's Early Start Initiative as Manifestation of Systematized Bullying

W. Gary Griswold

Darla J. Twale and Barbara M. De Luca (2008, 93) state that the unique societal characteristics of colleges and universities make them a "breeding ground" for workplace bullying. Likewise, Leah P. Hollis (2012, 3) indicates that bullying in higher education administration has negative effects that reach far beyond the individuals involved in specific incidents. These scholars and others who have examined incivility and bullying in higher education focus primarily on its manifestation in specific departments or campuses.

The purpose of this chapter is to broaden the application of this scholarship by examining an academic initiative imposed on the campuses of a large public university system. After first describing a new dimension of academic workplace bullying, I will examine the process by which a trustee-level mandate was prepared, announced, and enforced throughout the system and how, despite widespread faculty resistance on individual campuses and in statewide organizations, various uncivil methods were used to ensure the trustees' desired result.

I will then provide a reflection on how the mandate impacted my specific campus, where I became the WPA responsible for the writing segment of the program and where campus administrators, incredulous as to the inappropriate nature of the mandate, eventually embraced bullying behaviors themselves as they realized the mandate would not be going away. I conclude with exploring possibilities for addressing such large-scale institutionalized bullying.

DEFINITIONS

As has been made evident in other chapters in this volume, workplace bullying, especially in an academic setting, can be defined in various

DOI: 10.7330/9781607328162.c010

ways, depending upon the exact behaviors exhibited and the context in which the acts occur. The academic bully "might interrupt every time you speak at a committee meeting. Or roll his eyes at your new ideas. Bullies may spread rumors to undermine a colleague's credibility or shut their target out of social conversations. The more aggressive of the species cuss out co-workers, even threatening to get physical" (Fogg 2008, B10).

Complicating matters further is the reality that bullying is not an equal-opportunity issue. In contrasting the terms *harassment* and *bullying*, Hollis (2012, 1) explains that "harassment is when the target is from a protected class . . . while bullying is a class-free assault on the target. The former is illegal under the Title VII Civil Rights laws; the latter, bullying, is still legal in the United States." More specifically, there is legal recourse for harassment "if, and *only if*, you are a member of a protected status . . . and you have been mistreated by a person who is *not* a member of a protected group . . . and it is completely legal unless race, age, or another status group membership characteristic can be claimed." It is estimated that only 20 percent of instances of bullying fall under this latter category (Workplace Bullying Institute n.d., emphasis in original).

To this mix we must add the widely held assumption that all interactions in higher education are based on civil and clearly reasoned discourse. College and university administrators might not even acknowledge that such bullying activity exists (Lester 2013, ix), or it may be "tacitly accepted by the organizational leadership" (Vega and Comer 2005, 101). This is especially true of the subtler forms of bullying.

In this discussion I shall focus on a variety of bullying that has been referred to by Brianna C. Caza and Lilia M. Cortina (2007, 336) as "a form of 'milder' mistreatment" that occurs more frequently than aggressive bullying: workplace incivility. Although aggressive bullying might be "more memorable," incivility can likewise have a significant negative impact on individuals and organizational efficacy (Caza and Cortina 2007, 347).

Lynne M. Andersson and Christine M. Pearson (1999, 456) characterize the latency of incivility:

> A distinguishing characteristic of incivility, however, is that the intent to harm—as perceived through the eyes of the instigator, the target, and/or the observers—is ambiguous. One may behave uncivilly as a reflection of intent to harm the target, or one may behave uncivilly without intent (e.g., ignorance or oversight). Furthermore, the instigator may intend to harm the target, yet he or she may not even be conscious of such intent. Unlike instigators of aggression, instigators of incivility can easily deny or bury any intent, if present . . . With incivility, the intent is not transparent and is subject to varying interpretation.

Andersson and Pearson (1999, 458) further indicate that such behaviors can later lead to more direct manipulation, claiming that "an important aspect of workplace incivility is that it can be a factor in the formation and escalation of conflict spirals in organizations." They call this ongoing and widening of such behaviors the "incivility spiral." Put another way, incivility begets incivility.

Applying Andersson and Pearson's construct to the system-wide bullying examined here, I identify a new dimension of academic workplace bullying that I call Academic Systemic Incivility (ASI). ASI is defined as a multi-level, top-down administrative behavior that uses low-intensity bullying tactics to achieve a specific end or ends without regard to academic employee (faculty or professional staff) expertise or resistance.

THE SYSTEM-WIDE SCENE

In 2010, the California State University (CSU) Office of the Chancellor mandated in Executive Order 1048 that as of the summer of 2012, before enrolling at one of the system's twenty-three campuses, "incoming CSU freshmen who have not demonstrated proficiency in English and/or mathematics will be required to begin remediation prior to the term for which they have been admitted" (California State University, Office of the Chancellor 2010b, 1). Inspired by residential, non-mandatory, multi-week summer programs that many CSU campuses had in place for a number of years (e.g., Summer Bridge and Jump Start), the Early Start mandate required that each campus offer, at minimum, a one-unit educational activity that allowed all incoming students to comply with the requirement that they begin—but not necessarily complete—remediation.[1] As previously alluded and as we shall see later, there was significant resistance to the mandate.

THE BULLIED SPEAK

Before examining specific ASI behaviors of CSU administration in developing, implementing, and assessing the Early Start initiative, a look at the resolutions passed by the CSU system-wide Academic Senate in the past two decades will be illustrative, since they document faculty concerns that echo the plaints of many individuals who have been targets of subtle bullying and mobbing by administrative personnel: changes in processes with little or no consultation, receiving no response or a hostile one when raising objections to management's actions, being given inaccurate or misleading information, and public shaming of individuals.

In 2000, long before Early Start was a glimmer in the CSU trustees' eyes, the CSU Chico's Academic Senate, in Resolution AS-2489-00, felt the need to request that in working with the Academic Senate CSU and trustees, the chancellor should establish ways to ensure "greater faculty involvement in shared governance at all levels . . . greater and more timely interaction with faculty representatives as initiatives are planned, developed, and implemented . . . [and] candid and effective communication during decision making including explanations when decisions are contrary to faculty recommendations." In addition, the senate also called for "improved and more explicit procedures" to keep shared governance active (Academic Senate of the California State University 2000, 1). Later in the document, it seems that the senate is doubtful about these requests being addressed, stating that "the faculty seek tangible evidence that the Chancellor and the Board of Trustees truly understand their concerns" (Academic Senate of the California State University 2000, 1).

Another Academic Senate resolution, issued in 2008, foreshadows the CSU administration's use of ASI in implementing Early Start. Concerning "future initiatives/committees that impact curriculum," the resolution states that "the membership of any committee, taskforce, or any other group that may be formed as a result of system-wide initiatives will include significant faculty representation" (Academic Senate of the California State University 2008b, 1).

Finally, in Resolution AS-2960, the senate essentially calls out the administration for its tactics and labels its behaviors:

> Recent decisions related to educational policy and faculty rights by the CSU and campus administrations contravene the principle of a culture of collegiality and suggest a powerful and strategic bypassing of truly collaborative shared governance as defined by statute and the BOT's [Board of Trustees'] policies. The result, we believe, is a "culture of compliance" where decisions are made and announced to the faculty under the guise of consultation rather than regularly engaging faculty in decision making at the formative stages . . . Yet, such an approach is contrary to the way decisions have historically been made within the Academy. (Academic Senate of the California State University 2010, 1–2)

The resolution further notes "the frequent absence of Trustees and the Chancellor from [Academic Senate of the CSU (ASCSU)] meetings" and the "introduction of initiatives without prior review by the ASCSU in accordance with previously standard practice" (Academic Senate of the California State University 2010, 2).[2]

Such were the concerns of the CSU Academic Senate, and we will see how these perceived behaviors did indeed manifest themselves in the evolution and implementation of the Early Start mandate.

EVOLUTION OF THE MANDATE

In his September 19, 2007, presentation to the Office of the Chancellor's Committee on Educational Policy on "Remediation Policies and Practices: Overview and Prospects," Executive Vice Chancellor and Chief Academic Officer Gary W. Reichard reported on a June 2007 "survey" of CSU campuses that was intended to be "an effort to discover how students are being prepared to achieve full college-level proficiency in English and in mathematics after matriculating to CSU." He claimed that this survey "provided a snapshot of several important, innovative, and promising approaches to remediation" (Reichard 2007, 10).

The programs he referred to were multi-week, voluntary, and often residential preparation programs (i.e., the federally funded Summer Bridge and CSU-funded Jump Start) provided to a subset of incoming first-year students. He concluded his report with the recommendation that CSU strengthen such programs: "Survey results point to the potential value of an 'early start' on remediation via a summer experience prior to the initial fall term, especially for first-generation college students with remedial needs that might require more than an academic year of coursework to overcome" (Reichard 2007, 16).

Trustee Herb Carter, chair of the Committee on Educational Policy and a primary agent in the evolution and forced implementation of the Early Start mandate, would later explain further in an Office of the Chancellor promotional video: "The thing that got my attention right away is that in the [Educational Opportunities Program] there's a Summer Bridge that brings students in early, gives them the kind of preparation they need to be successful in the fall. And I started to think, well maybe there's something there we can do with Early Start in terms of remediation. It's important that we get something done there, so this is good for the faculty, it's good for the students, it's good for the state of California" (California State University, Office of the Chancellor 2014).

Subsequent to Reichards's report, the trustees called on the chancellor to convene a system-wide conference on remediation. So on October 30 and 31, 2008, a gathering labeled a "statewide conference" was held at the Crowne Plaza Hotel in Los Angeles. Its title was "Proficiency in the First Year at the University."

The conference did indeed look at a broad array of CSU campuses' efforts at preparing students for college-level mathematics and writing courses, including the aforementioned Jump Start and Summer Bridge programs that had been under way at my campus for a number of years. It is interesting, however, that although the stated focus of the gathering was to examine successful instructional approaches throughout CSU, attendance was by "provost nomination only."

Of the 143 attendees, those whose titles suggested that they were instructional faculty (lecturer, assistant, associate, or full professor in mathematics or English/composition/writing) included 43 individuals, or 30 percent of the participants (though nothing guaranteed that these individuals were directly involved in the teaching of developmental writing or math). Another 16 people (11 percent) had specific titles indicating that they were involved in developmental instruction (e.g., director/coordinator of developmental math or writing). Together, this group totaled 59 individuals (41 percent), which included the 23 presenters. The remaining attendees, 84 people, or 59 percent, were campus or chancellor office administrators: provosts, deans, vice chancellors, and similar titles (California State University, Office of the Chancellor 2008).

And although the title suggested that the conference goal was to examine a variety of programs and approaches taken at CSU campuses, later comments by Reichard to the Trustees' Committee on Educational Policy suggest that a certain path had already been determined. Reichard (2009, 1) stated that the conference was held in response to the Board of Trustees' call "to identify and disseminate particularly effective practices, especially including 'early start' programs." However, of the thirty-two presentations, only five discussed anything related to "early start"–style programs (California State University, Office of the Chancellor 2008). Nonetheless, Reichard (2009, 1), not surprisingly, reported that the conference had discovered that "the most intriguing were those [presentations] that described successful remediation programs . . . the so-called 'early start' programs."

The question remains, though, whether the participation described above constituted adequate faculty consultation as called for by the ASCSU. Indeed, it can be argued that having 40 percent of those attendees at this conference be faculty involved in "remedial" programs is significant consultation. However, we must remember that this event's stated purpose was rather broad: "Designed to showcase strategies that result in more effective and efficient ways to bring students to academic proficiency, the Developmental Mathematics and English Conference '08 offers opportunities to discuss and reflect on student progress in prebaccalaureate courses, sharpen awareness of resources throughout and within the CSU system, and provide a basis for future CSU policy options" (California State University, Office of the Chancellor 2008).

Neither the conclusion that "early start"–style programs were the most promising nor the subsequent "policy action" that mandated implementation of Early Start was decided with any input from CSU faculty. Further, no evidence exists that English and mathematics faculty were consulted in any significant way until the executive order mandating Early Start was announced.

THE (EXECUTIVE) ORDER IS GIVEN

On June 11, 2010, CSU chancellor Charles B. Reed issued Executive Order 1048, which stated that "each CSU campus will design a program for incoming freshmen to develop proficiency in mathematics and/ or English before they enroll as matriculated freshmen" (California State University Office of the Chancellor 2010, 2). This order, along with a subsequent Early Start Policy and Clarification and Guidance (California State University, Office of the Chancellor 2010a) issued the following October, provided these minimal requirements for each campus's Early Start program:

- For the summer of 2012, each campus must offer, for students who do not place into GE [general education]-level math or English, a "proficiency activity."
- These required proficiency activities are intended for students to begin remediation, not complete it.
- This activity might be a workshop, course, or program.
- At a minimum, the proficiency activity must be at least a 1-unit (15-hour) course. "Regular" 3-unit courses may also be developed.
- The proficiency activity may be offered online.
- Any student admitted into any CSU may take this activity at any campus. Reciprocity between all campuses is required.
- There are three outcomes (i.e., grades) that students may earn: 0–did not participate, 1–participated, and 2–participated/remediation completed. For English, 2012 and 2013 Early Start will be required only for those in the lowest quartile of the EPT [CSU English Placement Test], and beginning summer 2014, all students who do not place into GE-level composition must participate.

As can be seen in table 10.1, these minimal requirements were a far cry from the design of the Summer Bridge and Jump Start programs on which the Chancellor's Office and Trustee Herb Carter claimed Early Start was based.

RESISTANCE IS FUTILE

Even before Executive Order 1048 had been officially announced, CSU faculty became aware of Early Start through the discussions going on

Table 10.1. Characteristics of Summer Bridge and Jump Start programs versus those of Early Start
    The last characteristic, whether students self-selected to participate, is particularly significant in the success of the Summer Bridge and Jump Start programs. In a report to CSU Long Beach's Early Start Planning Committee, our campus WPA wrote, "The Jump Start program has been effective in part because relatively well prepared and highly motivated students choose to enroll" (Williams 2010, 1, emphasis in original).

Characteristic	Summer Bridge	Jump Start	Early Start
Duration?	4–6 weeks	7 weeks	1 week
Is sup. instruction and/or tutoring provided?	Yes	Yes	No
Social activities included?	Yes	Yes	No
Campus orientation included?	Yes	Yes	No
Is the program residential?	Yes	No	No
Must be taken at campus student will attend?	Yes	Yes	No
Do students self-select to participate?	Yes	Yes	No

within the Office of the Chancellor's Committee on Educational Policy, and they began to voice objections collectively. They continued to do so at individual campuses as the summer 2012 deadline approached. In April 2009 the CSU English Council forwarded a position to the CSU Board of Trustees and Chico's Academic Senate. Not having the advantage of the present analysis, the council said its members who were in attendance at the Proficiency in the First Year conference the previous fall were "delighted" with the Office of the Chancellor's and Board of Trustees' apparent interest in new approaches to preparing and placing first-year students in composition programs: "There seemed to be genuine recognition that first-year students' reading and writing experiences need to be contextualized in the college experience, that students need the opportunity to enter the discourses of the university, to understand themselves and the rhetorical practices they bring with them in this new context and [to gain] an appreciation for the innovative credit-bearing stretch courses that provide these sorts of opportunities for students" (English Council, California State University 2009, 1).

This delight was short-lived, however, as the council went on to state that it was "so disheartened to hear of the subsequent developments in the CSU Educational Policy Committee meeting concerning writing proficiency, and, more specifically, of the mandatory Early Start program" (English Council, California State University 2009,1). The resolution explained that carefully crafted voluntary summer programs like Summer Bridge and Jump Start were effective with students who have the resources and motivation to participate in them; in contrast, mandatory summer programs set up "yet another exclusionary barrier" for students who lack the time and resources to attend prior to the semester's start. Next, the council called on the chancellor's office to "abandon simplistic notions of proficiency" as well as "the obsession with where and when students receive particular types of educational experiences" (English Council, California State University 2009 1–2). The CSU Academic Senate followed suit that same month with its resolution, Opposition to Impending Implementation of Mandatory Early Start Programs (Academic Senate of the California State University 2008a). Each body issued an additional resolution as the details of Executive Order 1048 emerged, and the official document was made public in the summer of 2010.

As faculty returned to their campuses that fall and heard about the mandate, they began to voice their objections through their respective campus senates. Below is a list of CSU campus senates that developed and approved resolutions opposing implementation of Early Start (Academic Senate, CSU Channel Islands 2010; Academic Senate, CSU Dominguez Hills 2010; Academic Senate, CSU Fullerton 2010; Academic Senate, CSU Humboldt 2010; Academic Senate, CSU Long Beach 2010; Academic Senate, CSU Los Angeles 2010; Academic Senate, CSU San Francisco 2010; Academic Senate, CSU San Jose 2011; Academic Senate, CSU San Luis Obispo 2010; Academic Senate, CSU Sonoma 2010; Faculty Senate, CSU Northridge 2012; Faculty Senate, CSU Sacramento 2010; Faculty Senate, CSU San Bernardino 2009):

San Bernardino: September 2009
Los Angeles: March 2010
Fullerton: May 2010
San Luis Obispo: June 2010
Dominguez Hills: September 2010
Humboldt: November 2010
Sacramento: October 2010
San Francisco: October 2010
Sonoma: October 2010
Channel Islands: November 2010
Long Beach: December 2010
San Jose: February 2011
Northridge: March 2012

Over the course of three years, then, two entities representing the interests of faculty and more than half of the system's campuses raised concerns about the Early Start initiative. The response from the chancellor's office and the Board of Trustees was mostly silence, and they continued to move forward with implementation of the mandate. At one point, however, faculty concerns were brought forward to the chancellor and the trustees in a public forum.

On July 13, 2010, Teri Yamada, a faculty member at CSU Long Beach and that campus's California Faculty Association (CFA) president, addressed the Board of Trustees on behalf of the CFA, the CSU faculty union.[3] Yamada presented concerns expressed by faculty and staff regarding Early Start's pedagogy and possible adverse effects on student access, equity, and diversity. She concluded by asking for "mutual respect" and directly requested that the new program not be implemented (California Faculty Association, 2010). Herb Carter, then chair of the trustees and, as we have seen, a proponent of Early Start, responded with a "rebuke" to Yamada and the other faculty present, stating "it is your job to make it work" and admonishing them to "come to the next meeting with positive comments" (California Faculty Association, 2010; Academic Senate, CSU Stanislaus 2010, 14).

ASI was in full effect here, using silence and unresponsiveness to experts' concern as well as public hostility and shaming. Interestingly, other evidence confirms this analysis. Research conducted by Julia C. Duncheon (2015) likewise shows that campus implementation of Executive Order 1048 was carried out with little regard for faculty objections. Following the summer 2012 implementation of the Early Start mandate, Duncheon examined twelve campus approaches to implementing Early Start. In addition to studying the campuses' Early Start documents, she conducted interviews with CSU personnel ranging from chancellor's office representatives to campus senior administrators, department chairs, and actual classroom instructors. One of the key conclusions of this study was that faculty members generally opposed the Early Start mandate and that "shared opposition to the program motivated outright resistance to implementation initially" (Duncheon 2015, 157).

If the faculty with the expertise to design and administer programs, usually WPAs, did not get onboard, she states, they "were told that if they would not design an Early Start program, someone else would." Duncheon (2015, 162) further reports that one faculty member was threatened by his administration that if his department did not create an Early Start program, then the task would be outsourced to Pearson publishing. A statement by one faculty member interviewed sums up the two unsavory possibilities: "Our choices were to let someone completely unskilled and untrained in reading and writing instruction be at the helm of this particular project, or for us to design what we thought was the least objectionable thing we could do'" (Duncheon 2015, 162).

But Duncheon (2015, 165) also suggests that such coercion, resulting in what she calls "reluctant compliance," though perhaps immediately satisfying administration's wishes, does not necessarily close the question: "They [faculty] participated only because they perceived they had no choice. This finding is reflective of the challenge of top-down policymaking in large public systems. Simply because the implementers comply with a mandate does not mean they embrace the policy in the manner desired by legislators."

Duncheon examined only about half of the CSU campuses' Early Start programs, and indeed some faculty and departments refused to participate at all, resulting in the program being established entirely outside of the existing departmental structure. At the October 2014 meeting of the CSU English Council, one CSU WPA informed me that when his department refused to design an Early Start program, the campus's Office of Faculty Affairs placed it under the supervision of staff in the Learning Assistance Center and hired teaching associates to be the instructors.

MEANWHILE, BACK AT CSULB

My experience as a faculty member who was asked by campus administrators to provide advice on creating an Early Start program, first as the English department assistant chair and later as the individual to coordinate the writing component, would follow a path similar to what Duncheon describes. The initial meeting of CSU Long Beach's (CSULB's) Early Start Planning Committee included the faculty coordinators of first-year composition and first-year mathematics instruction, department chairs and assistant chairs from English and mathematics, associate deans from the College of Liberal Arts and the College of Natural Science and Mathematics, the university administrator who chaired the meeting, and an assortment of folks from the university's advising and enrollment management segments. As we went over the documents that outlined the basic requirements (i.e., Executive Order 1048 and Early Start Policy Clarification and Guidance), a variety of sounds indicating incredulity emanated from the group ("what?" "really?" "uh," "sigh"). One of the associate deans, of Asian descent, remarked on the lack of specificity concerning what exactly the mandate was asking us to do, stating "it's remedial dim sum." The university administrator chairing the meeting, who was in charge of Early Start planning and implementation on our campus and was responsible for providing the chancellor's office with a report of what our plan would be, stated that his hope and that of administrators from other campuses was that "this will just go away."

As the months went on and it became evident at my campus that Early Start was not going to go away, the committee still held on to the possibility that it was worthwhile to raise objections and concerns and included such language in the initial draft of CSULB's Mandatory Early Start Plan: "It is not clear that the ESP [Early Start program] will actually help . . . we are aware of no hard evidence that *mandatory* Early Start will help more students complete their remediation or improve their graduation rates. Many campuses, including CSULB[,] have had success with small numbers of *self-selected* students succeeding in *voluntary* summer programs . . . Many fear that mandatory Early Start may potentially hurt some students . . . We are terribly concerned about the uneven impact this may have on underrepresented and low-income students" (Early Start Implementation Team, California State University 2010, 7, emphasis in original).

The "voluntary summer programs" referenced here are Summer Bridge and Jump Start, both of which, as we have seen, were cited as inspiration for the Early Start mandate but both of which included much more than the Early Start minimal requirements. The English department's WPA, who for a number of summers directed the successful Jump Start program, had, in fact, been objecting to the use of Jump Start data in justifying Early Start ever since the implementation committee began meeting. But as campus administrators started to realize that their masters at the system-wide level would not be backing down, they began to be less and less tolerant of dissent. The WPA continued voicing his objections and publicly criticizing the Early Start concept and the campus officials who were forcing it forward, including the presiding university administrator. He ultimately resigned from the committee.

About a month later, the English department chair and I were meeting with a College of Liberal Arts administrator. What I now refer to as "the Great Scourge of 2012" was under way when CSULB's central administration, under the aegis of fiscal necessity, cut three-quarters of the faculty assigned time for departmental advising and program coordination. We sat across the table as this administrator informed us about what would be cut. Our units for coordination of our writing program, which once supported multiple WPAs but had dwindled to nine units, were to be cut again, resulting in a meager six units a semester for someone to supervise a program of approximately 150 sections of writing courses yearly. But what was truly shocking was the message this administrator passed along to us from Academic Affairs: we could have the six units, but with the stipulation that the WPA (who we call our "composition coordinator") could not be our current incumbent, the one who had spoken out against Early Start.

We asked, of course, why that was so, and the administrator, of course, proffered no explanation, but we all had a pretty good idea of what the reason was.

Since the person who had been the appropriate choice to coordinate our inaugural summer of Early Start was no longer in the picture, our department chair was asked to suggest someone else. She told me she thought I should do it. At first I was aghast. Why would I want to oversee a program that even our campus administration initially thought was a bad idea? Would I give my implied sanction by agreeing to coordinate the implementation of an academic program that had been developed with little faculty consultation and no regard for disciplinary expertise? Should I supervise a program over which our campus administration had directly interfered in departmental business? Absolutely not!

But as time went on, the chair and others pointed out the distasteful reality that Duncheon (2015) established in her study: I could agree to supervise Early Start and at least make sure qualified faculty would be assigned and that there was some level of appropriate coordination and assessment. If I refused, then the administration—as Duncheon illustrated and recent events had confirmed—would feel free to take matters into its own hands.

Ultimately, I told myself that, in Duncheon's (2015, 165) words, although I was coerced into compliance, it did not mean I would have to "embrace the policy in the manner desired by legislators." And so I agreed to do so, which is why I am able to tell this story of ASI and Early Start, which is probably not the one the creators and enforcers of the mandate would tell.

IMPLICATIONS, CONCLUSIONS, AND POSSIBILITIES FOR CHANGE

I hope these varied scenes from a system's efforts to impose an instructional mandate have illustrated that subtle bullying behaviors are manifested not just by individuals and groups in specific departments or institutions but that they can be normalized into the everyday operation of various levels of system administration.

What is particularly alarming is ASI's magnitude of effect. Far greater than an individual faculty member being ignored, silenced, and mobbed by one or more individuals in a particular department or office in a single institution, ASI, as illustrated by Early Start's implementation, negatively affects larger numbers of individuals and chips away at the ever-eroding concept of shared governance. Because it occurs over time at various levels of administration with varying levels of awareness, ASI can be particularly hard to identify except in retrospect, as has been done here. Therefore, many of the methods and approaches discussed elsewhere in this volume for challenging academic workplace bullying may not be applicable or effective in dealing with ASI. Yet while the challenge of ASI is formidable, the worst course of action is to do nothing. As Andersson and Pearson (1999) have illustrated, if not addressed, incivility grows into an ever larger set of spirals.

So what can be done? Since ASI is a distributed, multi-level type of bullying, I believe it can only be contained and eliminated by no less than a change in a system's academic culture. Twale and De Luca (2008, 164) call for the development of proponents of social change in academia they call "servant leaders": "These people would be in a position to deal with incivility and bully cultures in ways that autocratic or laissez-faire style leaders could not do as effectively. Servant leaders are empathetic listeners who push for openness, greater awareness, and persuasion. They do not need to be in administrative positions to lead. They often see the bigger picture beyond the bounds of time in order to envision change that will occur in the academic culture and the organizational structure as a result of change processes."

Though it might sound as though I am suggesting that we all stand by and wait for these academic messiahs to appear, what I am actually saying is this: those who can change the academic culture are already here. As we serve on university and department committees, as we participate in statewide academic governance, and each time we gather to evaluate promotion files, faculty have opportunities to be servant leaders by challenging incivility, be it manifested by power inequities, silencing, withholding of information, or any other low-grade tactic. In the face of hostility, arrogance, and indifference, we must do so in an open, reasoned, and civil manner, thereby contrasting the inappropriate approaches taken by others and serving as role models to the greater campus and system community.

Granted, for many of us, this is new territory. While as faculty we are usually quite comfortable speaking with authority about matters of scholarship and pedagogy, for the most part, we follow the lead of the

administration in terms of campus- and system-wide policies and procedures. However, as we have seen, the various levels of administration
are more and more willing to interfere in our instructional domain.
Therefore, while I cannot provide specific guidelines for confronting
ASI, I do have some suggestions that I believe hold promise.

Use Tenure for the Good of All Stakeholders

Many years ago, when I was a graduate student, a senior professor mentor constantly stressed to me that tenure should not be so much about
protecting oneself as it is about protecting others. In other words, we
who are fortunate enough to be tenured have the responsibility to make
sure the voices of those who do not have such a shield—contingent
faculty and staff—are heard. Poorly conceived fiats like Early Start may
certainly be a slap in the face to our role as subject-matter experts, but
often they have more serious day-to-day effects on our less protected
colleagues.

Use Technology to Our Advantage

Many instances come to mind when students have used cell phones,
digital cameras, and other handheld devices to document the inappropriate behavior of other students, faculty members, and others and
then used social media to disseminate what took place. Now I must
admit that for faculty to do likewise in documenting ASI may have serious legal and ethical considerations. However, it is easy to foresee situations where the ability to specifically cite exact wordings, backed up by
audio/video if necessary, might be very useful. I often think that actual
video/audio of Trustee Herb Carter telling Teri Yamada and others
that the faculty objecting to Early Start should be quiet and do as they
have been told—perhaps viewed at every Academic Senate at each CSU
campus—might have slowed or even stopped the top-down snowball of
the Early Start mandate, thus saving thousands of work hours and millions of dollars devoted to an ill-conceived program.

Increase Student Involvement and Awareness of Faculty Viewpoints

At my campus and I suspect elsewhere, students are becoming more
and more involved in committees and councils that make important
decisions regarding academic and fiscal policies. Usually, these students are representatives of the official student governments, and they

often interact more with administration than with faculty. Would it not behoove us to make sure we spend time with these student officials to make sure they are getting the faculty side of the story?

For that matter, why not invite other students, perhaps those we know to be insightful, critical thinkers, especially to meetings where there is a likelihood that ASI activity will take place? I am not talking about large groups but perhaps one or two "student guests" who are there at the invitation of a faculty representative. At many campuses, my own included, most meetings of the Academic Senate and its councils and subcommittees, except when discussing personnel matters, are considered open; while guests may not have the opportunity to speak, they will have the opportunity to witness and take what they witness back to their constituents. I believe this last tactic of strategic student involvement may be the most promising, since student collective action is one of the most powerful forces on any college or university campus.

Although a favorable outcome may not result every time, I contend that if enough of the academic community embraces the role of servant leaders and the approaches I have outlined, then, just as we have seen incivility grow within our various work levels and contexts, new sets of behaviors will begin to spread ever wider to all levels of a system. But instead of spirals of incivility, these will be swirls of an equitable, open, and civil academic culture.

NOTES

1.   I recognize that "remediation" has long since been established by developmental education scholarship as an inappropriate and pejorative term. However, it is used throughout this chapter because such is the parlance used consistently by the CSU chancellor's office and Board of Trustees.

2.   Ironically, the CSU Academic Senate released a resolution praising the chancellor's office for its efforts in examining workplace bullying. Doing so seems like praising the fox for guarding the henhouse.

3.   Fortunately, Professor Yamada, who along with a number of other faculty and staff was scheduled to address the trustees about Early Start at 3:30 p.m., was at the chancellor's office to attend earlier meetings, since the meeting of the Committee of Educational Policy was, without warning, moved up to 1:30. As a result, only a few Early Start resisters were able to attend.

REFERENCES

Academic Senate, CSU Channel Islands. 2010. Resolution on Mandatory Early Start Program: Resolution #SR 10-02. https://senate.csuci.edu/resolutions/2010-2011/.

Academic Senate, CSU Dominguez Hills. 2010. Resolution on the Implementation of Mandatory Early Start Programs: 10-8. http://www.csudh.edu/academic-senate/reso lutions/.

Academic Senate, CSU Fullerton. 2010. Resolution of Concern about the Implementation of Mandatory Early Start Programs: ASD 10-69. http://www.fullerton.edu/senate/pub lications_policies_resolutions/.

Academic Senate, CSU Humboldt. 2010. Resolution on the Mandatory Early Start Programs: 10-10/11. www2.humboldt.edu/senate/agendas/packets/10-11-02packet .html.

Academic Senate, CSU Long Beach. 2010. Resolution on Mandatory Early Start Programs. http://web.csulb.edu/divisions/aa/grad_undergrad/senate/resolutions/.

Academic Senate, CSU Los Angeles. 2010. Resolution on the Implementation of Mandatory Early Start Programs. http://www.calstatela.edu/academicsenate/documents.

Academic Senate, CSU San Francisco. 2010. Resolution on Mandatory Early Start: #RF10-280. http://senate.sfsu.edu/documents/resolutions/RF10-280.

Academic Senate, CSU San Jose. 2011. Sense of the Senate Resolution in Opposition to the Implementation of Mandatory Early Start Programs: SS-S11-2. http://www.sjsu .edu/senate/sen_res/.

Academic Senate, CSU San Luis Obispo. 2010. Resolution on Mandatory Early Start Programs: AS-714-10. http://digitalcommons.calpoly.edu/.

Academic Senate, CSU Sonoma. 2010. Resolution on Mandatory Early Start Programs. http://web.sonoma.edu/senate/resolutions/.

Academic Senate, CSU Stanislaus. 2010. August 20, 2010 Minutes. https://www.csustan .edu/sites/default/files/FacultyHandbook/GeneralFaculty/minutes/August-20-2010 .pdf.

Academic Senate of the California State University. 2000. Early Faculty Involvement in California State University (CSU) Initiatives: Resolution AS-3051-11/FA. http://www .calstate.edu/acadsen/.

Academic Senate of the California State University. 2000 Shared Governance in the CSU: Resolution AS-2489-00/FGA. http://www.calstate.edu/acadsen/.

Academic Senate of the California State University. 2008a. Opposition to Impending Implementation of Mandatory Early Start Programs: Resolution AS-2895-09/APEP/ AA. http://www.calstate.edu/acadsen/.

Academic Senate of the California State University. 2008b. Shared Governance Academic Freedom and Principles Governing System-Wide Initiatives with Curricular Implications: Resolution AS-2845/FA. http://www.calstate.edu/acadsen/.

Academic Senate of the California State University. 2010. Objection to Unilateral Decision Making and the Pursuit of a "Culture of Compliance" in the CSU: Resolution AS-2960-10. http://www.calstate.edu/acadsen/.

Andersson, Lynne M., and Christine M. Pearson. 1999. "Tit for Tat? The Spiraling Effect of Incivility in the Workplace." *Academy of Management Review* 24 (3): 452–71. https:// doi.org/10.5465/amr.1999.2202131.

California Faculty Association. 2010. July 13 CSU Trustees Meeting. www.calfac.org/news -release/.

California State University, Office of Academic Affairs. 2010. California State University, Mandatory Early Start Plan. http://www.calstate.edu/eo/EO-1048.html

California State University, Office of the Chancellor. 2008. "Proficiency in the First Year at the University: A Statewide Conference." https://www.calstate.edu/acadprog/Dvlp MathEnglish/Conf/index.shtml/.

California State University, Office of the Chancellor. 2010a. Early Start Policy Clarification and Guidance, October 1, 2010. http://www.calstate.edu/AcadAff/codedMemos/.

California State University, Office of the Chancellor. 2010b. Executive Order 1048. http:// www.calstate.edu/eo/EO-1048.html/.

California State University, Office of the Chancellor. 2014. *An Early Start Is a Smart Start.* http://earlystart.csusuccess.org/.

Caza, Brianna C., and Lilia M. Cortina. 2007. "From Insult to Injury: Explaining the Impact of Incivility." *Basic and Applied Social Psychology* 29 (4): 335–50. https://doi.org /10.1080/01973530701665108.

Duncheon, Julia C. 2015. "Writing Remediation, Faculty Perspectives, and the Challenge of Implementation." In *The Problem of College Readiness*, ed. William G. Tierney and Julia C. Duncheon, 143–77. New York: State University of New York Press.

Early Start Implementation Team, California State University. 2010. Mandatory Early Start Plan. Long Beach: California State University.

English Council, California State University. 2009. Position Statement: Mandatory Early Start Programs. https://csuenglishcouncil.wordpress.com/.

Faculty Senate, CSU Northridge. 2012. Resolution of Protest Concerning the Development and Implementation of Mandatory Early Start Programs in Writing. https://www.csun .edu/faculty-senate/policies/.

Faculty Senate, CSU Sacramento. 2010. Resolution Regarding Mandatory Early Start Programs. https://senate.sfsu.edu/resolutions/.

Faculty Senate, CSU San Bernardino. 2009. Resolution on the Implementation of Mandatory Early Start Programs: FSD 09–17. http://www.calfac.org/sites/main/.

Fogg, Piper. 2008. "Academic Bullies." *Chronicle of Higher Education* 55 (3): B10.

Hollis, Leah P. 2012. *Bully in the Ivory Tower: How Aggression and Incivility Erode American Higher Education.* Wilmington, DE: Patricia Berkly, LLC.

Lester, Jaime. 2013. "Preface." In *Workplace Bullying in Higher Education*, ed. Jaime Lester, vi–xiv. New York: Routledge.

Reichard, Gary W. 2007. *California State University Remediation Policies and Practices: Overview and Prospects, a Report to the Committee on Educational Policy.* Long Beach: California State University Board of Trustees, Office of the Chancellor. https://www.calstate.edu/Acad Prog/DvlpMathEnglish/documents/EdPol_A-Item3_09182007-acc.pdf.

Reichard, Gary W. 2009. *Proficiency in English and Mathematics: A Report to the Committee on Educational Policy.* Long Beach: California State University Board of Trustees, Office of the Chancellor. https://www2.calstate.edu/csu-system/board-of-trustees/past-meetings /2009/Documents/may-12-2009-educational-policy.pdf.

Twale, Darla J., and Barbara M. De Luca. 2008. *Faculty Incivility: The Rise of the Academic Bully Culture and What to Do about It.* San Francisco: Jossey-Bass.

Vega, Gina, and Debra R. Comer. 2005. "Sticks and Stones May Break Your Bones, but Words Can Break Your Spirit: Bullying in the Workplace." *Journal of Business Ethics* 58 (1–3): 101–9. https://doi.org/10.1007/s10551-005-1422-7.

Williams, Mark. 2010. "Implications of a Mandatory Early Start Summer Program at CSULB." Internal report to the CSULB Early Start Planning Committee. Los Angeles: California State University.

Workplace Bullying Institute. n.d. Home page. http://www.workplacebullying.org.

11

"I CAN'T AFFORD TO LOSE MY JOB"
A Chapter Dedicated to All Those Who
Found It Too Risky to Contribute

Anonymous

We reserve this space for them.

DOI: 10.7330/9781607328162.c011

ABOUT THE AUTHORS

SARAH ALLEN is an associate professor in the English department at the University of Hawai'i at Mānoa, where she serves as a specialist in rhetoric and composition. Her current book project offers a theory of inspiration in writing centered on Nietzsche's concept of the Dionysian. Her first book, *Beyond Argument: Essaying as a Practice of (Ex)Change* (2015), was published with Parlor Press and WAC Clearinghouse. She has placed articles in *Rhetoric Review, Rendezvous Journal of Arts and Letters,* and *Educational Philosophy and Theory;* she also has book chapters in *Writing Spaces: Readings on Writing* (Parlor Press) and *Research Writing Revisited: A Sourcebook for Teachers* (Heinemann).

ANDREA DARDELLO is an assistant professor of English at Frederick Community College, where she teaches social justice–themed writing courses and facilitates conversations to build cultural competency skills among faculty and administrators. Her pedagogy emphasizes storytelling as a tool of empowerment and an agent of change for students. She is also a licensed professional coach and founder of the I'm a KeepHer Sister Empowerment Circle, a monthly meet-up designed to provide women with a safe space to seek and speak their truth. She is the self-published author of *Oh, Yes She Did! A Real Woman's Guide to Authentic Communication.*

BETHANY DAVILA is an associate professor of rhetoric and writing at the University of New Mexico, where she co-founded (along with Cristyn L. Elder) the Stretch and Studio Composition program. Her research focuses on the social construction of linguistic difference, written standardness and racial privilege, and instructors' perceptions of student writers based on written language features. Her publications appear in *Written Communication, WPA: Writing Program Administration, Composition Forum,* and *Composition Studies.*

HARRY DENNY is an associate professor of English and the director of the Writing Lab at Purdue University. Harry's scholarship focuses on writing center theory and practice, cultural studies, and research methods. Harry is the author of *Facing the Center: Towards an Identity Politics of One-to-One Mentoring* and a co-editor of the forthcoming collection *Out in the Center: Public Controversies, Private Struggles* (with Anna Sicari, Rob Mundy, Lila Naydan, and Richard Severe), both of which are published by Utah State University Press.

CRISTYN L. ELDER is an associate professor of rhetoric and writing at the University of New Mexico. She serves on the executive board of the Council of Writing Program Administrators (CWPA) and the executive committee of the Conference on College Composition and Communication. She is also a cofounder of WPA-GO (the CWPA Graduate Organization) and *Present Tense: A Journal of Rhetoric in Society.* Her research interests include writing program administration, composition pedagogy, and writing across the curriculum with a focus on marginalized student populations. Her publications appear in *WPA: Writing Program Administration, Composition Forum, Composition Studies, Across the Disciplines,* and the *Writing Center Journal.*

DAWN FELS taught composition at several universities, most recently at the University of Pittsburgh. Her research and publications focus on the teaching and learning of writing, writing center praxis, and the labor conditions of writing center workers.

BRE GARRETT is the director of composition and an assistant professor at the University of West Florida. Bre's research intersects composition pedagogy, rhetorical theory, and writing program administration. She has published work on embodied composing and rhetorical theory in *The New Work of Composing* and *Computers and Composition*. She is currently working on projects related to curricular design and embodied pedagogies. Her recent book chapter, "Corporeal Rhetoric as Embodied Action: Composing in/through Bodily Motion," argues that bodies perform as rhetorical spaces. She has two forthcoming pieces on writing studio curricular design and forthcoming chapters that strategize embodied leadership practices in writing program administration.

W. GARY GRISWOLD is an associate professor of English at California State University, Long Beach. He is the founding director of CSULB's writing center and the Writer's Resource Lab, and he currently serves as the English Department's assistant chair and the director of its Professional Writing Certificate program.

AMY HECKATHORN is a professor of rhetoric and composition at California State University, Sacramento. She served as the writing programs coordinator for fifteen years, streamlining and modernizing the undergraduate and graduate writing curriculum. Her research interests include program administration (published in *Historical Studies of Writing Program Administration*), placement and assessment, curriculum design, and pedagogy.

AURORA MATZKE is an associate professor and the writing program director at Biola University. Her research appears in various feminist and administrative edited collections, as well as journals such as *Computers and Composition* and the *Journal of Business and Technical Communication*. Focused on open-access initiatives and community partnerships, Aurora's work often gives her the opportunity to work alongside diverse K–16 educators. Her current research examines how writing program administrators might successfully work against hegemonic, sexist, and racist teacher evaluation practices in the academy.

STACI PERRYMAN-CLARK is an internationally known scholar who has published widely in rhetoric and writing studies. She is associate dean of the Lee Honors College and an associate professor of English at Western Michigan University. Perryman-Clark is the author of *Afrocentric Teacher-Research: Rethinking Appropriateness and Inclusion* (Peter Lang, 2013); co-editor of *Students' Right to Their Own Language: A Critical Sourcebook* (NCTE and Bedford/ St. Martin's, 2014); the 2015 recipient of the WMU College of Arts and Sciences Faculty Achievement Award for Excellence in Research, Scholarship, and Creative Activities; and the 2018 recipient of the College of Arts and Sciences Faculty Achievement Award for Excellence in Diversity and Inclusion.

SHERRY RANKINS-ROBERTSON is an associate professor of rhetoric and writing at the University of Arkansas at Little Rock. Sherry's scholarship has appeared in *Kairos*, *Computers and Composition*, the *Journal of Basic Writing*, *Academe*, and the *Journal of Writing Assessment*, along with diverse edited collections. Sherry served as one of the co-editors of *WPA: Writing Program Administration*. With Nicholas Behm and Duane Roen, Sherry is an editor of *Applications for the Framework for Success in Postsecondary Writing: Scholarship, Theories, and Practice* (Parlor Press, 2017). Her recent book is an edited collection with Joe Lockard titled *Prison Pedagogies: Learning and Teaching with Imprisoned Writers* (Syracuse University Press, 2018).

SHIRLEY K ROSE is a professor of rhetoric and the director of writing programs in the Department of English of the College of Liberal Arts and Sciences at Arizona State University. She is a past president of the Council of Writing Program Administrators, and she is the director of the WPA Consultant-Evaluator Service. She has served as a peer reviewer for the Higher Learning Commission of the North Central Association of Schools and Colleges for the past decade. At ASU, she is past president of the Tempe Campus

Faculty Assembly. She regularly teaches graduate courses in writing program administration and has published articles on writing pedagogy and on issues in archival research and practice. With Irwin Weiser, she has edited four collections on the intellectual work of writing program administration, including *The WPA as Researcher, The Writing Program Administrator as Theorist, Going Public: What Writing Programs Learn from Engagement*, and *The Internationalization of U.S. College Writing Programs.*

EREC SMITH is an associate professor of rhetoric at York College of Pennsylvania. He publishes on a range of topics, including political rhetoric, "Rhetoric in Buddhism," and fat studies in several journals including *College Composition and Communication*, the *Journal of Assembly on Expanded Perspectives in Learning*, and *Praxis: A Writing Center Journal*. He has chapters in edited collections such as *The Making of Barack Obama: The Politics of Persuasion* (co-edited with Matthew Abraham), *The Politics of Size: Perspectives from the Fat Acceptance Movement*, and *President Trump and His Political Discourse: Ramifications of Rhetoric via Twitter*. Smith is the author of *Fat Tactics: The Rhetoric and Structure of the Fat Acceptance Movement* (Lexington Press).

INDEX